Charles E. Schiller, William-H. Brehaut, Pierre R. Lafrenaye, Marcus Doherty

Correspondence, Documents, Evidence and Proceedings

in the enquiry of Messrs. LeFrenaye & Doherty, commissioners, into the

office of the Clerk of the Crown and Clerk of the Peace, Montreal

Charles E. Schiller, William-H. Brehaut, Pierre R. Lafrenaye, Marcus Doherty

Correspondence, Documents, Evidence and Proceedings
in the enquiry of Messrs. LeFrenaye & Doherty, commissioners, into the office of the
Clerk of the Crown and Clerk of the Peace, Montreal

ISBN/EAN: 9783337273101

Printed in Europe, USA, Canada, Australia, Japan

Cover: Foto ©Suzi / pixelio.de

More available books at **www.hansebooks.com**

CORRESPONDENCE,

DOCUMENTS,

EVIDENCE AND PROCEEDINGS

IN THE

ENQUIRY

OF

MESSRS. LAFRENAYE & DOHERTY, COMMISSIONERS,

INTO THE OFFICE OF THE

CLERK OF THE CROWN AND CLERK OF THE PEACE:

MONTREAL,

FOLLOWED BY THE

REMARKS OF MESSRS. DELISLE & SCHILLER

ON

SO MUCH OF THE REPORT OF THE COMMISSIONERS AS HAS BEEN ALLOWED TO TRANSPIRE,

AND THE

REMARKS OF MR. BREHAUT

ON THE LETTER ANNOUNCING TO HIM THE CAUSES OF HIS DISMISSAL,

AS THE WHOLE APPEARED IN THE MONTREAL GAZETTE.

MONTREAL:
PRINTED BY M. LONGMOORE & CO., AT THE MONTREAL GAZETTE JOB OFFICE.

1861.

CORRESPONDENCE.

MONTREAL, 22nd Dec., 1863.

To the Editor of the MONTREAL GAZETTE :

SIR,—Would you be pleased to publish the following letter which I addressed to the Provincial Secretary on the 15th instant ; also a letter received this day from the Government intimating that my Commission of Sheriff has been revoked ; together with my reply thereto :

SHERIFF'S OFFICE,
Montreal, 15th Dec., 1863.

SIR,—I feel it to be my duty to call the attention of the Government to an article which appeared in the newspaper *Quebec Mercury*, of the 10th instant, charging the keeper of the Montreal Gaol with fraud in his accounts for medical comforts furnished to the prisoners, and Dr. Beaubien, the Physician of the gaol, and myself with having been privy to it.

It cannot fail to be remarked that these calumnies are promulgated at a time when it is publicly known that the report of the Commissioners on my conduct as late Clerk of the Crown, and of the Peace, is under the consideration of the Government, and when it is reported that I am about to be dismissed from the office I now hold.

The writer of the article in question quotes from official documents obtained from the Department of the Minister of Finance ; and although I feel assured that neither that officer, nor the Government are responsible for the article, seeing that it is usual when such charges are made against public officers, to afford them an opportunity of being heard before the accusations are rendered public through the channel of the Press ; yet I feel that I have reason to complain of its publication, as it is evidently intended, by quoting in this way from public documents, and bringing charges affecting my character, to prejudice public opinion against me, and lead the public the more readily to accept my dismissal from office, if such is the case.

With reference to those charges, I can only say that I never refused to recognize the authority of the Prison Inspectors ; and as evidence of this, I will refer to two letters I had the honor of addressing to the Government, upon this very subject ; dated respectively the 15th November, 1862, and the 10th October, 1863. I will quote from the letter, where, referring to that subject, I say :

"I took the liberty, by my letter of the 15th "November, 1862, of calling the attention of "the Government to the subject in question, "and of explaining the cause why some of "those regulations had not been observed, and "of requesting instructions on the matter in-- "volved, for my guidance, but, so far, I have "not received any. It will be seen by the "correspondence referred to, that the diffi- "culties involved in the execution of some of "those regulations were submitted for the "consideration and decision of the Govern- "ment, by my predecessor in office, the late "Mr. Boston, and that he, likewise, was never "instructed as to the course he should follow "in the matter.

"In so far as I am concerned, I can only "say that, however anxious I may be to give "the fullest possible effect to the regulations "of the Board of Prison Inspectors, I am un- "willing to assume the responsibility of doing "so, pending the decision of the Government "on the subject referred to."

This will, I think, conclusively establish how unjust and unfounded is the assertion of the writer in the *Mercury*, in that particular.

Exception is also taken, in the article in question, to the manner in which I have paid the Gaoler's accounts for "medical comforts," which it is said has been done without scrutiny or check whatever on my part.

This I most emphatically deny. The accounts of the Gaoler contained nothing more than the usual recognized charges fixed by an order in Council, and were precisely the same as have heretofore been paid by my predecessor in office for years past, with the knowledge and sanction of the Government.

The accounts were not paid without a careful examination, and they were, besides, certified to be correct by Dr. Beaubien, the Gaol

f

Physician, and their accuracy attested by the oath of Mr. McGinn in the usual way.

It will hardly be believed that a gentleman of the high character and standing of Dr. Beaubien would append his certificate to fraudulent accounts, or that a person of Mr. McGinn's known integrity would make false and fraudulent ones and attest them by his solemn oath. The character of these gentlemen stands too high in this community to be affected by such accusations without better evidence than is afforded in the article I refer to

Taking the whole article together, it is but too evident, that it is written more with a view to disparage me at this particular juncture, than to expose frauds.

I have the honor to be, Sir,
Your most obedient servant,
A. M. DELISLE,
Sheriff.

Hon. A. J. Fergusson Blair,
Provincial Secretary, Quebec.

Letter of the Assistant Secretary, Mr. Delisle.

SECRETARY'S OFFICE,
QUEBEC, 21st Dec., 1863.

SIR,—I am commanded by the Governor General to inform you that His Excellency has been pleased, by an instrument bearing date 19th December instant, to revoke the Commission appointing you Sheriff of the District of Montreal. Tancrède Bouthillier, Esq , is appointed in your stead. You will please deliver over to him all books, records, papers and things pertaining to that office.

I have the honor to be, Sir,
Your most obedient servant,
(Signed,) E. PARENT,
Asst.-Secretary.

A. M Delisle, Esq., Montreal.

Mr. Delisle to the Provincial Secretary.

MONTREAL, 22nd December, 1863.

SIR,—I have the honor to acknowledge the receipt of your letter of the 21st instant, informing me that His Excellency has been pleased, by an instrument bearing date 19th December instant, to revoke my commission appointing me Sheriff of the District of Montreal, and that Tancrede Bouthillier, Esq., is appointed in my stead. Requesting me further to be pleased to deliver over to him all books. records, papers and things pertaining to that Department. I beg in answer to state that I shall, as desired, hand over to Mr. Bouthillier all the books, records, papers and things belonging to the said office. As the cause of the revocation of my commission is not stated and that I feel extremely anxious to be informed upon that subject, as it must, I presume, be the result of the investigation made by Messrs. Lafrenaye and Doherty, the Commissioners who have enquired into the charges made against Mr. Brebaut, Mr. Schiller and myself by Mr. C. M. Delisle, may I request to be furnished with the report of the Honorable the Attorney General to the Executive Council upon that subject, as well as upon the petition I had the honor of addressing to His Excellency on the 5th November last, accompanied by copies of letters from Joseph Doutre, Esq., Q. C , to the said C. M. Delisle, and the order and proceedings of Council had thereupon.

May I also take the liberty of requesting to be furnished with a copy of the report of the Commissioners, Messrs. Lafrenaye and Doherty.

I have, &c.,
A. M. DELISLE.

Hon. A. J. FERGUSSON BLAIR,
Provincial Secretary, Quebec.

I also take the liberty of sending to you for publication the whole of the evidence taken by the Commissioners, Messrs. Lafrenaye and Doherty, in order that the public may judge how far the revocation of my commission, as Sheriff of this District, by His Excellency the Governor General, was justified. Until I am made aware of the grounds of my removal from office, (after nearly thirty-six years of faithful service,) I must refrain from making further observations.

Your obedient servant,
A. M. DELISLE.

PRELIMINARY DOCUMENTS.

(*Petition of Mr. A. M. Delisle.*)

PROVINCE OF CANADA,
DISTRICT OF MONTREAL.

To His Excellency, &c.

The Petition of Alexandre Maurice Delisle, of the City of Montreal, Esquire,

RESPECTFULLY SHEWETH:

That by letter from the Honorable the Provincial Secretary, under date the 27th January last, copy of a communication from Mr. Charles M. Delisle, preferring certain charges against your petitioner, and William H. Brehaut and Charles E. Schiller, Esquires, was transmitted to him with a request that your petitioner would be pleased to make such remarks thereon as he might see fit, for the information of your Excellency.

That your petitioner on the 2nd February following answered the said charges by a general denial of their truth, and an offer to submit to the most thorough investigation, if the Government desired it.

That a Commission was, subsequently, issued on the 18th February last, appointing Pierre Richard Lafrenaye and Marcus Doherty, Esqrs, Commissioners, to investigate certain charges of malversation of office against your Petitioner and the said W. H. Brehaut and Charles E. Schiller, and the Commissioners called upon your petitioner and the other gentlemen above named to answer twelve distinct charges which your petitioner did, by his plea of "not guilty," as will appear by the proceedings of the said Commissioners.

That in submitting the said charges to your petitioner in writing, the Commissioners also notified him that he would be called upon to answer such further charges as might be preferred against him *from day to day* during the said enquiry.

That your petitioner thereupon called the attention of the Commissioners to the fact that their Commission limited their enquiry to charges actually made, and not to such as might thereafter be brought from *day to day* against him, but being desirous that his conduct should undergo the most rigid enquiry, he merely called attention to the fact, without making it the matter of a special objection.

That your Petitioner, when the said charges were made, had reason to know that the said Charles M. Delisle, urged by other parties, was actuated by hostile feelings towards him, and a

desire to ruin his good fame and character, and thus procure his dismissal from the office of Sheriff, which he holds, and this because your petitioner positively declined to compound a series of the most grave criminal offences of which the said Charles M. Delisle had been guilty. That your Petitioner was soon confirmed in the opinion he had formed as to the malevolent intentions of the said Charles M. Delisle, by becoming acquainted with the fact that the said C. M. Delisle, both before and after the issuing of the said Commission, had entered into a correspondence with Joseph Doutre, Esquire, Advocate, of the City of Montreal, to bring and urge such charges against your Petitioner, which the said Joseph Doutre accordingly did. That the Commissioners extended their investigation to other charges than the twelve above mentioned, (evidently made by the said Charles M. Delisle,); and the evidence revealed the revolting fact that the offences charged, in some cases, had not been committed at all, while in others they had been committed by himself. That your Petitioner is deeply greived thus to advert to one so closely allied to him; but he feels bound to do so in self-defence. And your petitioner begs to assure your Excellency that although that unfortunate individual is his half brother, the wreckless conduct he has held has been such, that your petitioner has been compelled, long ago, to estrange himself from him, and for nearly a quarter of a century back has held no communion with him whatever.

That your petitioner, relying on his entire innocence, did not choose to embarrass and protract the said enquiry by submitting to the Commissioners such evidence as would have proved the charges brought against him to be the result of a preconcerted combination to injure and ruin him.

That the said investigation having been brought to a close, your Petitioner deems it necessary and proper to lay before your Excellency copies of certain letters from the said Joseph Doutre to the said Charles M. Delisle, written prior to and during the said investigation; also copies of seven indictments found against the said Charles M. Delisle for forgery, since he has absconded from this Province, all of which are annexed to the present petition.— That a perusal of the said documents will, your Petitioner trusts, satisfy your Excellency of the unfair means which were resorted to to operate his ruin, and that the motives which prompted them were dictated by other feelings than a desire to see strict and impartial justice done in the premises.

That the original of the said Joseph Doutre's letters are in the possession of the said O. E. Schiller, and your petitioner has that gentleman's authority to say that they can be furnished if desired.

Wherefore your petitioner respectfully prays, that when your Excellency shall be called upon to consider the Report and proceedings of the said Commissioners, your Excellency may also be graciously pleased, simultaneously, to consider the documents hereunto annexed. And as in duty bound, your Petitioner will ever pray,

A. M. DELISLE.

Montreal, 5th Nov., 1863.

———

Letters of Mr. Joseph Doutre, Q.C., to Mr. C. M. Delisle.

—

(Translation.)

MONTREAL, 22nd December, 1862.

SIR,—I have transmitted to the *Pays* the last letter but one that I received from you. It would have been published at once if I had insisted, but the editor was of opinion that the object which your letter had in view would be more certainly attained by communicating with the Government, and I put off its publication for a few days. You will understand that in the position you occupy, your evidence would be raceived with a proper mistrust. Before hazarding a thing of this kind, it would be requisite to know what evidence, besides your own, could be furnished in case of an enquiry. Will you, therefore, be so good as to indicate what proof, written or oral, could be obtained on each of the points mentioned in your letter, susceptible of either the one or the other kind of proof? I only see in all this a matter of public interest, and I need not consider either your animosities or my own recollections of injury. If a Commission should sit, I will communicate all the information that you furnish me.

Yours, &c.,

(Signed,) JOSEPH DOUTRE.

C. M. Delisle,
Ogdensburgh.

———

SIR,—I have received your letter of the 12th inst. I really do not know when the enquiry will be proceeded with touching the Peace Office. I can say nothing, because I know nothing, about the possibility of your being heard as a witness. I shall probably have nothing to do with the enquiry, beyond suggesting to the gentlemen charged with it what I consider ought to be done. I am persuaded that nobody thinks about arresting you under the extradition treaty,—your brother less than any one.

Yours, &c.,

(Signed,) JOSEPH DOUTRE.

Mr. C. M. Delisle,
Ogdensburgh.

MONTREAL, 19th March, 1863.

SIR,—The Commissioners (P. R. Lafrenaye and Marcus Doherty) have commenced work. Their intention is to notify you to attend as a witness, not with the idea that you will come, but in order to obtain information in detail, which you could give in a letter. I would not advise you to trust to the protection that a subpœna might afford. My object in writing is to put you on your guard, so that you may not be frightened if you receive a subpœna. You ought, either before or after receiving a subpœna, to write a letter to the Commissioners, giving them circumstantial detail upon all points, with the names of the witnesses. I cannot make use of the information which you have communicated for reasons which it would take me too long to explain. You must, therefore, begin anew. I have not indicated your present residence to any one; but the Commissioners presume that you are in Ogdensburgh from the date of the letter you sent to the Government, and which is in their hands as the basis of the accusations.

Yours, &c,

(Signed,) "JOSEPH DOUTRE."

Mr. C. M. Delisle,
Ogdensburgh.

———

MONTREAL, 21st March, 1863.

SIR,—On receiving your letter of the 19th instant, I saw Meyers who told me he had written to you to say there was nothing to fear on the score of what you wrote to me. The object of those who thus try to terrify you is transparent. They are afraid that your proximity to Montreal may give rise to information that may compromise them. Now you understand that for the same reason, they will take good care not to bring you back to Montreal, where you could give daily information to the Commissioners ; so I think you need not concern yourself about these threats. Set about furnishing to the Commissioners, without delay, the detailed information you have communicated to me. I have ascertained that the subpœna has been addressed to the Sheriff of Prescott, and you will have received it before now. The reason why such information is desired is this :— The Commissioners wish to act upon instructions and data, that they can show if necessary without exposing themselves to the accusation of receiving their information by indirect means. You need not date your letter to the Commissioners. Send it to me, and I will take care they get it. Give in detail all the facts you are acquainted with, and the names of the witnesses to each fact.

Yours, &c.,

(Signed,) JOSEPH DOUTRE.

MR. C. M. DELISLE,
Ogdensburgh.

MONTREAL, March 28th, 1853.

SIR,—I have this moment come from the country. On my arrival I went to the Court House and asked Johnson how the matter stood. He told me it was true that he had drawn four bills of indictment, and that they would be laid before the Grand Jury in a day or two. I was not able to find out who was at the bottom of this. On that head I can only make conjectures, and here they are. I think that A. M. D. perceiving that the threats he had used had not had the effect of keeping you away had recourse to these means to frighten you; but I am persuaded that nothing will be done with these bills. The direct action of Government is required to procure your extradition, and the motive that makes your brother wish so much to keep you at a distance will make him take very good care, (if he is at the bottom of the matter, as I imagine,) not to solicit Government intervention. The enquiries that Meyer and others have made of Schiller, to find out if anything was being done against you, have made both Schiller and your brother believe that you are so much afraid of a prosecution that you will keep your distance the moment such prosecution would be commenced. However, on all this, I repeat, I have only suppositions. I will not take upon myself the responsibility towards you of inspiring a confidence with no other foundation but conjectures. As to what you ask respecting the possibility of obtaining your pardon from Government, I can say nothing about it. If the enquiry which is being made about the Peace office results in the discovery of serious frauds, it is possible that in consideration of the service you would have rendered to society you would obtain mercy from the Government, and the bills of indictment would, in that case, instead of prejudicing you be of great service in facilitating and justifying the interference of the Crown. In order to be more distinct on this head, suppose these bills should be found by the Grand Jury, nothing would be easier than for the Crown officer to authorise a *nolle prosequi*, if he had instructions from the Attorney General. In this way I see how the Government could act, while I perceive no legal or practical way of obtaining your pardon otherwise. Without wishing to take the responsibility of advising you; I would say, that if I were in your situation I would keep quiet. The commission will go on at a good rate now. They have been furnished with the pay lists, and all the information and documents necessary. Already enormous irregularities have been discovered under the head of stolen goods unclaimed.

Yours, &c.,
(Signed,) JOSEPH DOUTRE.
Mr. C. M. Delisle.

MONTREAL, 30th March, 1863.

SIR,—I ascertained this morning that it was your brother and Schiller who took the initiative in the prosecutions directed against you. On this ground I feel sure that they will take good care not to demand your extradition. I send you the *Herald* of this morning, containing the proceedings of the Court on Saturday. The motion made by Mr. Johnson, that process do issue, is a motion of course having nothing to do with extradition. I think your enemies would be very much disappointed if you were to come and give yourself up; still less are they likely to go and fetch you.

Yours, &c.,
(Signed) JOSEPH DOUTRE.

MONTREAL, 6th April, 1863.

SIR,—I received your letters of Wednesday and Friday last. The information you have given the Commissioners is only known to them and to me, which accounts for the mission of your brother John. If you can give the following information, send it directly to the Commissioners :—1st. Who stole the case of brandy ? 2nd. The water-pipes? 3rd. The piece of cloth ? 4th. Who was the proprietor of these articles ? 5th. When were they stolen ? 6th. When did Schiller go to New Orleans ? As a general thing, communicate directly with them on all that concerns the enquiry.

In haste, yours, &c.,
(Signed) JOSEPH DOUTRE.

MONTREAL, 8th April, 1863.

SIR,—The contents of the indictments against you are as follows :—

1. Note of 30th Nov., 1861, $200, endorsed De-Lorimier.
2. Note of 6th Dec., 1861, $175, endorsed C. E. Schiller.
3. Note of 4th Dec., 1861, $80, endorsed C. E. Schiller.
4. Note of 4th Dec., 1861, $250, endorsed C. E. Schiller.
5. Note of 29th November, $50, endorsed C. E. Schiller.
6. Note of 2nd December, $93, endorsed Coursol.

This morning the Commissioners are going to examine Hands. The question, whether the enquiry ought to be public or private, was discussed during the whole day, and will be decided to-morrow morning. I was present. It is A. M. D. who contends that the proceedings ought to be private. I think the decision will be in favor of publicity. I shall have all published as fast as it transpires. You ought now to be satisfied that I have not been deceived in my anticipations. I think you have everything to gain by marching stoutly in the direction I have indicated. The Members of Parliament go off to-night I have seen a good number of them, and I think there is no danger for the Government. When you have done as I have directed, I will give effect to it on my own responsibility. If you make up your mind to do it, do not forget to mention the visit of your brother John, and do all you can to bring Johnson into this affair. He is doing all he can against you. He has just published a letter in the *Witness*, in the interest of the accused. I send it to you; but you must let me have it again, as I shall want it. I am hard at work to try and give all this a tendency that may be favorable to you. When you have any doubt as to my rectitude of intention or judgment, you will be at liberty to act as you please. It is not by words that I would inspire you with confidence. Even in case of a change of Government, I should consider things at a point when no Government will have the audacity to recede. In the letter which called forth Mr. Johnson's reply, the author of which I do not know, the motive of presenting the bills is clearly indicated. Now dot your i's.

Yours, &c.,
(Signed) JOSEPH DOUTRE.

The above was written when I received your letter. I want you to copy your letter over again, with the additional page herewith annexed:

[The following is in Chs. Delisle's handwriting.]

N.B.—D. sent me the letter which appeared in the papers in his hand-writing, and got me to copy it over.

MONTREAL, 26th April, 1863.

SIR,—I saw Mr. Ryan on his return from Ogdensburg, and since I heard from you. I have long felt how sad your position is. Unfortunately I can do nothing to relieve it. As to the idea you express of returning to Montreal, I dare not advise you on so delicate a subject. In order to ascertain how you would be received by the party most interested in the cause of your absence, (Malo) I asked him what he would do if you came back. He commenced by telling me that he took no active part in the proceedings against you. That Schiller warned him that he would have to go before the Grand Jury, and that, accordingly, some days afterwards he received an order to attend. As to what he would do in case of your return, I could get nothing satisfactory out of him. He said he did not know what he might do. It is possible that your return would entail no evil consequences, but it is also possible that it might turn out otherwise. I cannot take upon myself the responsibility of advising you. The enquiry would be much more complete if you were here. A great many facts must remain in obscurity, and if I only consulted my own wishes to see this affair cleared up, I should tell you to come, but as I should probably be powerless to protect you in case of accident, I do not wish to expose myself to the reproach of advising your return. Hands' deposition is now in the possession of the Government. I think it is the most serious case of all, as it compromises the three accused persons, and I do not see how they can get out of it. Rene would say nothing about the water pipes, except that he saw you throw some into the privy. His deposition revealed nothing. Several points crept out accidentally. The matter of stolen and unclaimed property will bring out nothing except a complete disorganization in that department.

I was going to close this letter; but I have received one from you, asking my opinion of the charges made against you and your co-heirs for commission in administering the estate of your father. I do not think you can succeed in this matter, not because your action would be barred by lapse of time, but because, after being of full age, you consented to pay for a service which perhaps would not have given your brother a right of action, but for the payment of which there might perhaps exist a natural obligation—which would be presumed from the fact of payment.

Yours, &c.,
(Signed)   JOSEPH DOUTRE.

Letter of Mr. Delisle to Provincial Secretary.

MONTREAL, December 21st, 1863.

SIR,—I had the honor of transmitting to you with my letter of the 5th November, last, a petition to His Excellency the Governor-General, accompanied by copies of certain letters from Joseph Doutre, Esq., Q.C., to Mr. C. M. Delisle, and to request that the same might be submitted to His Excellency for his consideration, simultaneously with the report, &c., made by Messrs. Lafrenaye and Doherty, Commissioners, named to enquire into certain charges brought against me. I have since obtained the accompanying extracts of letters from the said C. M. Delisle to Mr. C. E. Schiller, in reference to the same subject, which I beg to enclose, and to request they may also be submitted to His Excellency the Governor General for his consideration.

I have, &c.,
(Signed,)   A. M. DELISLE,

Hon. A. J. Fergusson Blair,
Provincial Secretary, Quebec.

Extract of a letter from Mr. C. M Delis'e to Mr. C. E. Schiller, without date, received 25th July, 1863.

MY DEAR SCHILLER,—There is one thing of which I wish to caution you all, it is this :—Doutre, I know, has forwarded a copy of Hands' deposition, as given before the Commissioners, to the Government. As I have said before, I sincerely regret all I have done, and I now wish to do all in my power to save you from any danger, if there be any. If I can do anything, either by a correspondence in the newspapers, or otherwise to do you all some good, I will do it, only say what you want me to do. Adieu,

CHARLES.

Extract of a letter from Mr. C. M. Delisle to C. E. Schiller, and without date, received on the 27th July, 1863.

MY DEAR SCHILLER,—During Sherman's absence to Montreal, I managed to get a Mr. Charley Baldwin, the agent of the Grand Trunk here, to pass his word that I would appear, to-day, before the Magistrate. I did so because I felt certain that my family would settle with Sherman. This morning I saw Sherman, and he told me you had offered to give $20 notwithstanding the *mean way* I had treated you all. When I heard him say so, it made me cry to think that you should be so good-hearted still.

My dear Schiller I ask your pardon and that of all others for having done what I did do.— I never would have done that if it had not been for all Doutre's *fine promises.* Even that letter which was published in the *Pays* was written by him and copied by me. If you choose I will send you all his letters.

Copy of a letter from Mr. C. M. Delisle to Mr. C. E. Schiller, without date, received 5th August, 1863.

PRESCOTT.

MY DEAR SCHILLER,—I have just got an anonymous letter telling me that if I sent you all Doutre's letters something would be done for me. I offered to do it, and I want to be honest with you and Alexander. I sincerely regret what I have done and ask both your pardon ; I therefore send you all Doutre's letters, although some of them compromise me, still I send them. I would more particularly refer you to the one of the 28th March and one of the 8th April. The hopes which Doutre had held out to me, in my position, caused me to do what he asked, but pardon me for it all. I throw myself at your knees and ask forgiveness. The last two nights I have slept in a field near the railroad, and I am starving. If anything is done, 1 want some clothes, for how can I go to N. Y. naked. I would much rather go home. I want to be honest with you all. I am sorry for what I have done. I also sent he paper I signed at Rouse's Point, although it is not asked. I am acting honestly with you, do the same with me, and I hope that the promise made me in the letter I got to-day is not a trick, like the promise Gale made me. But dear Schiller it is in your power to get my good brother, who I have maltreated, to forgive me and get me back to my children. I have suffered enough, I assure you. Anything you may want to know I will tell honestly. Don't let Doutre know I sent you his letters, for he may turn round and injure me. The way the whole thing commenced was this : Last summer I saw Sivallier (the old Sergeant of Police) and he told me that Doutre had asked him if he knew where I was, that he (D.) would give much to know. He induced me to write to D, because he said he knew the *Rouge party* would save me. I did so. You see the promises he made me. If anything is done come and see me here. But if my poor brother will pardon me let him give me as much as will keep me from starving till the next term, and then have *Nolle Prosequi* entered on the bills.

I hope dear Schiller you will bring me back. You will do it, I know, for it is in your power and that of A. M. D.

May God bless you all.

N.B.—Now mind get Alex. to write me a kind letter, in which he will say he forgives me.

Extract of a letter from Mr. C. M. Delisle to Mr. C. E. Schiller, without date, received August 7th, 1863.

MY DEAR SCHILLER,—Doutre's manuscript was sent back to him. I attempted to keep it, but he wrote back for it, and I sent it to him.

Write and get my poor brother to do so, and tell me if anything will be done for me. Ob Lord! I only wish you could see me for a moment, with an old flannel coat all torn and pinned together. I am worse than a beggar!— Tell Alexander to write a brotherly letter, it will give me courage. Tell him to write, not to fear, I will send him back his letter if he chooses, but let me know if anything will be done to bring me home. Let Johnson do as much for me as he did for Asselin. Write immediately; don't fear anything. Above all I want a pair of pants and some boots, and, if possible, a coat. Has my brother forgiven me ? You don't say a word about that.

Yours,

CHARLES.

SECRETARY'S OFFICE,
QUEBEC, 6th November, 1863.

SIR,—I have the honor, by command of His Excellency the Governor General, to acknowledge the receipt of your letter of the 5th instant, and to state that the same will be submitted to His Excellency the Governor General, in connection with the report of the Commissioners appointed to enquire into the offices of the Clerk of the Crown and Clerk of the Peace, Montreal.

I have the honor to be, sir,
Your most obedient servant,
(Signed)   E. PARENT,
Asst.-Secretary.
A. M. DELISLE. Esq.,
Sheriff, Montreal,

(Letter of Assistant Secretary to Mr. Delisle.)

SECRETARY'S OFFICE,
Quebec, 27th Jan., 1863.

SIR,—I have the honor to enclose to you herewith a copy of a letter from Chs. M. Delisle, Esq., preferring complaints against you, and to request that you will be pleased to make such remarks thereon as you may be prepared to offer, for the information of His Excellency the Governor General.

An early reply will oblige.

I have the honor to be, Sir,
Your most obedient servant,
(Signed)   E. PARENT.
A. M. Delisle, Esq , &c. &c. &c.,
Montreal.

(Statement of Mr. C. M. Delisle.)

OGDENSBURG, State of New York, U. S., December 19th, 1862.

To His Excellency the Right Honorable Lord Monck Governor General of Canada, &c , &c.

The complaint of Charles M. Delisle, of the city of Montreal, and now residing in the United States :

RESPECTFULLY SHEWETH:

That your complainant was for many years employed as Chief Clerk to the Police Magistrate in Montreal ; that during the whole of the time he was employed, he always enjoyed the esteem and confidence of his superiors and the public generally ; that he always discharged his duties to the entire satisfaction of the Government and every one else ; that up to the 7th December, 1861, his conduct and character was always irreproachable; that having committed an offence against the laws of the country he was forced to become a refugee in the States ; that on the evening of the 10th of December, 1861, Charles Edward Schiller, Deputy Clerk of the Peace for the District of Montreal, came to see complainant at Rouse's Point and stated to him (complainant) that he (Schiller) had been sent to see him (complainant) and to tell him (complainant) that Alexander Maurice Delisle, Esquire, had undertaken and promised to arrange and settle his affairs, so that I might go home and return to my family, and that in order to accomplish that arrangement it was necessary that complainant should sign a power of attorney authorizing him (the said A. M. Delisle) to draw my salary from the Government through the hands of C. J. Coursol, Esq., for the time and space of five consecutive years, so as to guarantee him (A. M. Delisle) of his disbursements. That, moreover, the said Complainant, delivered up all the money he (Complainant) had, said Schiller promising that the said money would be applied to the settlement of Complainant's affairs. That Complainant then signed the said power of attorney in favor of A. M. Delisle, which power of attorney was in the handwriting of W. H. Brehaut, Esq. Complainant further states, that he gave and delivered to the said Schiller the said power of attorney, together with the sum of $500 to be applied as promised by him. That on the following morning said Schiller left Complainant with the express understanding and promise on his part, that the moment he would reach Montreal, his (Complainant) affairs would be settled and paid by him (Schiller) and and the said A. M. Delisle, and that then he (Complainant) would be able to return to his home. That notwithstanding that Complainant conformed himself to all the propositions and conditions of the said Schiller and A. M. Delisle, they have not settled his affairs, but they have left him in the States, and refuse in any way to account for the $500 which they got from Complainant.

That complainant having for many years had occasion to see what was going on in the Department of the Clerk of the Peace in Montreal, he is in a position to prove by documentary evidence and by verbal testimony, that those public officers (very lately too) have by means of false returns, false names and signatures and false pretences, fraudulently obtained a considerable amount of money from the Government. That moreover one of them has embezzled some of the Government monies. That large frauds have been carried on by them in the way of postage. That some of the Government stationery in their office has been sold to a second party. That some *unclaimed stolen goods* have been taken, carried away and unlawfully appropriated to the use of one of those officers, the deputy. That a quantity of stationary belonging to the Government, such as blank books, paper, ink, &c., were used for the schooling and education of children. That they speculated in Government monies, by drawing £125 a year allowed for a clerk, and paying that clerk only £60 a year and pocketing the balance. That C. E. Schiller in his capacity of Superintendent of Crown witnesses, has for

many years past falsely and fraudulently obtained large sums of monies from Government, by over-charging the actual cost of the service of subpœnas. That the said Schiller, every time that he swore to the correctness of his accounts committed perjury. That the said Schiller has at the very least defrauded Government of £125 to £150 a year for many years past. That the complainant can prove many other facts of frauds against that Department, which he will be ready to do at any time Your Excellency may see fit to call upon him to do so.

That complainant would most respectfully pray that a Commission be appointed to enquire into these complaints, and that justice may be done.

(Signed,)   C. M. DELISLE.

[COPY.]

Secretary's Office,
    Quebec, 27th January, 1863.

Mr. A. M. Delisle's Reply.

—

MONTREAL, 2nd February, 1863

SIR,—I have the honor to acknowledge the receipt of your letter of the 27th ultimo, enclosing copy of a complaint made by Mr. Charles M. Delisle against the Clerks of the Peace at Montreal, charging them with having practiced frauds against the Government, and requesting me to offer such remarks thereon as I may be prepared to make.

I have for some time past ceased to belong to the office in question, but, on my own behalf, and as regards the office of Clerk of the Peace while I was at the head of it, I can only remark upon these charges that they are utterly devoid of any foundation in truth.

It may be proper to add that Mr. C. M. Delisle is a fugitive from justice, an absconding felon, whose statements are utterly undeserving of consideration; but, if the Government attach any importance to them, and desire to investigate the charges in question, I shall at any time be prepared to submit to and to facilitate the most thorough enquiry.

I have the honor to be, Sir,
    Your most obedient servant,
        (Signed,)   A. M. DELISLE.

The Honorable Provincial Secretary.

EVIDENCE AND PROCEEDINGS.

MONTREAL, 4th March, 1863.

ALEXANDER M. DELISLE, ESQ.,

Late Joint Chief of the Peace, and Clerk of the Crown in the District of Montreal.

Sir,—Having been appointed by His Excellency the Governor General, by commission, bearing date at Quebec on the eighteenth day of February last, past to investigate certain charges of malversation of office, recently made against the late Joint Clerk of the Peace, and Clerk of the Crown at Montreal,— Messrs. Delisle and Brehant, and their Deputy, also Charles Schiller,—and to enquire into the organization of said offices, as referred to in said Commission, we beg leave to inform you that we will, on the 9th day of March instant, at ten o'clock in the forenoon, in the Grand Jury room in the Court House, in the City of Montreal, proceed with such investigation, and in the discharge of the duties devolving upon us as such Commissioners, and we hereby notify you to be then and there present, in order to furnish such information as you may be possessed of, to facilitate the objects of the said investigation and enquiry, and to answer or explain such charges as may then and there, and from day to day during the sitting of the said Commission, be preferred against you as such late Joint Clerk of the Peace and Clerk of the Crown, at Montreal aforesaid.

We remain, Sir, yours respectfully,
(Signed,)   P. R. LAFRENAYE, Com,
               M. DOHERTY, Com.

MONDAY, 9th March, 1863

Present :

PIERRE R. LAFRENAYE,
MARCUS DOHERTY, Esquires,
               Commissioners.

Messrs. Delisle, Brehaut and Schiller appeared, when the Commissioners read their Commission to them, as well as the following charges, to which they were allowed until Saturday next to answer.

COPY OF THE COMMISSION.

(L. S.)   PROVINCE OF CANADA.

His Excellency the Right Honorable Charles Stanley Viscount Monck, Baron Monck of Ballytrammon, in the County of Wexford, Governor General of British North America, &c., &c., &c.

To all to whom these presents shall come, or whom they may in anywise concern. Greeting.

Whereas certain charges of malversation of office have been made against the late Joint Clerk of the Peace, and Clerk of the Crown at Montreal, Messrs. Delisle and Brehaut, and their Deputy, also Charles Schiller, and whereas it has been deemed advisable that the charges so made should be thoroughly investigated, and that a full enquiry should be made into the organization of those offices, *now know ye* that under and pursuant to the provisions of the thirteenth chapter of the Consolidated Statutes of Canada, entitled, "An Act respecting Inquiries concerning Public matters and Official Notices," the authority in me thereby vested, and by and with the advice and consent of Her Majesty's Executive Council for the said Province, I have nominated, constituted and appointed, and by these presents do nominate, constitute and appoint, Pierre Richard Lafrenaye and Marcus Doherty, of the City of Montreal, in the District of Montreal, Esquires, to be *Commissioners* to investigate the charges so brought against the above officers, and to enquire into the organization of those offices ; *and I do hereby authorise* and empower them, the said Pierre Richard Lafrenaye and Marcus Doherty, as such *Commissioners*, to summon before them any party or witnesses, and to require them to give evidence on oath, orally or in writing, (or on solemn affirmation, if such parties be entitled to affirm in Civil Matters,) and to produce such documents and things as they, the said Pierre Richard Lafrenaye and Marcus Doherty, may deem requisite to the full investigation of the matters and things aforesaid.

To *have* and to *hold* the said office of Commissioners for the purposes aforesaid unto them, the said Pierre Richard Lafrenayo and Marcus Doherty, during pleasure, and I do hereby require that the said Commissioners do report the result of the above-mentioned investigation, with all convenient speed, to the Governor of the said Province, for the time being.

Given under my hand and Seal at Arms at Quebec, this Eighteenth day of February, in the Year of Our Lord, One Thousand Eight Hundred and Sixty Three, and in the Twenty Sixth Year of Her Majesty's Reign.

By Command,   (Signed,)   MONCK.
        (Signed)   E. PARENT, Assist.-Sec.

Charges of malversation of office, which have been made against the late Joint Clerk of the Peace and Clerk of the Crown at Montreal, Messrs. Delisle and Brehaut, and their Deputy, also, Charles E. Schiller :

1stly. That by false returns, false names, false signatures and false pretences, the late Joint Clerk of the Peace and Clerk of the Crown at Montreal, Messrs. Delisle and Brehaut, and their Deputy, also,

Charles Schiller, have fraudulently obtained a considerable amount of money from the Government.

2. That one of them has embezzled some of the Government monies.

3. That large frauds have been carried on in the way of postage.

4. That some of the Government stationary in their office has been sold to a second party.

5. That some unclaimed stolen goods have been taken and carried away, and unlawfully appropriated to the use of one of those officers, the deputy.

6. That a quantity of stationary belonging to the Government, such as blank books, paper, ink, &c., were used for the schooling and education of children.

7. That they speculated on Government monies by drawing a sum of £125 a year allowed for a clerk, and paying that clerk only £60 a year, and pocketing the balance.

8. That Charles E. Schiller, in his capacity of Superintendant of Crown Witnesses, has, for many years past, falsely and fraudulently obtained large sums of money from Government, by overcharging the actual costs of the services of subpœnas.

9. That the said Charles E. Schiller, every time that he swore to the correctness of his accounts, committed perjury.

10. That the said Charles E. Schiller has, at the least, defrauded the Government of £125 to £150 a year, for many years past.

11. That the said Charles E. Schiller has been in the habit of making a profit upon the fees charged by constables for the service of documents emanating from the office.

12. That the said Charles E. Schiller has also been accustomed to take credit for the payment of mileage upon the service of subpœnas, where such subpœnas had been sent by post, and no mileage had accrued.

(Signed,) P. R. LaFrenaye,
M. Doherty,
Montreal, March 9, 1863. Commissioners.

The said charges having been read, the parties were allowed until the 14th instant to answer them.

SATURDAY, 14th March, 1863.
Mr. Delisle, Mr. Brehaut and Mr. Schiller severally appeared.

Answer or plea by Mr. Delisle to the charges in writing, read over and handed to him on the 9th instant:—" I am not guilty of the charges made against me, and shall, in proper time, be prepared to establish my innocence. I will add that I am prepared to furnish the Commissioners any aid and assistance in my power to elucidate the truth in reference to the said charges during the investigation to be made."

By Mr. BREHAUT.—General denial of the charges, with the expression of his readiness to afford the Commissioners every assistance in his power in the production of any documents he may have in his possession, as Joint Clerk of the Peace.

By Mr. SCHILLER.—I deny all the charges against me, and am prepared to give the Commissioners all the aid in my power in carrying out the enquiry.

Mr. DELISLE directed the attention of the Commissioners to the fact that the above notice called upon them not only to answer the charges actually made, but also to such as *might* "*from day to day*, during the sitting of the said Commissioners, be preferred against them," which was unauthorized by the Commission.

MONDAY, 16th March, 1863.
William F, Philips, Esq., is sworn in to act as Clerk or Secretary to the Commissioners.

Adolphe Bissonette, Joint High Constable of Montreal, appeared, and being duly sworn states:—I am 33 years of age. I was appointed Joint High Constable by commission, dated the 10th day of December, 1861, with Mr. Benjamin Delisle, who held that office previously for a number of years, over twenty, I suppose.

I have now in my possession books showing the disposition of the stolen goods, commencing 2nd January, 1861, pertaining to the office, in which a record was kept of stolen and unclaimed goods, which were in the possession of the High Constable since said date. So far as I have examined, I find that no books or records of such goods have been kept in the said office previous to the date above specified, and have no knowledge of the nature or extent to which such goods had been previously received there, except from time to time. When acting as Sub-Chief of Police it was my duty to deliver such goods into said office. This may have happened twenty or thirty times in the course of a year, for the space of six or seven years.

In the discharge of my duty as such Sub-Chief and Serjeant of Police, I from time to time paid into said office sums of money stolen or supposed to be stolen. I have no means of ascertaining to what amount, inasmuch as I never took receipts therefor. I paid such sums, and delivered into the hands of the High Constable, Benjamin Delisle, by order of the Inspector and Superintendent of Police,—being at one time Colonel Ermatinger, and afterwards Mr. Coursol. What became of all such monies and goods I am not aware, but I know that the greatest part of such goods were delivered to their owners after trial, and that I witnessed their delivery. Since 1854 or 1855, previous to this, I have no knowledge. I have no means of ascertaining how often I was a witness to the delivery of such goods to their owners. I considered it my duty after each case was disposed of by trial, to see that the goods and money were returned to their owners, when so ordered by the Court.

I have examined the vault of our office as Joint High Constable, and find that there are unclaimed goods specified in the statement thereof, made up to the 27th January, 1863, now shown to me by the Commissioners, and which I herewith produce, marked No 1. I do not know how long the whole of the said goods have been in the vault; some of them were brought there since I was appointed to the office.—It is our duty as such Joint Head Constable. to keep those goods until an order issues from the Court to sell them.

There was no such order issued since I was appointed to the office, and I have no knowledge of how such goods were disposed of previous to my appointment to office.

I have been in possession of the key of the vault in which said goods are kept, since the end of the Court of Quarter Sessions held in February, 1862, when it was handed over to me by Mr. Benjamin Delisle, my partner, as such Joint High Constable. Since I have had the key, no one has had access to the said vault except myself.

Before that Mr. Benjamin Delisle had the key of that vault, to my knowledge. I cannot say if any one had access to said vault before that time, except Mr. Benjamin Delisle; but I do not believe any one else had.

It is not to my knowledge, either before or since I was appointed Joint High Constable, that anyone ever took any of the said goods away, or appropriated them to their own use.

[The examination of this witness is continued until to-morrow at 2 P.M.]

WEDNESDAY, 18th March, 1863.

The evidence of Mr. Adolphe Bissonette is resumed and continued as follows :—

I never saw but one key for the said vault. Besides myself as Sub-Chief of Police, all policemen who arrested robbers and theives, also delivered the articles stolen to the said High Constable, Mr. Benjamin Delisle. I have no recollection of how the vault was kept in the old Court House by the Head Constable, Mr. Benjamin Delisle, who had the keeping of the goods. The first that I produce relating to stolen goods, begins by the following entry :—

Montreal, 2nd January, 1861.

No. 7.
The Queen
v.
Oscar Barcelo.
Arson.

} The following Goods were this day placed in my custody by Mr. Alfred Porry, of Montreal, as being the property in this case :— One Piece of Grey Cotton.

(Signed,)   BENJAMIN DELISLE,
                          High Constable.

The last Pages of said book contain the following entry :—

Montreal, 18th December, 1861.

No. 23?.
The Queen
v.
S. Lemay,
F. Martel.
D. Lapierre.

} The following articles were this day placed in my custody by Louis Lacroix, as being the stolen property in this case, to wit :—Three pairs of woollen stockings, property of —

Received from Benjamin Delisle, Esq., High Constable for the District of Montreal, the articles above mentioned, in the case of the Queen vs. —

(Signed,)   MADAM S. GAUTHIER,
Louis Lacroix, Witness.

Montreal, 17th December, 1861.

There are 239 entries in the said book, some of them being entered on the back of the first 17 pages thereof.

The second book, which I now produce, contains 9 entries relating to stolen Goods, begins by the following entry :—

Montreal, 18th January, 1862.

No. 24?.
The Queen
v.
Thomas Allcock,
alias Irwin.

} The following articles were this day placed in my custody by John O'Leary, Detective of Montreal, as being the stolen property in this case, to wit :—One Gold Plated Watch, No. 896; one Silver Chain; three pair of Goggles for the eyes.

(Signed,)   DELISLE & BISSONETTE,
                          High Constables.

Received from Messrs. Delisle and Bissonette, High Constables for the District of Montreal, the articles above mentioned in the case of the Queen against —

(Signed,)   CHARLES ROY.
— Witness.

Montreal, 20th March, 1862.

This last book is now the one which I use for making my entries whenever any stolen goods are brought into my possession. These are the only two books containing entries of stolen and unclaimed goods, pertaining to the office of Joint High Constable; and I cannot produce any other book but these two belonging to the said office, as I have no other but those two in my possession, and I never saw any others in the office.

The statement which is now shown to me by the Commissioners, and which is herewith produced marked No. 1, is a list of articles which remained un-claimed in the custody of the said Joint High Constable up to the 27th January, 1863.

The statement now shown me by the Commissioners marked No. 2, is a list of articles delivered to the owners by the H. C. since the 1st January, 1861, to 27th January, 1863.

The statement now shown to me by the Commissioners, and which is herewith produced, marked No. 3, is a list of articles in the custody of the High Constable for the Courts of Queen's Bench and Quarter Sessions. These three statements are certified by Messrs. Delisle and Bissonette, Joint H. C., up to the 27th January, 1863.

Cross-examined by Mr. Delisle.

Question.—When were you named Joint High Constable ?

Answer.—On the 10th December, 1861.

Q.—On what day did you take your oath of office, and when did you assume your duties as Joint High Constable ?

A.—I was sworn on the 24th Dec., 1861, and entered upon my duties on the 2nd January, 1862.

Q.—Were you not so appointed on an application made to the Government by Mr. Benjamin Delisle, the then H. C., requesting your appointment ?

A.—Yes.

Q.—Had Mr. Benjamin Delisle previously spoken to you on that subject, and are you aware of the reasons why he desired to have you named jointly with him ?

A.—Yes.

Q.—Will you please state those reasons, and what passed between Mr. B. Delisle and yourself upon that subject ?

A.—The reasons given by Mr. B. Delisle were, that he was very old, (being then aged 73 or 74 years,) and that he thought if he had me as his partner, that the duties would be better performed; that the Constables he had in his employ were not doing their duty properly, and thought that if he had a young man with him the business would be done correctly.

Q.—What number of constables had Mr. Benjamin Delisle in his employ at that time, and please state their names ?

A.—He had two; one named William Hands, and the other Louis Lacroix.

Q.—Did you, since entering your office, dismiss the two constables, and if so for what reason ?

A.—I dismissed Hands because he would not do what I desired him to do; in fact he wanted to be more High Constable than myself; he also refused to execute warrants in Griffintown. As to Lacroix, I found him to be a man of bad character; and also I was informed that he once caused a subpœna to be served by another person, and made the return of it himself, and besides that he was a drunkard.

Q.—Do you know if those two men entertain an ill feeling against the department ?

A.—I know that they entertain an ill feeling towards me.

Q.—Do you know how Mr. Benjamin Delisle paid those two officers, was it by a fixed salary or otherwise ?

A.—It was not by a salary; they were paid so much for executing a warrant or a subpœna, or any other service.

Q.—What fee was Mr. Benjamin Delisle entitled to for the execution of a warrant, and what allowance did he make to those two constables for performing that service ?

Question rejected by the Commissioners for several

reasons, and amongst others the following :—Because it is foreign to the enquiry now in question being involved, neither in the charges nor in the defence filed, and tends merely to investigate the manner in which the High Constable for the District of Montreal, appointed under the Great Seal of the Province of Canada, has discharged his duties ; an enquiry wholly foreign to the objects of the Commission and the duties of the Commissioners, and because the question is immaterial and irrelevant.

Q.—How many years have you been employed in the Police, both in the Corporation Police and the Government Police ?

A.—Since the 13th August, 1854.

Q.—Up to what time were you employed in the Corporation or City Police ?

A.—Up to the 1st January, 1862.

Q.—Whilst in the City Police, did you not frequently take prisoners and stolen goods to the Police Office, and did you see other members of the Force do the same thing ?

A.—Yes.

Q.—To whom were those goods invariably delivered ?

A.—Always to the High Constable.

Q.—By whom were such koods produced in Court during the trials of parties accused of stealing them ?

A.—By the High Constable ; and I never saw any other officer produce such goods during trials when I was present in Court, and I was there most of the time.

Q.—Did you ever in your experience know of any case where goods were given in charge of the Clerk of the Peace or his Deputy ?

A.—No, never to my knowledge.

Q.—How many Constables or Peace Officers were attached to the City Police, and how many to the office of High Constable ?

A.—There were eighty two in all attached to the City Police, and two to the office of High Constable.

Q.—What period of time have you reference to ?

A.—From 1855 to 1862.

Q.—Were not the Goods so brought to the Police Office confined only to such as were claimed, and for which parties were to be tried for stealing them ?

A.—Yes ; and there was an order from the Police Committee that all unclaimed goods should be delivered to the Chief of Police, and sold for the benefit of the Corporation.

THURSDAY, 19th March, 1863.

Cross-examination of A. Bissonette continued by Mr. Delisle.

Q.—Were those goods accordingly sold as ordered ?

A.—Yes.

Q.—Can you say how often they were sold ?

A.—To my knowledge twice ; but they may have been sold oftener.

Q.—Can you say what amount such sales produced ?

A.—I cannot say.

Q.—Do you know if the same system is still followed by the Corporation with reference to unclaimed goods ?

A.—Yes.

Q.—Who is the present Chief of the City Police ?

A.—Mr. Guillaume Lamothe.

Q.—Then, Sir, if any such sales presently take place, they are made under the directions of Mr. Lamothe ?

A.—They are made under the orders of the Police Committee, by directions of Mr. Lamothe.

Q.—Do you know what became of the proceeds of the sales of such unclaimed goods made under the orders of said Police Committee.

A.—To the best of my knowledge the proceeds were paid to the City Treasurer.

Q.—Did not the City Police, under the orders of the Police Committee, retain all unclaimed goods, and occasionally cause them to be sold as you have mentioned ?

A.—All unclaimed goods in my possession, while I was attached to the City Police, which were not identified, and were not to be produced at the trial of criminals, were handed to the Chief of Police.

Q.—Is it to your knowledge that the same rule or course was followed by all the other members of the City Police with reference to the class of unclaimed goods referred to in your last answer ?

A.—There were strict orders to the force to do so, and to my knowledge I saw such goods handed to the Chief of Police several times.

Q.—Have cases of that kind recently, and since your appointment as Joint High Constable, occurred where unclaimed goods have been so kept by the City Police ?

A.—In the case of the Queen against John Prangley and his brother, I know that several articles that were not claimed at the time when the depositions were taken against the accused, were taken from the Police Office to the office of the Chief of the City Police, and such goods were not entered in my books, as I had no control over them, and did not form the subject matter of any trial.

Q.—Did the Clerks of the Peace or their Deputy ever assume the possession or control of the unclaimed goods in your possession ?

A.—No. As to the possession, they never assumed the possession of them ; and as to the control, I never delivered any goods except under the order of the Judge, the Crown Prosecutor, or the Clerk of the Court after trial. I refer to what occurred during my incumbency in office as Joint High Constable with Mr. Benjamin Delisle.

Q.—Is not our office the Peace Office on the 2nd flat of this building, up stairs, and are not all the duties connected with the department done there, except when the Court sits below ?

A.—Yes.

Q.—Can you not state positively that no unclaimed goods were ever removed from the vaults by any one but yourself as High Constable ?

A.—Yes.

Cross-examined by Mr. Schiller.

Q.—You have said that you were in attendance on the Court of Q. B. and Quarter Sessions and Police Office since 1855. Did you ever, during that time, see me present at the High Constable's office when goods were received or delivered, or did you ever see me handling any of them ?

A.—I may have seen Mr. Schiller present once or twice when goods were so received or delivered, but I am positive that he never had anything to do with them.

Q.—In all cases where you brought goods or monies, did they turn out all correct at and after the trial of the parties accused ?

A.—Yes, decidedly so. I never saw one article missing.

Q.—Since you are in charge of the stolen goods as High Constable, did you ever perceive that anything was deranged or disturbed in the said vault ?

A.—No.

Re-examined by the Commissioners.

The Corporation has been disposing of the unclaimed stolen goods, to my knowledge, since the year 1855. I believe there is no law authorizing the Corporation to do so. I do not know if the Joint Clerk of the Peace ever remonstrated with the Corporation regarding such a practice. The goods were brought before the Magistrate, and, oftentimes, only those that were claimed, and the remainder was taken back to the Police Station for further investigation, in case the owner thereof should appear. That is, all goods taken by the Police under suspicion of having been stolen, were primarily brought to the Police Court, as also the party accused of stealing, when in custody, and after preliminary investigation before the Magistrate. If there was no case made out, the goods in question were taken back to the Police Station to see if an owner came forward to claim them, and the party arrested was discharged. For example, when the Prince of Wales was at Montreal in 1860, I arrested two parties on suspicion of being pickpockets. On their person was found three gold diamond studs, and a gold breast-pin. When brought before the Police Magistrate, no owner claimed those articles. Mr. Coursol, the Police Magistrate, told me to keep those articles in charge, to see if I could not find an owner. Sometime afterwards I was brought before the Police Committee, and ordered to deliver over those articles to the Chief of Police, so that they might be sold for the benefit of the Corporation. And I accordingly did so, and handed them over with other articles to the Chief of Police.

There is a difference between the Police and the Peace Office, and my reason for stating so is, that Mr. Coursol has his own clerks, and the Joint Clerks of the Peace have also their own. I understand that I am and act under the instructions of the different Courts of Criminal Jurisdiction. It is true and to my knowledge that the Clerk of the Peace is the Clerk of the Police Court when in Session, and as such receives all fines, and superintends the execution of all judgments therein rendered. Hands refused to execute warrants in Griffintown, but I cannot recollect in what cases; and he wanted to be more master than myself.

[Evidence closed.]

Benjamin Delisle, Joint High Constable, sworn, &c. I am aged seventy-four years, and am the uncle of Mr. A. M. Delisle.

I was named High Constable for the District of Montreal in 1830 or 1831, and have acted as such ever since, and for about the last two years conjointly with Mr. Adolphe Bissonette.

I kept no books nor accounts of stolen goods which came into my possession, but have some receipts for such goods, showing when I delivered them to the owners after trial.

I have no account sales respecting such stolen goods. There was one sale made of such goods unclaimed during my term of office, which took place some time ago, and which is the only one I remember during my time of office.

The book now produced by Mr. Schiller was not kept by me, but I had access to it. The best part of it is in the handwriting of Mr. René Cotret. The first entry in the said book appears as follows :—

1843. Dec. 23. The Queen *vs.* George Desloriers, Larceny. One pair of moleskin trowsers, property of Gilbert Hazel.

The last entry in the said book appears as follows :

1857.	Larceny. Delivered to Wm.
July 15. The Queen *vs.*	Hands, 1 black Frock Coat, 1 pair of black Pantaloons, &c.
John Hagarty.	&c., given to H. C. by

WM. HANDS.

This book was never kept by me. This book is a record of the names of the parties arrested, and the offences with which they were charged, and the goods found in their possession, handed over to me by the different constables therein mentioned, and by the police.

FRIDAY, 20th March, 1863.

Evidence of Mr. B. Delisle continued.

I had the key of the vault in which stolen goods were placed, and when they were wanted for trial, I produced them. I cannot say how long I had the key. In the old Court House there was a vault for the purpose of depositing stolen goods. The stolen goods were deposited in that vault, and I used to produce them when required. I am not aware that there were two keys to that vault. I used sometimes to lock that key in my desk, and in the day time was in the habit of hanging it up in my office. Generally I used to accompany persons who went to the vault for goods. It very seldom happened that I sent other parties to get goods in that vault. When I did they were persons I could depend upon, but I cannot recollect their names. As to the entry concerning one gold locket entered in the said book as having been given to me by Wm. Hands in the case of John Hagarty, on the 15th July, 1857, I can give no account from memory, but will, with your permission, look over the vouchers in my possession to ascertain, if possible, how it has been disposed of. I cannot presently produce any voucher to show to whom I returned the said locket; but I shall make a search for the receipt, which I must have taken for it. As to the entry in the said book of the 22nd June, 1857, in the case of the Queen against John Albreck respecting a hand organ, of the value of £50, therein mentioned as being the property of one Laurent Castoner, I produce a receipt given to me on the 20th Oct., 1857, by that man, which is as follows :—

The Queen *vs.* John Albreck.	Larceny. A small organ, the property of Laurent Castoner, given by me to C. Coulombe and Simard, of

the Police, on the 22nd June, 1857.

"Received the above organ from the High Constable, 20th October, 1857.

Witness,   (Signed,)
W. Tetu.   LAURENT M. CASTONER."

As to the entry in the said book in the case of the Queen against Joseph Beaudry, bearing date 18th July, 1862, relating to a silk purse containing £22 10s. 0d. in half eagles, given to me by Charles Coulombe and J. B. Simard, I now produce a memorandum and receipt, which is as follows, viz. :—

The Queen against Joseph Beaudry. Larceny.

18 Half American Eagles, at 25s. each	£22	10	0
12 English Shillings	0	15	0
8 Coppers	0	0	4
	£22	5	4

[*N.B.*—An error in addition of 20s.]

On the back is written :

" Received the within amount of twenty-two pounds 5s. 4d., from Benjamin Delisle, Constable, on the 8th day of October, 1852.

(Signed,)   THEOPHILE HURTUBISE."

As to the entry in the said book in the case of the Queen against Eugene Bellefleur, of the 25th June, 1857, concerning one gold ring therein mentioned as being the property of Abraham Hoffnung, I produce a receipt which is as follows, viz.:—The Queen against Eugene Bellefleur, Larceny. One Gold Ring, the property of Wm. Hoffnung, given to me by Tobias Burke, of the City Police, on the 25th June, 1857.

(Signed,)   B. D., H. C.

"Received the above stated Ring, from Mr. B. Delisle, High Constable.

(Signed.)   A. T. BRAZEAU."

Montreal, 9th July, 1857.

As to the entry in the said book in the ears of the Queen against Alexr. McKenzie, of the 4th August, 1848, which is as follows, viz.:—About 150 lbs. weight of Copper Pipes, property of Joseph Knapp.

I produce an order and receipt, which is as follows:—

Montreal, 10th Nov., 1848.

SIR,—Will you be so good as to deliver to the bearer the brass cocks, stoppers, copper pipe, &c., the property which Alexander McKenzie was convicted of having stolen from the St. Mary Distillery, and oblige

Your most obd'nt Servant,

(Signed,)   JAMES LOGAN.

Benj. Delisle, Esq.,

High Constable.

"Received the articles within mentioned from Benjamin Delisle, High Constable in and for the District of Montreal. Montreal, 10th Nov., 1848.

(Signed.)   JAS. LOGAN."

per James Williamson.

As to the entry of the Queen against Thos. McLeod and al, of the 3rd July, 1848, concerning six brooches, nine pairs of ear-rings, and several other articles therein mentioned as being the property of Genevieve Homan. and of the Queen vs. Nathan G. Cross and al, of the 8th June, 1848, on a charge of counterfeiting, concerning 33 counterfeit Mexican dollars. 12 American half dollars, and several other articles; and also of the Queen against Eustache Chatter, concerning 18 dollars and one cotton shirt, the property of Etienne Vigneau. I have been unable to find any vouchers showing what disposition has been made of the same. As to the counterfeit coin, my duty was to show them to some authority before destroying them. I do not remember what became of the coin in question. I cannot say why the said book was stopped from and after the 15th July, 1857; nor can I say the reason why no entry appears in the said book from the year 1853 and for the year 1855, nor why there are only seven entries of cases in 1854, only one for the year 1856, and twelve for the year 1857. I do not know that any one ever removed or appropriated to his own use any of the goods entrusted to my care as stolen goods. It is not to my knowledge that any person has ever taken any such goods on the understanding that they would pay for them when they would be sold by auction.

———

SATURDAY, 21st March, 1863.

Indictments are produced by Mr. Schiller, Deputy Clerk of the Crown for the Court of Queen's Bench for 1856, and by Mr. Drehaut, of Indictments, found in Quarter Sessions for 1856, at the request of the Commissioners.

Benjamin Delisle's evidence is resumed.

As to the entry in the said book in the case of the Queen against James May and al, of 15th September, 1851, concerning the sum of £5 17s. 6d. in British shillings therein mentioned, as the property of William Tucker, I have not as yet been able to find any voucher showing how the same has been disposed of. As to the entries in the said book in the case of the Queen vs. Mark Scholes and al, 14th April, 1852, concerning one watch guard therein mentioned as the property of Philip Carrol, and one old silver watch, and one watch key, the property of persons unknown. And of the Queen vs. Martin Healy, 23rd January, 1852, concerning seventeen pieces of firewood therein mentioned, as the property of Prisque Gravel, and one traineau unclaimed; and of the Queen vs. Francis McNulty, 18th March, 1851, relating to one pack of clothes lines unclaimed, I have as yet been unable to find any vouchers showing what disposition has been made of the same.

A statement marked "A," now shewn to me by the Commissioners, and herewith produced and headed "List of unclaimed Monies now in the possession of the High Constable for the District of Montreal," and handed over by that officer to Mr. Schiller in September, 1859, showing that the sum of £27 5s. 7½d. was handed over to me as High Constable for the District of Montreal to Mr. Schiller, in Sept., 1859, but I have no recollection of that fact. I do not recollect whether that money ever went through my hands. I have no vouchers that I know in my possession to show that I paid that amount in a lump sum to Mr. Schiller. I might or might not. I might sometimes take receipts from Mr. Schiller for unclaimed monies handed over to him, but seldom. I cannot recollect any particular case when I took a receipt from Mr. Schiller. I cannot give any explanation concerning the last item of the said statement, which is as follows:—Vincenzo Montesi, (recognizance) £5 4s. 4d., and, in fact, I cannot give any explanation at all concerning that item. I do not see any dates to any of the items mentioned in said statement. The said statement is certified by Mr. Schiller as Deputy Clerk of the Peace, as I know his signature.

Cross-examined by Mr. Delisle.

Question.—Were not the stolen goods which were brought to the Police Office always handed over to you, and had you not the exclusive charge and keeping of them from your appointment to office in 1830 or 1831, up to the time Mr. Bissonette was named High Constable conjointly with you?

Answer.—Yes.

Q.—Did you not apply, long ago, to Government to be made some allowance for the onerous and responsible duty which you discharged in keeping and accounting for such goods, and what answer did you get?

A.—I applied some five or six years ago, but did not get anything.

Q.—Do you recollect if you submitted to the Court of Q. B. a list of the unclaimed stolen goods in your possession, in order to obtain the authority to sell them on the occasion mentioned in your examination in chief?

A.—Yes, I think I remember that.

Cross-examined by Mr. Schiller.

Q.—Do you recollect that the Court House was burnt on the 17th July, 1844, and that all the stolen goods were consumed on that occasion?

A.—I do perfectly.

Q.—You have said in your examination in chief that you hung the key of the vault where stolen goods were kept in your office. Do you mean that it was exposed to public view?

A.—No, not at all. I kept the key in a small cupboard locked up in the office in the day time, and took it home every evening.

Q.—Were your office and desk not broken open in the night during the time when the Prince of Wales was in Montreal?

A.—Yes.

Q.—Did I ever go in the vault where the stolen goods were kept alone?

A.—No, you did not generally go alone. You frequently came with me to point out the goods required for trials, and further, deponent saith not.

EXPLANATIONS given by Mr. Delisle and Mr. Brehaut with reference to the book of stolen goods referred to in Mr. Benjamin Delisle's examination. Messrs. Delisle and Brehaut made the following statement:—

"With reference to the book in question, we beg to "state that it forms no part of the books belonging to the "office of the Clerk of the Peace; that it was opened "and kept, as far as it goes, with a view of assisting "Mr. Benjamin Delisle, as he always had the exclu- "sive charge and keeping of the stolen and unclaimed "goods; that what is written in that book was done "with no other view than of aiding and being useful "to him, and that we disclaim any responsibility in "reference to it, inasmuch as we never, at any time, "were given or had the charge, custody, or keeping of "stolen or unclaimed property.

"That in point of fact, the books produced by Mr. "High Constable Bissonette before the Commission- "ers, and which have been opened and kept since "1861 by the High Constable, are substantially what "the book, first referred to, was intended to be, to "wit: a book for the use of the High Constable, and "not for the Clerk of the Peace.

"That in proper time we shall be prepared to es- "tablish not only that we never had the charge of "such goods, but that the nature of our office and of "our duties as Joint Clerk of the Peace rendered it "impractible that we should do so, and that the Act "6 Wm. 4, chap. 5 in the Consolidated Statutes, chap. "104, in so far as it relates to the Clerk of the Peace "is, and has ever been, inoperative.

(Signed,) A. M. DELISLE,
 W. H. BREHAUT."

Montreal, 21st March, 1863.

1863, } The Commissioners intimate that Mr.
April 2nd } Schiller received £50 in deposit in 1859, and that this sum has not been accounted for. It was in a case of

The Queen } Indictment found in Queen's Bench
vs. } in September, 1859, on an accusation
John Greene. } of stealing jewellery valued at £11 5s. 0d., the said sum of £50 having been deposited as security on the personal bond of the said Greene, taken by Mr. Coursol, the Inspector and Superintendent of Police.

SATURDAY, 4th April, 1863.

Mr. A. M. Delisle submitted the following statement, viz.:—

"Being called upon to explain how the proced- "ure, where recognizances were forfeited, was "had, under the 120 and 121st sections of chapter "99 of the Consolidated Statutes of Canada, and "if the lists of such recognizances were submitted "to the Justices of the Courts therein mentioned, "for the purpose of being forfeited, estreated, or "put in process in the terms of the said 121st sec- 'tion of said Act, I would remark that that branch

"of the duties of the office devolved upon me. "The course followed by the Crown prosecutors, "representing the Hon. the Attorney General, and "sanctioned by the Criminal Courts, precluded "any necessity for the submission of such lists, for "in all cases of default on such recognizances the "same were either declared to be forfeited at once, "or the default recorded, which involved a for- "feiture; that then copies of the said recog- "nizances, and of the orders made thereon by the "Court, were handed to the Attorney General, or "his representative and the necessary legal pro- "ceedings adopted for the recovery of the amounts "so forfeited to the Crown, whenever the Crown "saw fit to take action thereon, which was fre- "quently done.

"When forfeitures were recovered the amount "never came into the hands of the Clerk of the "Crown, or of the Peace, but was accounted for by "such Attorney General or his representative to "Government."

WEDNESDAY, 8th April, 1863.

Present:

Messrs. LAFRENAYE and DOHERTY.

Joseph Doutre, Esq., Advocate, entered the room, and claimed the privilege of being admitted, on the ground that he represented, or appeared on behalf of the Public.

"The undersigned urgently protest against any departure by the Commissioners from the manner of proceeding hitherto practised by them in this enquiry, by the admission of any one thereat, and which they understood, when the investigation was opened, was the course intended to be followed by the Commissioners, and which, so far, has been acted upon. They respectfully urge upon the Consideration of the Commissioners that they have been appointed under the Statute to collect and receive evidence for the information of the Executive Government of this Province only, and that their delegated authority does not extend beyond those powers. Any alteration by the Commissioners by which the public shall be permitted to participate in the enquiry, would be contrary to the intent of the Statute, and extremely unjust and injurious to the undersigned by subjecting them to public animadversion and reproach, without the means of protection, and compelling them to submit to public judgment without the legal advantage of a trial, and long before their defence can be made to appear. Like Grand Jurors, the Commissioners report their evidence to the Government to be acted upon, and any departure from this manner of conducting the enquiry, would and can only tend to prejudice the public mind against them; and that the admission of any one individual would necessarily warrant and justify the admission of the public at large, and thus frustrate the intention of the law, which manifestly intends that the Executive Government shall receive the *first* communication of the evidence taken in the enquiry."

Respectfully submitted.

(Signed,) A. M. DELISLE.
 W. H. BREHAUT.
Montreal, 8th April, 1863. · C. E. SCHILLER.

The Commissioners rejected the above protest. and admitted the public, and Joseph Doutre, Esq. and the

B

Reporters of the Montreal *Herald* and Montreal *Gazette*, and others, entered.

THURSDAY, 9th April, 1863.

William Hands, of Montreal, Grocer, is sworn, and says:—I know the parties Messrs. Delisle and Brehaut, and Schiller. I commenced the grocery business on 1st May, 1862, in the City of Montreal, and still continue that business. I am aged 48 years. Previous to this time I was employed as a Constable in the High Constable's office, Mr. Benjamin Delisle, and had been so occupied for about eleven years. My duties as such constable were the executing of warrants, the service of subpœnas, escorting prisoners to and from gaol. I was also, during this time, engaged during the Sessions of the Court of Queen's Bench in serving subpœnas of the said Court, running as messenger for the Crown Prosecutor, and taking charge of Petty Jurors when they were locked up at night.

I was paid by the Sheriff for keeping the Jurors, and by the Crown as Messenger.

For the execution of warrants, I was paid by the High Constable, Mr. Benjamin Delisle, and for services of subpœnas out of session. I was paid by Mr. Schiller only in cases of Assault and Battery disposed of in the Police Court; and by Mr. Benjamin Delisle for services in revenue cases ; and in cases of sailors' wages I was also paid by Mr. Schiller. I did nothing with regard to any other office, except as constable. Except that I acted as agent for Mr. A. M. Delisle in collecting house rents for twelve months. To the best of my belief this was the year before the late Mr. Harvey became clerk in the office of the Peace. Mr. Harvey succeeded me in the collection of these rents, and I saw him accounting for rents from time to time to Mr. Schiller. I had no fixed salary during my connection of eleven years with the office of the Peace as constable, as aforesaid, nor in any other capacity, except the year I acted as agent for Mr. Delisle. What I received from Mr. Delisle while engaged in collecting his rents, I was paid £10 in money for that year. I think it was Mr. Schiller who paid them to me. I was also to get a small house from Mr. Delisle, free of rent, in Visitation Street, for my services as such agent. There were several of them, and all were very cold, except one which was warm, but, however, I could not get that one. I had no other monthly or quarterly salary from any other source, except a small pension as having been, formerly, in the Irish Constabulary. The pension was paid to me through the Commissariat, at Montreal.

Q.—Is it or is it not true that during a part of the eleven years of your connection with the said office of the Peace, and more particularly during the year 1854 and part of the year 1855, you received from Government a regular annual salary paid to you quarterly, and at the same time that the salaries of the employees of the said office were paid?

A.—It is not true. I have never received nor been paid quarterly, nor otherwise, any sum or salary whatever from Government for my services in the office of the Clerk of the Peace, except once that I received twenty dollars from Mr. Schiller through Mr. Brehaut, as both were present, at the time, and intimated to me that it was a *Christmas present.* I was never nominated as a clerk in the Peace Office, that is, I never understood that I was appointed a clerk in said department, nor did I receive any salary as such, but used to fill subpœnas, and might copy some documents for Mr. Schiller when he called upon me. Mr. Schiller often put things in my way, that is, did me favors, and I did not like to refuse to help him when he was in a hurry. To the best of my recollection I signed, during my connection with the said office, the pay-lists forwarded to the Government specifying the salaries of the clerks in the Peace department. I think I so signed *twice* such pay-lists. Mr. Schiller asked me to sign them, and I did not know the motive. I only suspected at the time that Mr. Schiller had advanced the money to a former clerk, and that he wanted to draw it through me. I also thought that I was to be appointed a clerk myself, and this was one of the reasons that induced me to sign. Another reason was, that I did not think Mr. Schiller would ask me to do anything wrong. I never drew nor received the items of salary specified in the said pay-lists, and for which I so signed.

I do not remember the amounts of the items for which I so signed; it did not make much impression upon me at the time, as I did not expect to get the money at the time. Having examined the pay-list for quarter, ended on the 31st March, 1854, (of the office of the Clerk of the Peace,) being a statement of the salaries of the officers and clerks of the said office, and an exact duplicate of the same entered in the account current book, with the Provincial Government, from the 10th Sept., 1850, to 31st Dec., 1861, which forms part of the books produced before the Commissioners on the 14th March last past, with which I have now compared the said list, and in which I see that my name has been returned as an officer or clerk in said department, charging for me at the rate of £50 per annum, I declare that I never got a copper of it as clerk in or any other way, and it is now the first time that I knew that my name was entered on said book as clerk or officer in the office of the Clerk of the Peace for the District of Montreal.

The following is a copy of the said pay-list:—

DISTRICT OF MONTREAL,
Office of the Clerk of the Peace.

Name of Officer.	Nature of Office.	Period from 1st Jan. to 31st March.	Amount in Currency.
A. M. Delisle,	Clerk of Peace.	1st Jan. to 31st March. at £350	£97 10 0
W. H. Brehaut,	do. do.	do. at 350	87 10 0
C. E. Schiller,	Deputy. do.	do. at 125	31 5 0
L. D. R. Cotret,	1st Clerk.	do. to 28th Feb. at 125	31 5 0
George Baby,	2nd Clerk.	do. at 50	4 3 0
Wm. Hands,	2nd do.	1st March. at 8	8 6 8
Louis Malo.	Crier Qr. Sessions.	1st Jan. to 31st March. at 30	7 10 0
Commission on £96 15s. 5d., being net proceeds of account current, rendered for the Quarter ending 31st December, 1853, Voucher No. 1			9 13 6
Office Expenses, Voucher No. 1			1 16 0
			£298 19 6

The Commissioners now declare that the receipted pay-list for said quarter has not been transmitted to them from the office of the Honorable the Inspector-General of Public Accounts for this Province, although such receipted pay-list was asked for by their letter, dated the 14th March last, addressed to the Hon. Provincial Secretary; but that in lieu of such pay-list an acquitted warrant was transmitted to them, and which they now produce as forming part of this investigation, and by which receipted warrant it appears that the amount of said quarter, to wit: £268 19s. 6d. was paid to Messrs. Delisle and Brehaut.

The examination of the witness is continued as follows:—

I have just examined the unsigned pay-list for the quarter, ended 30th June, 1854, which appears to have been transmitted to the Government for payment, and upon the back of which it is certified by Joseph Cary, Deputy Inspector-General, that a warrant may issue for the payment of £284 1s. 1d. in favor of the said Clerk of the Peace, and by which I see that the sum of £50 is placed to my credit, or charged against the Government in my favor as an annual rate or salary as 2nd clerk in said office of the Clerk of the Peace, and in which my quarter's salary purports to be £12 10s. 0d.; and I have now to declare in reference to the said charge and pay-list, that I do not think I ever signed said list, and I am positive that I never re-received the sum of money set down to my name, nor any part of it.

FRIDAY, 10th April, 1863.

The evidence of Wm. Hands is resumed.

The last above-mentioned pay-list is in the words and figures following:—

list for this quarter has not been transmitted to them by the Government. In lieu thereof, an acquitted warrant was transmitted to them, and which they now produce as forming part of this investigation, and by which receipted warrant it appears that the amount of the said quarter, amounting to £284 1s. 1d., was paid to Messrs. Delisle and Brehaut, being the amount of the above pay-list for said quarter, an exact copy of which said unsigned pay-list is to be found at page 88 in the Account Current Book with the Provincial Government, from 10th Sept., 1850, to 31st Dec., 1861, which forms part of the books produced before the Commissioners on the 14th March last past, by the late Joint Clerk of the Peace.

Having just examined the pay-list for the Quarter ended 30th Sept., 1854, in which again I find myself entered as 2nd clerk in the office of the Peace, at a salary of £50 per annum, and by which it appears that I signed a receipt for the sum of £12 10s. 0d., purporting to be my quarter's salary as such clerk, I have to say in reference thereto that the signature Wm. Hands in said pay-list is my signature, but I never received the said amount of £12 10s. 0d., nor any part thereof. I have already stated my reasons why I signed such a pay-list. I recollect only two pay-lists that I signed, and this is one of them, and I think it was some time after Mr. Baby had left the office of the Peace that I signed such pay-list. The said pay-list is in the form following, to wit:—

Name of Officer	Nature of Office	Period from 1st July to 30th Sept. 1854	Rate per Annum	Total Currency
A. M. Delisle	Clerk of Peace	1st July to 30th Sept.	£350	£87 10 0
W. H. Brehaut	do.		350	87 10 0
C. E. Schiller	Deputy do.		125	31 5 0
L. D. R. Cotrel	1st Clerk		125	31 5 0
Wm. Hands	2nd Clerk		50	12 10 0
Louis Malo	Crier Qr. Sessions		30	7 10 0
	Office Expences	Voucher No. 1.		2 0 6
				£259 10 6

We hereby acknowledge having received the amount opposite our respective names, in full, of salary to date. (Signed,)

A. M. Delisle ... £87 10 0
W. H. Brehaut ... 87 10 0
C. E. Schiller ... 31 5 0
L. D. R. Cotrel ... 31 5 0
Wm. Hands ... 12 10 0
Louis Malo ... 7 10 0
Office Expences, Voucher No. 1 ... 2 0 6
£259 10 6

Name of Officer	Nature of Office	Period from 1st April to 30th June	Rate per Annum	Amount in Currency
A. M. Delisle	Clerk of Peace	1st April to 30th June	£350	£87 10 0
W. H. Brehaut	do.		350	87 10 0
C. E. Schiller	Deputy do.		125	31 5 0
L. D. R. Cotrel	1st Clerk		125	31 5 0
Wm. Hands	2nd Clerk		50	12 10 0
Louis Malo	Crier Qr. Sessions		30	7 10 0
	Office Expences	Voucher No. 1.		3 15 0
	Stationery	Voucher No. 2.		13 4 4
	Postage	Voucher No. 3.		16 2 4
				£284 1 1

We hereby acknowledge having received the amount opposite our respective names, in full, of salary to date. (Signed)

A. M. Delisle ... £87 10 0
W. H. Brehaut ... 87 10 0
C. E. Schiller ... 31 5 0
L. D. R. Cotrel ... 31 5 0
Wm. Hands ... 12 10 0
Louis Malo ... 7 10 0
Vouchers Nos. 1, 2 and 3 ... 26 11 1
£284 1 1

The Commissioners declare that the receipted pay-

This statement of pay-list appears to be a copy from the Account Current Book herein before mentioned, with which I have just compared it. In regard to the pay-list for the quarter, ended the 31st Dec., 1854, now shown to me, the signature "Wm. Hands" thereto set is my hand-writing; but I never received the £12 10s. nor any part thereof set in said pay-list against my name as 2nd Clerk in the office of the Clerk of the Peace. It was Mr. Schiller who asked me to sign said pay-list. I did not like to disoblige him, and did not think there was any bad motive for so doing. My impression was, that the Clerk of the Peace was after paying a salary in advance to a clerk who retired, and that I was got to sign it for the purpose of having the money refunded to the Clerk of the Peace from the Government. I also thought that I was, perhaps, going to get the situation myself.

Copy of pay-list:—

Name of Officer.	Nature of Office.	Period from 1st Oct. to 31st Dec., 1854.	Rate, &c.	Total.
A. M. Delisle,	Clerk of the Peace.	1st Oct. to 31st Dec.	£550	£97 10 0
W. H. Brehaut,	Deputy do.	do.	550	87 10 0
C. E. Schiller,	1st Clerk.	do.	125	31 5 0
L. R. D. Cotret,	2nd Clerk.	do.	125	31 5 0
Wm. Hands,	Grier Qr. Sessions.	do.	50	12 10 0
Louis Malo,	do.	do.	30	7 10 0
Office Expenses and Printing, Voucher No. 1				6 13 4
Stationery				14 17 2
Postage				4 9 0
				47 12 3
				£305 2 3

We hereby acknowledge having received the amount opposite our respective names in full, of salary to date.

(Signed,)
A. M. Delisle.
W. H. Brehaut.
C. E. Schiller.
L. D. R. Cotret.
Wm. Hands.
Louis Malo.
Vouchers Nos. 1, 2 and 3.

£305 2 3

I see also by the examination of the pay-list for the quarter ending 31st March, 1855, that I signed a receipt or receipted said for pay-list the sum of £12 10s. 0d., charged therein in my favor as 2nd Clerk as aforesaid; and have to declare, also, in reference to this pay-list, that I never was such clerk, and never received said sum of money nor any part of it. Said pay-list is also receipted by A. M. Delisle, W. H. Brehaut, C. E. Schiller, L. D. Rene Cotret, and Louis Malo. The signatures at the bottom of said pay-list are as follows:—A. M. Delisle, W. H. Brehaut, C. E. Schiller, L. D. Rene Cotret, Wm. Hands, Louis Malo. I am well acquainted with the signatures of Mr. A. M. Delisle, W. H. Brehaut, C. E. Schiller, L. D. Rene Cotret, for having seen them sign and write their names often in my presence, and I therefore declare that the signature A. M. Delisle set and subscribed at the foot of the said pay-list is in the hand-writing of Mr. Delisle; and that the signature W. H. Brehaut, set and subscribed at the foot of the said pay-list is in the hand-writing of Mr. W. H. Brehaut;

and that the signature of C. E. Schiller, set and subscribed at the foot of the said pay-list, is in the hand-writing of Mr. C. E. Schiller; and that the signature L. D. Rene Cotret, set and subscribed at the foot of the said pay-list, is in the hand-writing of Mr. L. D. Rene Cotret.

I have just examined the pay-list for the period from the 1st day of January to the 30th June, 1855, now shown to me by the Commissioners. It is receipted by me in connection with the other gentlemen above described, each for the item of salary therein specified against his name. I declare that I was not second clerk as therein specified for the period of time therein mentioned, nor that I was ever notified to me that I was a clerk, nor did I ever receive a copper of the salary therein mentioned, and with which the Government is charged in my name, and which, in this case, appears to have been so charged at the rate of £125 a year. The signature A. M. Delisle, set and subscribed at the foot of the said pay-list, is in the hand-writing of Mr. A. M. Delisle. The signature W. H. Brehaut, set and subscribed at the foot of the said pay-list, is in the hand-writing of W. H. Brehaut; the signature C. E. Schiller, set and subscribed at the foot of the said pay-list, is in the hand-writing of Mr. C. E. Schiller; and the signature L. D. Rene Cotret, set and subscribed at the foot of the said pay-list, is in the hand-writing of Mr. L. D. Rene Cotret. Copy of the said last-mentioned pay-list marked "A," is herewith produced with my deposition, and I now desire to state, in explanation, that the documents I alluded to in the commencement of my evidence as having signed as pay-lists, those were the signatures I alluded to as having signed, were those two pay-lists for the quarters ending 30th Sept., 1854, and 31st Dec., 1854. With regard to the two others for the quarters ending 31st March, 1855, and for the period from the 1st January to the 30th June, 1855, I signed them, not knowing whether they were pay-lists or not.

I was a constable, and acted as such during the whole of the year 1854, during which year I served, in the month of January two summonses, now shown to me, that is, in the cases of "The Montreal Turnpike Trustees vs. Ant. Vinet dit Souligny." The same against Joseph Lachapelle; the same against Joseph Vinet; the same against Joseph Borne; and Charles Coulombe against Noel Mareille, issued out of the Peace Office. In March, 1854, I perceive on looking at the records now shown to me, that I served a subpœna in the case of Cox vs. McLaren, acting as such constable as aforesaid; and also in the month of August of said year, I served as constable the summonses in the cases of the Deputy Revenue Inspector vs. J. B. Simard and Joseph Chapeleau. In the month of Sept., 1854, I perceive on looking at the records now shown to me, that I served the summonses, and served some subpœnas in the following cases, viz., issued out of the said Peace Office, to wit.: the Attorney General vs. Amable Prevost and al; the same vs. Jerome Grenier; the same vs. Ant. Bouthillier; the same vs. Andre Lapierre and al; the same vs. Gilbert Gauthier; Durnford vs. Martel; the same vs. Correstine; and also in the cases of Casey vs. John Palmer, Casey vs. Wm. Jackson.

In the month of Nov., 1854, I perceive on looking at the Records now shown to me, that I served as constable the summons and also a suubpœna in the case of the Harbor Commissioners of Montreal vs. Richard Norton, the same being issued out of the

Peace Office aforesaid; and also in the case of Philip Durnford, Revenue Inspector, vs. Thomas Dunn. I served as such constable a summons, a subpœna, and I executed a warrant of distress issued in that last-mentioned case, and deducted my fees out of the proceeds of the sale; and I also served in said month the summonses and some subpœnas in the cases of the Attorney General vs. Demerse; the same vs. Goyette; the same vs. Derome; and the same vs. Marcotte, and in the cases of Durnford vs. Jones; the same vs. Vandal; also in the cases of the Harbor Commissioners vs. Trudeau; the same vs. Contant; the same vs. Dudevoir; Casey vs. Burns.

I continued to act as such constable through the year 1855, during which year I served as many documents as by small fees managed to support my family. Perhaps I might have executed 200 or 300 warrants during that year, and I see that I served a summons in the case of the Attorney-General vs. James Smith, now shown to me, and which was issued out of the Peace Office in April, 1855

SATURDAY, 11th April, 1863.

William Hands re-appears, and continues his examination as follows, viz. :—

I have, from time to time, when acting as constable, arrested parties in the possession of stolen goods. I remember one case in particular, when I found a lot of money on the person of a woman. The High Constable was present, and I gave both money and prisoner up to him. The stolen goods so found by the constables were marked and handed over to the High Constable. Such stolen goods, however, were always produced and brought into Court with the persons arrested for stealing them. After the investigation of the prisoner's case, such goods were again returned to the High Constable.

With this deposition the Commissioners have produced the different pay-lists herein mentioned, and the papers accompanying such pay-lists for the quarters hereinbefore mentioned, and certain acquitted warrants hereinbefore mentioned and transmitted to them from the office of the Hon. the Inspector General to form part of this investigation, and for the purposes thereof, and which were given in communication to Messrs. Delisle, Brehaut and Schiller.

Cross-examined by Mr. Delisle.

Question.—As Clerk of the Crown did I not occupy separate rooms from the offices of the Peace and Police Office, and did I not transact my business as Joint Clerk of the Peace there?

Answer.—I have not known you to transact business as Clerk of the Peace in your office of Clerk of the Crown. I never saw you acting as Clerk of the Peace in the Police Office; but I know that you occupied separate rooms, except once that I saw you take a deposition in the Police Office. I always saw Mr. Schiller transact the business in the Peace Office, and the Court below.

Q.—Did any one speak to you about the evidence you were to give in this case, and if so, please to name the person or persons?

A.—Yes; two or three persons, and perhaps more, did speak to me on the subject. A clergyman spoke to me at my house, and took me into my room and spoke me privately. He asked was I to give evidence against Messrs. Delisle and Brehaut. I told him that I did not know, that I was not summoned; that I believed there was a Commission to sit. He asked me first what I had to say, and what the case was. I then told him that there was a gentleman in the office named Charles M. Delisle, who was a clerk in the office, and who, I believed, to be a very bad man; that he left the office and went away; that he wrote a letter to some newspaper in Montreal, which was published, and that my name was mentioned in it as being a clerk in the office, and a salary drawn for me by the Clerks of the Peace. I then told him I was never a clerk in the office, nor ever received a salary, with the exception of $20 that I got from Mr. Brehaut. I told him that if I was called up, I would tell the truth, and he told me to do so.

I don't know how he came there, or who sent him to me.

Since the publication of Mr. Charles Delisle's letter in the papers, and about the time that the clergyman called,—I think it was before, Mr. Brehaut called at my house about nightfall,—and asked me "Did any of those fellows come here to you?" "What fellows, Sir?" says I. "Why," says he, "Charley Delisle and Lacroix, and those fellows are conspiring against Mr. Delisle and me to injure us." "Sir," says I, "I have nothing to do with them, and I have not seen Mr. Charles Delisle since he left the office, nor neither do I want to have anything to do with them." He said that if any of them came about the place, to send them away. I said I would, that I had nothing to do with them; that I was not in contact with them. About a week afterwards I came to the Court House, and I think there was a Court sitting, because there were people in the passage. Mr. Schiller was coming up the stairs, and he asked me would I buy a cow. I said that I did not want one then, that I was going to buy one on the first of May. Mr. Brehaut also passed me then, and likewise asked me if I would buy a cow. I then thought there was something extraordinary in the question, and I do not understand what was meant then, nor do I now know what they meant. Then Mr. Brehaut called me into his room and asked me what I had to say if I was called on. I said that I had nothing to say, but that I signed two pay-lists, and that I received twenty dollars from him. "From me?" says he. "Yes, Sir, I think you were present (says I) when I received the money from Mr. Schiller, and Mr. Schiller said that it was a Christmas present from Mr Brehaut." He then said "Did I not receive more?" "No, Sir," says I; "I never received a copper but that, meaning the twenty dollars." "Well," says he, "I have your receipts for the entire amount." "If you have, then," says I, "they are a forgery." He then said, "how much would compensate you for what you did in the office?" "Well, Sir," says I, "I do not think that I am entitled to any compensation, for I did nothing that I would require payment for." Says he, "did you not fill some documents, and write in the office now and again?" "I did, Sir," says I, "fill some subpœnas and copied some documents, but it was very seldom." He then asked me what was my reason for signing the pay-lists. I said that Mr. Schiller asked me, and that I did not like to refuse him, and that I expected that he would have given me the situation of clerk at the time. He said that would, too, but that I was not capable of filling the register. Mr. Roy, a lawyer, the younger of two brothers who are lawyers, and who pleads in the Police Court below, and who is short and stout, also spoke to me, and asked me if I had signed the pay-list and received the pay as clerk. I told him that when he would be appointed on the commission, I would tell him all about it.

Q.—Did any one speak to you on the same subject before the publication of Mr. Charles M. Delisle's letter. If so please name the parties, and say what passed?

A.--Mr. Matthew Ryan spoke to me in the Court House, I suppose about five years ago, and asked me did I sign a pay-list and get money as acting Clerk. I told him I did sign two pay-lists, and got $20. Mr. Coursol also spoke to me about it two years ago. He said he was at the seat of Government for about a week. After his return he said he saw my name on the Returns as clerk, and asked me was I clerk. I said not. He asked me did I get any money for being clerk. I said I got no money, unless twenty dollars.

Q.--Did you not frequently act as a messenger for me?

A.--Yes, Sir, I frequently went to the Bank and the Post Office. I recollect being on duty for you when you were the President of the Champlain Railroad; I acted as a detective on that occasion for you.

Q.--You said that you received ten pounds a year for collecting house rents for me. Are you quite sure that that was the amount?

A.--I am not very sure; it was either ten or twelve pounds.

Q.--You have said that you belonged to the Irish Constabulary force in Ireland; when did you enter that Force?

A.--In October, 1831, being then eighteen years of age.

Q.--Where were you stationed?

A.--In the South Riding of the County of Tipperary. I was in a place called Donegall first, in Clonmel, Killcash, Nine Mile House, New Birmingham, the Commons, Golden, Banshee, Donisken. This last was the place where I retired from the Force, where I had been a sergeant for two years and a half. I got a pension of £17 10s. 0d. sterling per annum, for seventeen years, and some days' service.

Q.--When did you leave the force?

A.--In October, 1848.

Q.--Why did you leave it?

A.--My health was impaired, and I passed a Board of directors in Dublin Castle, who declared me unfit for service, and recommended me for a pension, which was granted on the same day.

Q.--When did you leave Ireland?

A.--I left it, to the best of my recollection, in July, 1849. Before leaving, I was Master of the Golden Auxiliary Work House, where I had 500 boys under my control, and which I resigned to come to America.

Q.--When did you arrive in Canada?

A.--About the latter end of August, 1849.

Q.--Where did you reside since your arrival in Canada?

A.--In Montreal, with the exception of three months.

Q.--What has been your occupation since you arrived in Canada?

A.--About two months after my arrival in Canada I got a place in the mounted Police at Laprairie, commanded by Captain Fortin. Being injured from riding, I was obliged to leave the force about a fortnight after joining, and afterwards I got into the Police Office at Montreal, where I remained until a few days after Mr. Bissonnette was appointed joint High Constable.

Q.--Then you belonged to the Irish Police when the state trials of Daniel O'Connell and Smith O'Brien took place?

A.--I think I was;

Q.--Did you directly or indirectly take any part in those trials?

A.--No, I never did.

Q.--Do you not draw your pension from the Commissariat in Montreal under another name than "William Hands"?

A.--I do. But it is the same name differently spelt, and I can be identified as the same party who served in the Irish Constabulary, and draw my pension from the Commissariat. When I first joined the force I spelt my name "Hans," and I so gave it at the time. I afterwards introduced the letter "d," and spelt my name Hands. However, I still draw my pension under the name of Hans, because that was the name I was discharged by.

Q.--What made you change your name from "Hans" to "Hands"?

A.--When I was a young boy I had cousins who spelt their names Hans. My father spelt his name Hands. I thought Hans appeared handsomer than Hands, and I wrote my name Hans.

Q.--Then tell us, if you please, how you were christened. Was it under the name of Hands or Hans?

A.--I suppose Hands, for it was so my father spelt it.

Q.--If you thought the name Hans handsomer than Hands, what made you change it in Canada to Hands?

A.--I got wiser and more sensible in Canada, and thought it proper to spell it as my father did.

MONDAY, April 13th, 1863.

The cross-examination of William Hands is continued as follows :--

Q.--Then, if I understand you, you at present make use of two signatures, William Hans and William Hands?

A.--Yes, I do, sir. In my return for my pension and in my ordinary business, and it is only in my return for a pension that I spell my name "Hans."

Q.--You left the Irish Constabulary on account of bad health, and yet you continued in the same kind of service in Canada for eleven years. Had your health improved in Canada, and was the climate more favorable to you?

A.--My health improved, and then I was not in the same service. I had night duty to perform, such as patroling, and also attending at fairs at a distance, and other severe duties, when I was in the Irish Constabulary.

Q.--Were you not stationed in Dublin during the State trials against Daniel O'Connel and al, in 1844?

A.--Never, Sir. I was never stationed in Dublin. I was in Dublin one or two nights at the time I passed the Board of Doctors, as before mentioned. I think it was about the middle of October, 1848.

Q.--Did you ever attend any political meetings for the repeal of the Union in Ireland?

A.--I never did, either on duty or otherwise.

Q.--Did you ever report to your superiors anything in connection with such meetings for the repeal of the Union?

A.--Never, Sir.

Q.--Did you ever procure evidence in connection with the State trials, directly or indirectly?

A.--Never, Sir.

Q.--Where were you stationed during the State trial of O'Connell in 1844?

A.--I cannot recollect the station I was in. To the best of my belief, in 1844 I was stationed in Golden.

Q.--In what year was Smith O'Brien tried, and where did his trial take place?

A.--I am not certain; but I think it was about 1848 or 1849; nor do I remember the place where he was tried.

Q.--Did it not take place before you left the Irish Constabulary in 1848?

A.--I do not know whether it was before or after I left the Constabulary force, that is, I can't recollect.

Q.--Were not the Police Force collected together on the eve of that trial?

A.--I believe they were.

Q.--Where were they assembled?

A.--They were assembled at headquarters in Tipperary, that is, for the sub-district to which I belonged.

Q.--Then you were among the number of those so assembled?

A.--Yes, Sir.

Q.--How long did you remain there with the Force?

A.--Until they were despatched to their stations again.

Q.--Did they not remain there until Smith O'Brien's trial was over?

A.--I do not recollect. I cannot say.

Q.--Did not the trial of Smith O'Brien take place at Clonmel, at a short distance from where you were stationed at Tipperary?

A.--Now I think I recollect that it was at Clonmel the trial took place, and it is distant from Tipperary about 18 or 20 miles.

Q.--Did you ever attend any political meeting connected with the trial of Smith O'Brien?

A.--Never, Sir.

Q.--Did you aid or assist in procuring evidence for that trial?

A.--Never, Sir.

Q.--Is not the pension you got, in whole or in part, for services rendered in the trials of either Daniel O'Connell or Smith O'Brien?

A.--It is no such thing, Sir. I got my pension for my services and good conduct.

Q.--Are such pensions as yours always granted for a similar amount of service to that you rendered?

A.--I held the rank of constable at the time I was discharged, which rank is equivalent to the rank of a sergeant in the army, and I was paid according to my rank and conduct.

Q.--Did you ever sign any other pay-lists besides the four upon which your signature appears?

A.--I never recollect to have signed any pay-lists except two, that is, to what I considered pay-lists.

Q.--Are you prepared to declare, Sir, that you ever signed pay-lists or receipts evidencing the payment of money, without reading them and knowing what you signed?

A.--I do solemnly swear that I did not know that they were pay-lists except the two, and I did not know for what purpose I was asked to sign them.

Q.--Had you not got the whole of the money received from Government in your name, when you signed the last pay-list dated 30th June, 1855, with the exception of a small balance?

A.--I never got a copper but the twenty dollars, and I did not get that as a salary; and if I did, Sir, would Mr. Brehaut afterwards ask me how much would I think would satisfy me for my services, as I have stated before?

Q.--Did you ever acknowledge, since signing the said last pay-list, dated the 30th June, 1855, that you had received the whole of the said amount, save a small balance; and did you ever execute or sign any paper, document, or receipt, evidencing that fact?

A.--Never, Sir; I never gave a receipt of that kind.

Q.--You have a wife and children, have you not?

A.--Yes, Sir, I have a wife and three children.

Q.--Have you not purchased property since you are in Montreal?

A;--Yes, Sir. I bought a small house at the corner of Shaw and Craig Streets, in the City of Montreal, for which I paid £170 cash, which I had accumulated since my arrival in Montreal., I had saved my pension, and it was principally with that money that I paid for the house.

Q.--Did not Mr. Charles Delisle soon after 1855 speak to you on the subject of the pay-lists you had signed, and did you not tell him all about it?

A.--I don't recollect it, Sir, and I don't think I did. My reason for thinking so is, that Mr. Charles Delisle is a man I did not think a great deal about, and that makes me think I never spoke to him about it. I never was a favorite of Mr. C. M. Delisle, or Mr. René Cotret.

Q.--Did you ever make a written deposition or statement in relation to the said pay-lists?

A.--Never, Sir.

Q.--When the twenty dollars you have alluded to as having been handed to you in the presence of Mr. Brehaut by Mr. Schiller as a Christmas box, it must have been, I suppose, about Christmas time or January when such presents are usually made?

A.--I think so, Sir.

Q.--Where was this money handed to you?

A.--I really do not recollect whether it was in the old Court House or this one; but I think it was in the old Court House, and I think Mr. Brehaut was standing by at the time.

Q.--Did you give any receipt for this money?

A.--I did not, but I was very thankful for getting it; but I am not at the present time.

Q.--You have sworn that since you signed the last pay-list dated 30th June, 1855, you had never received the whole of the amount mentioned therein, save a small balance, and that you never gave a receipt evidencing that fact. Please look at the receipt now shown to you, which is in the words, letters, and figures following, to wit:--

"Received from Messrs. Delisle and Brehaut, Clerk of the Peace, by the hands of William H. Brehaut, Esquire, the sum of five pounds cy., being the balance in full payment of salary, as second clerk in their office, up to 30th June, 1855, and for which I have signed the usual receipts in the pay-lists.

Montreal, 28th July, 1855.   WM. HANDS."

And say if the signature "Wm. Hands" subscribed to that receipt, is not in your hand-writing and your genuine signature?

A.--It is my hand-writing, but I never knew how it came there. To the best of my knowledge I never read this receipt before, and also that I don't think it was usual for clerks to give receipts of that description for salaries.

Q.--In whose hand-writing is the body of that receipt?

A.--It is in Mr. Brehaut's hand-writing.

[The said receipt is produced and fyled, marked B.]

Q.--When Mr. Matthew Ryan spoke to you, as you said, about five years ago, about your having signed pay-lists and got no money, did you not then perfectly well know that if what you have said in reference to said pay-lists were true, it was your duty to have informed the Government that gross frauds had been perpetrated in the Peace Office, and did you over do so?

A.--I did not, Sir; nor would I have done so, and those who knew more about the mysteries of the office have done so.

Q.--After having been seventeen years in the Irish Constabulary, and acted for about eleven years in Montreal as a police officer and a detective, can it be possible that you were ignorant that in signing the pay-lists adverted to, without doing any service as clerk, or receiving the money, you were lending yourself to a gross fraud, and becoming an accessory or party to it?

A.--I did not know at the time I signed them; but now I know I had no right to sign them, and if I knew as much then as I know now, I would not have signed them.

Mr. Delisle declares that he has no further questions to put to the witness; and Mr. Brehaut, on his own behalf, declares that he has no questions to put to the witness.

Cross-examined by Mr. Schiller.

I always found Mr. Schiller in his transactions with me, with regard to paying me for the services of subpœnas and summonses, issued out of the Peace Office, correct and honest. Mr. Schiller never speculated upon me, and never deducted anything from the amount it was my right to receive.

With respect to the subpœnas that I served in the Queen's Bench, (Crown side,) Mr. Schiller paid me six pence for each service, with which I was satisfied, as the High Constable only gave me five pence for the same service in the Quarter Sessions.

For the execution of a warrant at Point St. Charles, five shillings was the tariff; but I was only allowed one shilling and three pence, and on some occasions I had to go twice for this service.

Re-examined by the Commissioners.

Q.--Do you know any other person or persons, now in Montreal, who gets a similar pension as yours from the Constabulary Force in Ireland?

A.--I do, Sir. John Oxley, employed in the Water Police, and a man named McGuire, whom I knew at home; and one Michael Fitzgerald, who is at present in the City Police. John Oxley knows me well, and knew me at home.

Q.--Under what circumstances did Mr. A. M. Delisle employ you as a detective, as you have already stated, when he was President of a Railroad Company.

A.--There was a conductor on the cars from Montreal to Rouse's Point, whom he suspected of taking money from passengers on the cars, and appropriating it to his own use. He sent for me, and he told me that he wished to have that man detected, and, being smarter than I was, he laid a plan for the purpose of detecting him. He told me, when I would go on the cars, to buy a ticket, and afterwards to pay my passage to the conductor without showing the ticket, and to take notice if any other passenger paid him. I did so. I went to Rouse's Point, and returned the next day, paying my fare in the same manner. When I reached St. John's in my return, I saw a man who came into the cars at St. John's, paying the conductor some fare. I watched the man, and found he was an Irishman like myself. I got his name and the amount of fare he paid, and reported the whole circumstances to Mr. Delisle.

Q.--When Mr. Delisle sent you to the Banks, as you have stated, did he ever entrust you with any money whatever?

A.--I was entrusted, through Mr. Schiller, with sums varying from $50 to $200.

Q.--Have you ever got any certificate or certificates of good conduct from Messrs. Delisle and Brehaut, or either of them, and if so produce them?

A.--I have, and now produce to the number of three, which are now fyled and produced with the letters "C; D. E."

Q.--Have you got any certificate of good conduct from any other person or persons, and if so produce them?

A.--I produce one from the High Constable B. Delisle, and another from George R. Richards, Vice-Guardian of the Golden Auxiliary Work House, of which I have before spoken as having been master, marked respectively "F. & C." A pensioner from the Constabulary Force in Ireland does not require a certificate.

Q.--When you received only 6d. for service of subpœnas, as you have before stated, from Mr. Schiller, and 5d. from the High Constable for the same services in Quarter Sessions, were you entitled to more?

A.--I do not think so. With regard to the services performed, I thought I was entitled to more; but I also thought they had the perquisites of office, and could allow me whatever they pleased.

Q.--When you were allowed only 1s. 3d. for executing warrants at Point St. Charles, did you ever refuse at any and what time to execute such warrants, either at Point St. Charles, Griffintown, or elsewhere, for the reason of the lowness of this fee, or for any other reason?

A.--I did, Sir. After Mr. Bissonette coming to the office of H. Constable, he had a party of four or five to arrest in Griffintown in one warrant. In place of taking me with him, and giving me a share in this arrest, he went at night, I was informed, with the police, and arrested the parties, with the exception of one whom he could not find. He asked me, I believe, on the day following, to take the warrant to see if I could arrest the party whom he was after. I refused to take it, saying, as he had arrested the others, that he might take that person also. On another occasion I refused for this reason. There was a gentleman came to the office and got a warrant against his servant for larceny. When the warrant was paid, Mr. Bissonette thought it would be an easy matter to arrest her, and that he would pocket the whole fees. Finding that he did not know her whereabouts, he handed the warrant to me for execution, and I declined it under those circumstances.

Q.--Do you remember any circumstances attending your signing the receipt bearing date the 28th July, 1855, which has already been shown to you, and what and who induced you to do so?

A.--I do not; and if I did sign it it was at the suggestion of Mr. Schiller, without my knowing what the purport of it was; and if I did sign it it was for the $20 presented to me, as I have before stated. I am quite certain that I never received a copper more.

On reflexion, when I said above that I thought Smith O'Brien was tried at Clonmel, the circumstance was brought to my memory by Mr. Delisle mentioning Clonmel, and my knowing that he had been arrested at Thurles.

I have said above that I was not thankful now for the $20 above spoken of, because now knowing that the salary was drawn for me by influencing me to sign those documents, and that if they drew a salary for me, they ought to have given me more, and now thinking that there was an improper motive in making me do so.

I cannot say whether it is usual for clerks in the

Peace Office to give their receipts for their salaries to the heads of that department, separate and apart from the receipt which they give in the pay-lists themselves; but I know that the messengers give no receipts except signing the pay-lists themselves. I know this, because I have often seen Mr. Schiller pay them without taking receipts.

On this 14th day of April the witness re-appeared, and his examination was closed, and further sayeth not, &c., &c.

(Signed,) WM. HANDS.

Mr. Delisle and Mr. Brehaut, at the request of the Commissioners, now produce two letters, dated respectively 1st May, 1854, and 5th August, 1854, relating to the pay-lists in the office of the Clerk of the Peace at Montreal, to Joseph Cary, Dy. I. G., for the quarters ended 31st March and 30th June, 1854, respectively.

[TRANSLATED.]

Augustin Delisle, Esq., Notary Public of the City of Montreal, being sworn, saith:--

I have the charge of the Advocates' Library. I am aged sixty years. I am the uncle of Mr. A. M. Delisle. I was employed in the Peace Office at Montreal as a writer, and Mr. Delisle and Mr. Brehaut were then conjointly Clerks of the Peace. I do not exactly recollect the time, but I believe it was seven or eight years ago. Having then no employment, I spoke to Mr. A. M. Delisle, Joint Clerk of the Peace, to see if I could obtain something to do, but he did not then know I could be employed. I mentioned to him that I had heard there were Registers to be written up, and that if he would give me them to do, I would make them up. After some hesitation I obtained the work.

I do not recollect having made any condition as to price, and said that I would leave it to his generosity; and it was after this that I entered the office of the Peace as a writer, to enter in the registers the judgments of the Court of Quarter Sessions, which were a little in arrear. There may also have been, in arrear, judgments of the Criminal Court, but I do not recollect it. This was the only work at which I was employed. I worked in a separate room, and I was only disturbed once: Col. Ermatinger having taken that room, and I was then put to work elsewhere. I do not recollect precisely how long I was so employed; but it may have been six or seven months. I do not recollect having made any conditions, but I think I heard it said that I was to get one dollar a day. I suppose I may have received, at different times, about £60 or £65 for all the time I was so employed at the Peace Office.

I recollect receiving money from Mr. Brehaut, who observed to me that I was well paid; but I cannot exactly remember if Mr. Schiller also paid me money.

Question.--Do you or do you not know that you were to get an annual fixed salary, payable every three months by the Government?

Answer.--No, I did not know it.

Q.--Were you or were you not paid every three months regularly, the same as the other clerks in the office of the Peace?

A.--I cannot recollect if it was every three months; but whenever I wanted money I received it, either from Mr. Brehaut or Mr. Schiller. It is possible that I may have been employed nine months in the office of the Peace, instead of seven, as I have stated, as it is a long time ago that those events occurred, and that I did not make any notes of it at the time.

I was not ordinarily in the habit of signing the pay-lists. I had the hope of obtaining the place of cler which was then vacant, and it is as such that I signed the pay-lists. I only knew that there was then a place of clerk vacant, but I did not know which of them.

I was made to sign pay-lists. I was in hopes of getting the vacant place of clerk, and I cannot remember the number of pay-lists I signed.

I cannot remember if I signed the pay-list for the quarter ending 30th Sept., 1855. I see that my name is entered upon it as second clerk, for the period between the 1st July and 30th Sept., 1855, at a rate of £125 a year, forming £31 5s. 0d. for that quarter, which pay-list is as follows:--

Pay-List, for the Quarter Ending the 30th day of September, 1855.

			Rate per Annum.	Amount.
Alex. M. Delisle,	Clerk of Peace.	1st July to 30th Sept.	£350	£ 87 10 0
Wm. H. Brehaut,	do.	do.	500	125 0 0
C. E. Schiller,	Dy. Clerk of Peace.	do.	150	37 10 0
L. D. René Cotret,	1st Clerk.	do.	175	43 15 0
Auguste Delisle,	2nd Clerk.	do.	125	31 5 0
Louis Malo,	Crier Qr. Sessions	do.	30	7 10 0
Office Expenses, Voucher No. 1				1 17 9
			£334	£334 7 9

We hereby acknowledge having received the amount opposite our respective names in full, of salary to date.

(Signed,)
A. M. Delisle.
W. H. Brehaut.
C. E. Schiller.
L. D. René Cotret.
Auguste Delisle.
Louis Malo.

Montreal, Oct. 1, 1855.

(The Commissioners declare that the acquitted pay-list for the above quarter was not transmitted to them from the office of the Hon. Inspector-General of this Province, although applied for; but that in lieu of such pay-list, an acquitted money warrant was transmitted to them, which they produce to form part of this enquiry; by which acquitted warrant it appears that the amount for that quarter, £334 7s. 9d., was paid to Messrs. Delisle and Brehaut.)

Having examined the pay-list for the quarter ending 31st Dec., 1855, and which is now shown to me by the Commissioners, I see that my name is inscribed in it as second clerk for the period from the 1st Oct. to 31st Dec. 1855, at a salary of £125 a year, forming £31 5s. 0d. for that quarter; and at the bottom of the pay-list I see my signature thus, "Aug. Delisle."

Having taken communication of a third pay-list, for the quarter ending 31st March, 1856, now shown to me by the Commissioners, I observe in it my name as second clerk for the period from the 1st Jan. to 31st March, 1856, at the rate of £125 a year, payable each quarter, £31 5s. 0d.; and the foot of this pay-list is my signature, which I signed thus: "Aug. Delisle."

Q.--Have you received the amount of £31 5s. 0d., as appears in each of those three pay-lists, forming the sum of £93 15s.?

A.--I do not think I received that amount, but to the best of my knowledge the most I can have received is £70. I gave receipts either to Mr. Brehaut or Mr. Schiller for the sums I received. I signed the pay-lists in question in the hope of getting the place of clerk, which was then vacant. It is so long ago that I do not remember the circumstances ; but all I do know is, that I fully believed that the vacant place of clerk would be given to me, which I looked upon as certain.

I cannot recollect which was the largest sum I received at any given time.

It happened that during the first three months I was in want of money, and, I believe, that some was given to me in advance. I was never notified by Messrs. Delisle and Brehaut that I was to get a fixed salary. To the best of my memory I believe it was Mr. Schiller who made me sign the pay-lists. I received money on the day that I signed the pay-list dated 31st Dec., 1855 ; but I cannot recollect the sum in any way, and I give the same answer with reference to the pay-list which I signed on the 31st March, 1856. Every time Mr. Brehaut gave me money, I gave him receipts for what I received, and it is probable that if I drew money from Mr. Schiller, that I gave him receipts. I did not consider myself as clerk in the office, but I entertained the hope of becoming so. After the work I had begun was finished, I must have left after soliciting the place without success. I do not know who got the vacant place.

My christian name is Augustin, but I have always borne the name " Auguste," and it is so that my name appears in the pay-lists. I was perfectly satisfied when Mr. Brehaut told me that I was well paid.

I never had any settlement with Messrs. Delisle and Brehaut to ascertain if the sum of £93 15s. was really paid to me or not, to the best of my knowledge.

———

WEDNESDAY, 15th April, 1863.

The evidence of Mr. Auguste Delisle is continued.

Cross-examined by Mr. A. M. Delisle.

Question.--Although you are not very old, is it not true that your memory is not so good as it used to be formerly ?

Answer.--Certainly.

Q.--Will you examine the receipt now shown to you, which is in the words, letters, and figures following :--

" Received from W. H. Brehaut, Esquire, the sum of six pounds currency, in full settlement of all accounts up to this day." 2nd May, 1856.
£6 0 0. (Signed,) AUG. DELISLE.

And say if that receipt is not wholly in your hand-writing, and signed by you ?

A.--That receipt is entirely in my hand-writing, and the said receipt is produced and marked " A."

Mr. Brehaut and Mr. Schiller declare that they have no questions to put to the witness.

Re-examined by the Commissioners.

Q.--Do you remember under what circumstances and for what reason you gave the said receipt, and if you do detail all the circumstances ?

A.--I recollect none of the circumstances.

[Examination closed.]

Louis Dominique René Cotret, of the City of Montreal, Esquire, Advocate, sworn, saith : I am aged 39 years. I am not at present engaged in the prac-tice of my profession, but I am now in the office of the Judge of Sessions of the Peace, in and for the City of Montreal, and have been so employed since the latter end of Dec., 1861. My duties in that office consist of taking affidavits, filling up warrants, and all other documents required in that department. I also keep a book in which are entered all the cases as they issue from the office for the information of the Judge of Sessions ; but I keep no records, the said office not being a Court of record. The proceedings commenced in the said Police Court pass from our hands into those of the Clerk of the Peace and Clerk of the Crown.

The only connection that I see between our office and the office of the Peace is, that by an order in Council the Clerks of the Peace act as clerk to the Judge of the Sessions of the Peace in weekly and special Sessions, and make convictions and orders for the payment of money, when ordered in those Courts. The Peace department thus taking charge of the proceedings commenced in the Police Office, thereby come into possession of the records of such proceedings for such further return in reference thereto, as may be deemed proper. At least this is as I understood it.

It is to my knowledge that stolen goods have been brought, from time to time, to the said Police Office, with the parties accused of having stolen them. Such goods are produced with the prisoner in the Police Office before the Judge of Sessions, for the purpose of the examination. Such goods were brought either by the police or constables having the prisoners in charge ; and, after this examination, if they were claimed sufficiently to make a case, they were given up to the High Constable by the parties who produced them, and if not, they were restored to the parties from whom they had been taken.

The original papers issue from the Police Office, such as summonses and warrants, which are served and returned before the weekly or special Sessions, that is, they are returned into the department of the Clerk of the Peace, and the Police Office has nothing further to do with them. I have seen stolen goods above spoken of, in many instances, returned to the owners after trial, and so far as I have known applications to be made for their restitution, they were returned to their owners.

Q.--Will you please examine the indictment now shown to you, for larceny, filed 24th Sept., 1859, in the Court of Queen's Bench, (Crown Side) against Fran-çois Lucas, in which he is charged with having feloniously stolen 8 wine glasses, 2 boxes of figs, and one case containing 12 bottles of brandy, the property of Edward Leslie and Patrick Leslie, and say whether it is to your knowledge that the said Francois Lucas was convicted upon the said indictment, and that application was made by or on the part of the owners for the restoration to them of the said brandy and other articles specified in the said indictment, or for any of them after said conviction, or at any other time ?

A.--I remember that a complaint was brought on the part of the Messrs. Leslie against some one, but I cannot recollect who, and I believe that the party was convicted, but I am not sure, not being in the habit of attending the Criminal Court ; but I have no knowledge whether an application was made for said goods at any time. I have no knowledge of any brandy having been in question, except that mentioned in the indictment just spoken of. It is not to my knowledge that any one connected with the Peace

Office, or any one else, took away or converted to his own use metal spouts, or any goods of any kind. I remember seeing Mr. Chas. M. Delisle taking two iron spouts, which had been lying for a good while either in the passage or in a vault used as a dock, next to the passage, and throw them into the privy, they were about four feet long each. This is the only thing I saw done. Mr. Charles M. Delisle said jocularly that somebody would look for them. Those spouts had been lying loose there for some time, and I don't know to whom they belonged. I do not say that these spouts were stolen property, they may have been or not, I don't know. I am under the impression that two or three sales of stolen property took place while I was in the office of the Clerk of the Peace, in which office I had been for a period of eighteen years.

THURSDAY, 16th April, 1863.

Mr. Louis D. René Cotret re-appears, and continues his evidence as follows :--

In addition to what I have said yesterday in reference to the manner in which the business originating in the Police Court, and the proceedings thereon had passed into the department of the Clerk of the Peace, I wish to add that the Clerks of the Peace are bound by law to collect monies paid in the Police Office; and as they have no clerk there to collect those monies, we did it for their convenience and to oblige them, and handed over such monies, together with the papers drawn up in the Police Office, in order that they may ascertain whether we have accounted for everything, and to enable them to make their entries. I do not remember anything about four iron spouts, as being part of stolen goods at any time, having only been in the vault with the High Constable three or four times during the last twenty years, and this to assist him in finding goods to produce at trials during the sitting of the Court.

The High Constable, to my knowledge, had the charge of the key of the vault of stolen goods in the different buildings where that vault has been kept. I never heard that a piece of cloth (étoffe du pays), forming part of the stolen goods, disappeared, and could not be found on the day of sale. I see before me a book in which there are entries relating to stolen goods supposed to be brought to the Police Office, the first entry in which book is on the 23rd December, 1843. The first page is in the hand-writing of Mr. Schiller, I believe, and I have no doubt that it is. The second page, in part the hand-writing of Mr. Schiller, and in part of Mr. A. M. Delisle, as also the third and fourth pages. The fifth page is in the hand-writing, in part, of Mr. A. M. Delisle, in part of Mr. Schiller, and in part myself; 7th and 8th pages are partly in the hand-writing of Mr. Delisle, and partly of myself; the 9th and 10th pages are also in my hand-writing, and so are the 11th and 12th pages, with the exception of a receipt the hand-writing of which I cannot be sure of; the 13th and 14th pages are in my hand-writing, except one receipt, which is in the hand-writing of Mr. Schiller. At page 28 there is a receipt, on a flying sheet, in the hand-writing of Mr. Benjamin Delisle, to which I have affixed my signature as a witness. At page 40 there is a receipt in the hand-writing of Mr. Benjamin Delisle, H. C., dated 17th February, 1845, and signed by a man named Thomas C. Speer, in the case of Edward Mahan and al. At pages 43 and 44 the entries are in my own hand-writing. At page 46 there is a receipt in the hand-writing of Mr. Schiller, in

the case of I. B. Laplante, signed A. H. Dubrul. One Leandre Fortier was a clerk in the Peace Office in 1849, although I am not positive ; and the entry in the case of the Queen vs. Bridget Brennan, in said book, appears to me to be in the hand-writing of the said Fortier. My impression is, that the entry, in the said book, under date 7th March, 1851, in the case of the Queen vs. Martin Quinn, is in the hand-writing of Ed. Gagnon, who has been a clerk in the Peace Office.

My impression is, that the entry bearing date 7th February, 1852, in the case of the Queen vs. Edward Coyle, is in the hand-writing of the said Edward Gagnon. I believe that all the receipts on page 62 are in my own hand-writing. I cannot say positively whether I was present at the time that the articles mentioned in such receipts were delivered over to their owners, inasmuch as after having written out the receipts I might have been engaged on some other duties in the Peace Office. I was then a clerk in that office.

In many cases the articles have been delivered in my presence to their owners, but I cannot point out in which cases they have been so delivered. The said book does not contain any entries after the year 1857, 15th July. I have myself made the greater portion of the entries in the said book, and I was then a clerk in the Peace Office during that time. An order had been given to keep that book, but I do not know from whom that order emanated, and that order was given at the time I commenced making entries in that book in January, 1844. There is no other book, to my knowledge, in the Peace Office since the 15th July, 1857, up to the day that I left said Peace Office in the latter end of December, 1861.

I do not know of any book in the Peace Office in which an entry was made of the articles mentioned as having been stolen, in the case of the Queen vs. Frs. Lucas, hereinbefore alluded to. I find sixty-five entries in the said book relating to stolen goods, for the year 1851. I find 30 entries for the year 1852 in the said book; and the last entry for said year stops 5th August. I do not see any entry made in the said book for the year 1853. I find 7 entries made in said book for 1854. I do not see any entry made in the said book for the year 1855. I see one entry made in the said book for the year 1856. I find 12 entries in said book for 1857, the last of which is made on the 15th July. I find 122 entries in said book for the year 1844. I see, in said book, a receipt bearing date 22nd April, 1847, in the hand-writing of Mr. Benjamin Delisle, the High Constable, in the case of the Queen vs. George Barnett, and which receipt appears to be signed by one F. N. Desjardins per Jos. Pilon. I am well acquainted with the said book, as it is for the most part in my own hand-writing, and it was kept in the Peace Office aforesaid. I have appeared sometimes as a witness before the Criminal Courts, to prove the voluntary statement of prisoners, but I never appeared with regard to stolen goods, and whenever I appeared as such witness before such Criminal Courts, I was never paid as such witness, and I was never taxed as such.

I have a brother of the name of Eusebe René Cotret, he was a constable, as far as I can recollect, for about three years. I believe he commenced in 1852, and he was employed as such constable by Mr. Benjamin Delisle.

The warrants for the month of March, 1854, which are in the custody of the High Constable, are now shown to me, which said warrants have been produced by Mr. Bissonette, Joint High Constable. I find 12 of those warrants which bear the signature of "René" on the back thereof, and which I believe to be in the hand-writing of my brother, who was then acting as a constable. The mode in which the returns to said warrants were made at that time was as follows :--

"Executed at Montreal this ——— day of ——, 185--. (Signed,) RENE, Constable."

Which form of return is indorsed on the back of said warrants. The warrant in the case of Robert Horning, bearing date 10th March, 1854, for assault and battery, and endorsed "Misdemeanor," executed on the 10th March, 1854. I believe that the signature "Wm. Hands," signed on the back of the said warrant, is in the hand-writing of "Wm. Hands," who was a constable at the time. I find 16 warrants for March, 1854, and executed by the said Wm. Hands, as appears by said returns endorsed thereon; and I have no doubt the signature "Wm. Hands," written on the back of said 16 warrants, is in the hand-writing of the said Wm. Hands, whom I have frequently seen write. The said Wm. Hands was a constable at the time. I see other warrants issued same month, and purporting, by the signature thereon, to have been executed by Hands and René, who acted together as constables frequently.

FRIDAY, 17th April, 1863.

L. D. R. Cotret, Esq., continues his evidence as follows, viz. :--

The warrants which are now shown to me, to the number of ten, which were issued in the month of April, 1854, bear the signature of "Wm. Hands" on the back thereof, and which signature I believe to be in the hand-writing of Wm. Hands, who was acting as a constable; and the said warrants appear to have been executed by the said Wm. Hands, in the month of April, 1854. Having also examined nine other warrants, six of which issued under the signature of Col. Ermatinger, then Inspector and Superintendant of Police, in the month of April, 1854; and one of which under the signature of J. L. Beaudry, J.P.; and another under the signature of Js. McGill Des Revieres, J.P.; and another under the signature of J. A. Gagnon, J.P. They purport to have been executed in the month of April. 1854, as such constable, by the said Wm. Hands; and I have no doubt that the writing mentioning the execution of said warrants, on the back thereof, is that of the said William Hands. Fourteen other warrants are now shown to me, which were issued in the month of May, 1854, and which are headed "Peace Office," under the signature of Col. Ermatinger, then Inspector and Superintendant of Police for the City of Montreal; and on the back thereof I perceive the signature "Wm. Hands," which I have no doubt is the signature of the said Wm. Hands, then acting as a constable, and by the notes concerning the execution of warrants on the back thereof, and which are in the hand-writing of the said Wm. Hands, except one, which is in the hand-writing of Mr. Benjamin Delisle, H. C. It appears that the said Wm. Hands arrested the persons mentioned in the said warrants. There are 13 more warrants issued in the said month of May, which are now shown to me, and which appear to have been executed by the said Wm. Hands as constable.

Thirty-one warrants issued in the month of June, 1854, now shown to me, were all executed by the said Wm. Hands, as constable, in the said month. The are three more warrants which were executed by him in the month of June, 1854, and which had been issued in previous months; and there are two more which purport to have been executed in the said month of June, by said Hands and René, as constables. On the back of twenty of those warrants are to be found notes concerning their execution, in the hand-writing of the said Wm. Hands. Twenty-five warrants, issued in July, 1854, purporting to have been issued out of the Peace Office in the City of Montreal, being now shown to me, I declare that they purport to have been executed by the said Wm. Hands, as such constable; and on 19 of them I see, on the back thereof, a signature which I believe to be that of the said Wm. Hands, as having arrested the persons mentioned in the said warrants in the month of July, 1854. 29 warrants to apprehend issued in the month of August, 1854, purporting to have been issued from the Peace Office in the City of Montreal, and now shown to me, appear to have been executed by the said Wm. Hands, as constable, in the said month of August, and bear, on the back thereof, the signature "Wm. Hands," which I have no doubt to be in the hand-writing of the said Wm. Hands. Also a search-warrant and three other warrants to apprehend, issued in the said month of August, 1854, appear to have been executed by the said Wm. Hands, constable, from the memorandums on the back thereof. On the back of the said search-warrant the return is in the hand-writing of the said Wm. Hands, and signed by him as constable. Five more warrants for the said month, now shown to me, purport to have been executed in the same month of August by the said Wm. Hands, and another constable generally known by the name of René.

Twenty-eight warrants of arrest purporting to be issued out of the said office in the month of September, 1854, being now shown to me, I declare that they purport to have been executed by the said William Hands, as constable; and several of the said warrants bear the signature of the late Alexis Laframboise, Esq., then J. P.; others that of J. L. Beaudry, Esq., J.P., and Joseph Belle, Esq., J. P., and of other Justices of the Peace. These warrants all purport to have been executed in Sept., 1854, by Wm. Hands, constable.

Two search-warrants now shown to me, issued also in Sept., 1854. I state that my impression is, from the memorandum on the back of the said warrants, that they were executed by the High Constable, assisted by the said Wm. Hands.

A warrant of arrest and commitment, issued also in the month of September, 1854, under the signature of Col. Ermatinger, then Inspector and S. of Police for the City of Montreal, now shown to me, appears to have been executed by the said Wm. Hands, from the memorandum on the back thereof, in the hand-writing of Mr. Benjamin Delisle, High Constable. Another warrant of arrest, issued in the same month, appears to have been executed by said Hands and my brother. Fifteen warrants of arrest, issued in the month of Oct., 1854, bearing the heading "Peace Office," in cases of the Queen vs. Divers persons, charged with divers offences, and particularly assault and battery, being now shown to me. I declare that they appear to me to have been executed by the said Wm. Hands, as constable, in the month of Oct., 1854; and on 14 of those warrants the signature "Wm. Hands," on the back thereof, is, I believe, the signature of Wm. Hands, constable. There are two warrants for that month, purporting to have been executed by the said Wm. Hands and my brother. 29 warrents of arrest, issued in the month of November, 1854, in the case of the Queen vs. Divers persons, charged with divers offences, and more particularly of assault and battery, issued at the City of Montreal under the signature of different J. P.'s, being now shown to me. I declare that they purport to have been executed by the said Wm. Hands, as constable ; and twenty of them bear, on the back thereof, the signature of the said Wm. Hands, and I have no doubt it is his signature, knowing his hand-writing.

The mode of executing the said warrants was, arresting the persons therein charged of the offences therein mentioned, and bringing them before the Police Magistrate or other Justice of the Peace in attendance.

In looking over the warrant issued in the case of the Queen vs. Wm. Gray, on suspicion of murder, and which appears to have been executed at Huntingdon by the High Constable B. Delisle, I find a memorandum in the hand-writing of the said B. Delisle, showing that he was assisted in executing said warrant by the said Wm. Hands. It appears by the Bill of Expence made by Mr. Schiller, and annexed to said warrant, that the distance travelled in making said arrest was 20 leagues from the City of Montreal, and the said High Constable and Recors were absent four days in making said arrest. Twenty-two warrants of arrest, issued in the month of Dec., 1854, purporting to have been issued in the Peace Office at Montreal, for divers offences, in the case of the Queen vs. Divers persons, under the signatures of different Justices of the Peace, being now shown to me, I declare that they purport to have been executed by the said William Hands, as such constable, and bear, on the back thereof, the signature "Wm. Hands," which I believe to be in the hand-writing of the said William Hands, and subscribed to the execution thereof. On the back of a search-warrant issued in the same month, it appears, by the memorandum on the back thereof, in the hand-writing of Mr. B. Delisle, that the same was executed by the said Wm. Hands. Four more warrants, issued in the same month, appear to have been executed by the said Wm. Hands. (The Commissioners declare that the warrants hereinbefore mentioned, and those hereinafter mentioned, issued during the year 1855, were produced before them by Mr. Adolphe Bissonette, Joint High Constable.) Fifteen warrants of arrest issued in January, 1855, at Montreal, under the signatures of different Justices of the Peace, in the cases of the Queen against Divers persons, charged with assault and battery, principally, being now shown to me, I declare that they purport to have been executed in January, 1855, by the said Wm. Hands, as a constable ; and, on the back of 4 of them, I see the signature of Wm. Hands, which I believe to be his own hand-writing. I see, among the said warrants, one issued at Sorel, (Wm. Hy.,) to arrest a party therein named, and which appears to have been placed in the hands of the High Constable for execution, upon which I see endorsed in the hand-writing of the said B. Delisle the following entry :—

Hands went after the prisoner 5 leagues, 3s. .£0 15 0
Arrest....................................... 0 5 0
                                                    ———
                                                 £1 0 0

By Hands I understood that the said Wm. Hands is meant, there being no other constable of that name, at that time, connected with the office.

SATURDAY, 18th April, 1863.

The examination of L. D. R. Cotret, Esq., is continued as follows, viz. :—

Of the warrants issued in the month of February, 1855, I now see 9 purporting, by the return thereon endorsed, to have been executed by the said Wm. Hands, his name being subscribed to such returns. Five of said nine returns I believe to be so subscribed by the said Hands, in his own hand-writing.

Of the warrants of arrest issued as aforesaid, in the month of March, 1855, I now find, upon examination, that nine of them purport, by the endorsed returns of execution, to have been executed in that month by the said Wm. Hands, acting as such constable, five of which returns of execution are made and signed by the said Wm. Hands, to the best of my knowledge, as I know his hand-writing. All the said warrants purport, on the face of them, to have issued from the Peace Office.

I see two other warrants, issued in the same month, which purport to have been executed by the said Hands, and another constable named Rene.

In the month of April, 1855, I see eight warrants issued as aforesaid, and purporting, by these returns, to have been executed in that month by the said Hands, three of which returns I have no hesitation in saying, are made by the said Hands, and signed by him "Wm. Hands." The other five bear endorsements in the hand-writing of High Constable Delisle, intimating that they were executed by the said Hands. Two other warrants issued in this month, purport to have been executed by Hands and René.

Of thirteen warrants issued in the month of May, 1855, I find that eleven were executed by constable Hands. The other two bear endorsement in the hand of the said High Constable, showing that they, also, were executed by him and the said Wm. Hands. I see also two search-warrants, issued in the same month, both of which were executed by Hands and René ; one of them at Long Point, 6 miles from the City of Montreal, and upon which a special return is made by said Hands, as constable, to the best of my belief. I see, in the said month, also, a warrant of arrest in the case of the Queen vs. Frs. Bizaillon and al, in which it appears, by the High Constable's notes thereon written, that he paid constables £3 10s. 11d., and in which said Hands' name is entered as having executed said warrant. Said Bizaillon and others lived at that time at St. Timothé, and the distance travelled and the time and expences involved appear endorsed on the back thereof. Of thirteen warrants issued as aforesaid, in the month of June, 1855, all purporting to have been executed by said constable Hands, I have no hesitation in saying that he did so execute ten of them in that month, the returns of such execution being in his hand-writing, and signed by him as constable, that is, I have no doubt of it.

I see that in this month a search-warrant and a commitment issued, on the back of both of which is endorsed the name "Hands," which is the only evidence I see that the said constable Hands had anything to do with them.

Four other warrants of arrest now shown to me purport, by the endorsement of the execution thereof, to have been executed in the said month of June, by Hands and René.

Being shown and having examined the Account Current Book with the Provincial Government, from

10th Sept., 1850, to 31st Dec., 1861, (which forms part of the books produced before the Commissioners on the 14th March last past,) I declare that I see regularly entered what appears to me to be duplicates of the pay-lists furnished from quarter to quarter to the Government, by the Joint Clerk of the Peace for the District of Montreal. And at the foot of the pay-list for the quarter ending 31st Dec., 1850, I see original signatures, which are as follows :--(Signed,) A. M· Delisle, W. H. Brehaut, C. E. Schiller, L. D. René Cotret, Ed. Gagnon. The three first are respectively the signatures and in the hand-writing of A. M. Delisle, W. H. Brehaut, and C. E. Schiller ; the 4th is my own signature, and the 5th I believe to be that of Edouard Gagnon, who was formerly a clerk in the Peace Office ; but I cannot swear positively to his signature. My impression is, that he must have been a clerk at that time ; but as I took no memorandum or notes of the time that he was there, I cannot speak positively as to whether he was then a clerk or not in that department.

(The Commissioners produce a statement No. 6, which forms part of the papers to them transmitted from the office of the Minister of Finance, which purports to be an Inventory of the Stationrey, blank forms and blank books, in the hands of the Clerks of the Peace, on the 9th day of Sept., 1850, when the Act 13th and 14th Vic., Cap. 37, came in force, and wherein it is mentioned that such stationery, blank forms and blank books, have been and were then used for the benefit of the special fund.) Having nothing to do with the books of the said Peace Office during the time I was a clerk in the said office, I cannot speak about the stationery nor the books of the said office, nor can I state anything about the postage. I am not aware whether there was a franking privilege for postages of letters in the said office or not. I cannot remember when the said Edouard Gagnon left the Peace Office, and when Mr. George Baby replaced him, as I did not keep any memorandum in writing of those facts, not being interested therein.

MONDAY, 20th April, 1863.

Louis D. R. Cotret, Esq., continues his evidence as follows, viz. :--During the time I was Clerk of the Peace Office, the clerks employed there, that is, under clerks, were not frequently changed. To the best of my recollection during the said time there was one Leandre Fortier, Edouard Gagnon, George Baby, and, I believe, Auguste Delisle, Alfred Harvey, Senr., and Alfred Harvey, Jnr. These are all I can remember having been occupied in the office during my connection therewith, which connection terminated in Dec., 1861. I am not aware whether constable Hands, above spoken of, acted as Mr. Delisle's agent for the collection of rents. I have no personal knowledge that Mr. Harvey, Senr., above named, and now deceased, acted as such agent.

Since the month of Sept., 1850, as far as I can recollect, the said clerks, in the Peace Department, were paid sometimes by Mr. Schiller, but oftener by Mr. Brehaut, either by cheque or in money ; and as their receipts, they signed the pay-list forwarded before they received the money, and, after its receipt, again signed a duplicate of such pay-list in the Account Current Book, of which I have already spoken, up to 31st Dec., 1853. Having examined the said book on Saturday last, I see thereby that said clerks gave their duplicate receipts as aforesaid in manner aforesaid, and this is how I gave receipts for my sa-

lary, to the best of my recollection, up to the 31st Dec., 1853.

Subsequently I signed the pay-list on receiving the money ; and such receipts, on the pay-lists, were the only receipts given, to my knowledge, or that I ever gave. When I said that I believed Mr. Auguste Delisle was a clerk, I said so because I was not present at his engagement, and did not see him sign the pay-lists ; but I know that he worked daily in the Peace Office for about a year, as nearly as I can recollect. He used to make up registers and copies of documents that were required from the office. Having examined the pay-lists of the office of the Clerk of the Peace for the quarter ended 30th Sept., 1854, the 31st Dec., 1854, the 31st March, 1855, and also the pay-list for the period from the 1st Jan. to the 30th June, 1855, now produced and shown to me, and subscribed, respectively, A. M. Delisle, W. H. Brehaut, C. E. Schiller, L. D. René Cotret, Wm. Hands, Louis Malo, I say that I have no hesitation in saying that I believe the said signatures to be those of the said several parties just mentioned, and in their own several and respective hand-writing, having frequently seen them write and sign their names, all except Hands and Malo, whom I have sometimes seen sign their names ; and I have no doubt that the latter two signatures are those of Hands and Malo.

Cross-examined by Mr. A. M. Delisle.

Q.--Are you or are you not aware that after the fees were funded in 1850, Mr. Brehaut and myself assumed different branches of the duties of Joint Clerk of the Peace ?

A.--I do not know any of arrangement made between you ; but I know that Mr. Brehaut seemed to have particular branches of the department, and you others.

Q.--Will you please describe, as you saw and understood it, the various duties so discharged by Mr. Brehaut and myself ?

A.--Mr. Delisle took the Criminal Courts, and Mr. Brehaut had the general management of the office, that is, as a general rule ; but Mr. Brehaut sometimes took the Criminal Court, and Mr. Delisle worked in the office, taking affidavits or something else.

Q.--Did Mr. Brehaut ever hold the Criminal Courts except in my absence from town ?

A.--I would not be positive in saying that.

Q.--Did I not occupy distinct and separate offices from the offices of the Peace and the Police Office, and were not those offices the apartments of the Clerk of the Crown, which office I held likewise ?

A.--I know that such has been the case since we are in the new Court House ; but I don't remember whether you occupied distinct offices in the old one.

Q.--Who had the charge of the finances of the office of the Clerk of the Peace since 1850, and by whom were you paid ?

A.--I received my salary from Mr. Brehaut most of the time, and sometimes Mr. Schiller would hand it to me as coming from Mr. Brehaut. The greater part of the time I was paid by cheques from Mr. Brehaut, as near as I can remember. I state further that I was always regularly paid.

Q.--You have said that you saw me, sometimes, working in the office, taking affidavits, and something else. How often did it happen ?

A.--Not very often.

Q.--With reference to the book relating to stolen goods, produced at this investigation, of which you have spoken, was it not opened for the use of the High Constable, and do not the entries therein evidence that that was its intended use?

A.--I cannot say for whom it was opened; but from the fact that the H. Constable had and has the stolen goods in his possession, it would lead one to suppose that it was for the H. Constable's convenience.

Q.--Do the Joint Clerk of the Peace at present keep a book of that description?

A.--No, they do not.

Q.--Do not the Joint High Constable, Messrs. Delisle and Bissonette, keep a book for entering stolen goods, and is the book they keep not substantially the same as the one referred to?

A.--Yes, Sir.

Evidence of Louis D. René Cotret in cross-examination by Mr. A. M. Delisle.

Question.--Can you explain why the book in question appears to have been so irregularly kept?

Answer.--I can explain it in this way; sometimes there was too much work for me to do in the Office to allow me to make the entry in due time, and then the papers were set aside and the book forgotten.

Q.--Were the irregularities apparent on the face of that book, intended to conceal anything or to do anything wrong?

A.--No such thing.

Q.--When stolen goods were brought by the Police or by Constables, were they not invariably so brought before the Police Magistrate or Justices of the Peace at the Police Office and never at the Peace Office?

Q.--I know the goods were brought before the Police Magistrate; but before we occupied the new building there was only one allowed for the public business, and I don't know by what name you should call it. I don't know if there was, formerly, any distinction between the Police Office and the Peace.

Q.--Were not all the stolen goods brought before the Police Magistrate or Justices of the Peace sitting, invariably and without distinction, consigned to the care of the High Constable?

A.--They were, Sir, if they were claimed as stolen goods.

Q.--When they happened not to be claimed or identified what became of such goods?

A.--Sometimes when they were found in possession of suspicious characters they were given over to the High Constable, and sometimes they were restored to the parties in whose possession they had been found.

Q.--Has it ever occurred, to your knowledge, that stolen goods consigned to the keeping of the High Constable were not forthcoming when required?

A.--No Sir.

Q.--Did you ever hear of any complaint on the part of owners or claimants of such goods that they could not get their property?

A.--I did not, Sir.

Q.--If such a thing had happened would you not most likely have heard of it?

A.--It is more than likely.

———

TUESDAY, April 21, 1863.
The evidence of Louis Dominique René Cotret, Esq., continued.

Mr. Delisle declares that he has no further questions to put to the witness.

Cross-examined by W. H. Brehaut.

Question.--Have you not seen Mr. Hands employed to go messages, fill up or copy papers, or do other things for our department, not connected with his duty as a Constable?

A.--I have.

Mr. Schiller declares that he has no questions to put to the witness.

Edward Carter, Esq., Clerk of the Crown and Joint Clerk of the Peace, for the District of Montreal, is sworn, and deposes as follows, viz.:--

I know the parties hereinbefore mentioned. I was appointed to the office of Clerk of the Crown and Joint Clerk of the Peace on or about the 22nd March, 1862, and took the oath of office on the 24th of the same month. My appointment was consequent on the vacancy created by the appointment of Alex. A. Delisle, Esq., to the Office of Sheriff for the said District.

Question.--Will you favour us with your views upon the organisation of the Offices of the Clerk of the Peace for the District of Montreal?

Answer.--So soon as the term of the Queen's Bench, which commenced on the day I took the oath of office, had terminated, as also other sittings of the Quarter Sessions, which followed immediately after, I was enabled to turn my attention to the organisation and working of the Department of the Peace Office. I very soon became convinced that the system which prevailed of carrying on the business of the department was very bad, and such as to be extremely disagreeable to the chiefs of the department and likely to entail responsibility upon them, which the utmost caution could not avert. I refer chiefly to the fact that, whilst the Clerks of the Peace had nominally two Clerks in their Department, in reality but one of them was employed in doing the work which, properly, devolved upon the Clerks of the Peace, the other being placed in another department, namely, the Police Office, to assist the Police Magistrate's Clerk in the performance of the duties which properly belonged to the Police Magistrate. The anomaly thus produced was that in the Police Office, where two Clerks were actually employed issuing summonses, warrants, subpœnas, and other proceedings, and in receiving the fees of office payable thereon, one of these Clerks being appointed by the Police Magistrate, was in nowise accountable to us as Clerk of the Peace, not subject to our our control, and the other Clerk being appointed by us, was equally irresponsible towards the Police Magistrate and less subject to his control than he would have been if appointed by the Police Magistrate himself. This want of proper organization and control over so important a department as that of the Police Office, where considerable sums for fees of office and fines were, at all hours of the day paid, satisfied me of two things,--1st, that the work of the department would never be satisfactorily performed. Secondly, that monies might be received in that office which should be paid over to the Clerk of the Peace or their Deputy, and yet, occasionally, either intentionally or by neglect, never be so paid over or accounted for without its being in the power of the Clerk of the Peace to detect or become aware of such fraud or neglect. For this reason, that the proper performance of their duties required a personal attendance in their own offices, situated in another story of the Court House, and so entirely disconnected from the Police Office as to render it impossible for them to have any supervision over the Clerks in the Police Office. I also found that the circumstances of the Police Magistrate having one Clerk subject to his orders, in conjunction with one of our own, subject to our control, gave rise to another difficulty, namely, the proper distribution of the work and labor performed in that department, resulting in a difference arising between the Police Magistrate and the Clerks of the Peace as to what constituted the proper duties appertaining to our respective Offices. This matter was brought under the consideration of Government by a letter from the Clerk of the Peace, of date 27th May, 1862, addressed to the Honble. the Provincial Secretary, and by letter from the Police Magistrate, written about the same time. A subsequent letter was sent by the Clerk of the Peace on the 2nd June following, accompanied by a memorandum, in which the position assumed by the Clerk of the Peace was fully set forth, and which, in substance, was that they were public officers and not bound to attend upon the Police Magistrate, or to assist him in the performance of his ministerial duties, such as the preliminary enquiries, held by him, into all misdemeanors and felonies, and in the issuing of the initiatory proceedings in all cases of summary convictions and orders. That a Clerk had been assigned to assist him in the performance of these particular duties, relying for the support of this position, not only upon the law, which required the active participation of the Police Magistrate in the performance of those duties ; but also upon an order in Council of the 8th May, 1841, in which it was, amongst other things, stated as follows :-- "The " Committee are of opinion that whatever necessity " might have formerly existed for the performance " of duties out of Session by the Clerks of the Peace " in Quebec, Montreal, and Three Rivers, it is proper " that those duties should be now performed by the " Magistrates to whom they legally and properly be- " long, or by Clerks to be provided for those who are " stipendiary and who are supposed to be constantly " employed."

Other correspondence took place with the Government at a later period, on the same subject, as well with the Clerk of the Peace as with the Police Magistrate ; but the matter was not finally determined until the 17th day of February last past, date of a letter addressed by the Provincial Secretary to the Clerk of the Peace, as also to the Police Magistrate, communicating the decision of His Excellency the Governor General in Council, which, in effect, sustained the views urged by the Clerk of the Peace, inasmuch as by article " 3," it was amongst other things decided that for the future " there shall be but two " Clerk allowed in the Office of the Judge of the " Sessions of the Peace, of whom the present Clerk " may be one. . . . . And that the Judge of the " Sessions of the Peace be informed that he will be " expected to perform his ordinary duties out of Ses- " sions by the means of such Clerk." This decision has had the effect of accomplishing a very desirable object, the separation of the department of the Clerk of the Peace from that of the Police Office, and to render the Judge of the Sessions of the Peace responsible for the proper duties of the latter office, which duties from their peculiar nature required his constant attendance there. It also placed the Clerk employed there under his exclusive control and supervision so necessary for the proper performance of the duties of any public department. This order of Council was carried out, the Clerks of the Peace were left with but one Clerk, and the Judge of the Sessions appointed as his second Clerk, one Mr. Des Rosiers.

It is necessary I should mention that in so far as fines and fees of office are concerned, something more remained to be done with a view of accomplishing a perfect system of accounting for such fines and fees as may, from time to time, be paid into the Police Office.

And for this reason, that the collection, by the Judge of the Sessions or his Clerks, of all fees payable upon summonses, writs, &c., issued by him, is inseparable from the performance of all the duties out of Sessions, the responsibility of which exclusively devolves upon the Judge of the Sessions by the order in Council last referred to.

The Commissioners will please observe in view of the said Order in Council, that the Clerks of the Peace could never, under any circumstances, be made responsible for the honesty or punctuality of the Clerks of the Police Office, over whom they have no control whatever in respect of properly accounting for the monies they might receive.

Under the Order in Council, the Clerks of the Peace have nothing to do whatever in the Police Office, excepting when the Judge of the Sessions acts judicially in holding special or weekly Sessions under the provisions of the Sec. 85, chap. 103, of the Consolidated Statutes of Canada, and then it is that as public officers they assist the Judge of the Sessions in the holding of those Courts. In view of this provision of Law, the Order in Council last referred to, has imposed no other duty on the Clerk of the Peace than that of preparing all orders, convictions and judgments rendered at such Sessions.

It is evident, therefore, that instead of following the system now adopted with reference to the monies paid into the Police Office, namely, one or other of the two Clerks or both bringing to the Deputy Clerk of the Peace, small sums of money such as 5s., 10s. or 15s. in the afternoon of each day, saying that it was for a warrant, a summons, or a subphœna, and the Deputy entering it in his daily Cash Book ; that some other system, affording a proper check and a means of determining whether all monies received in the Police Office should be introduced.

Payments of monies in the way above stated, without a proper record being kept and without receipts being given by the Officers of the Departments into which the monies are paid in favor of the officers of other departments, from whom they are received, affords no check whatever, and in the event of a defalcation, an inquiry thereupon would be rendered extremely difficult, if it did not preclude altogether, the possibility of ever discovering the guilty party. I would, therefore, respectfully suggest to the Commissioners, as a remedy for this existing defect in the present organization.

1stly. That an Entry Book be kept in the Police Office, not only of every case that originates there, but also of every proceeding adopted in such case, such as the issuing of summonses or warrants, entering into recognizances, and issuing of subpœnas, mentioning in the money column the amount received on each proceeding, with the initials of the Clerk who received the money, in an adjoining column, to indicate by whom the money was received.

2ndly. That as cases may arise in which the Judge of the Sessions should have the power of issuing a summons or warrant without exacting the fees as in cases of extreme poverty, so that a failure of justice might not ensue, an entry should be made in another column of the cause for the issuing of such proceedings without exacting a fee, such entry to be attested by the signature of the Judge of the Sessions. This would afford the best clue to the detection of any deficiency and at the same time attest in authentic form in what cases this discretionary power of the Magistrate had been exercised.

3rdly. That not only the fees upon the initiatory proceedings, that is to say, before the hearing of the cause, should be collected by the Clerks of the Judge of the Sessions; but also all fines imposed and subsequent fees, that is to say, those payable upon the proceedings upon the hearings and afterwards should also be collected by them.

The reason will strike the Commissioners as a very obvious one, namely, that it is better the department charged with the collection of fees upon the first proceedings also, who should keep proper books of them, should continue to collect all other fees incident to the same cause as well as the fines imposed. Any other rule would lead to complications and confusion by having a portion of the fees collected in our department and another department.

4thly. That the fees as well as fines and penalties so collected, should be retained and paid over to the Clerk of the Peace, with a return or statement, in writing, distinguishing the fees of office and fines in the same manner as other Magistrates throughout the District are obliged by law to make their returns to the Clerk of the Peace.

This, in effect, is carrying out the recommendation contained in the Order in Council of the 8th May, 1841, in another form and which is to this effect :— "And as the Clerks of the Peace are required by law to keep a Register of all convictions before Magistrates in Montreal, Quebec, and Three Rivers, the Committee recommend that the Police and other Magistrates, acting in those cities, be instructed to furnish the Clerk of the Peace monthly with lists of those convictions, &c., &c."

5thly. That the returns so made by the Judge of the Sessions be in duplicate, taking a receipt upon one of them from the Clerk of the Peace or their Deputy, for the payment of the amount mentioned in such return and leaving the other duplicate with the Clerk of the Peace.

6thly. That the Clerk of the Peace be required to keep a record of the monies so paid to them, taken from such returns to consist of two books, the one entitled, "Building and Jury Fund," according to form I now produce marked A, which form includes the classification of the different funds payable to the Sheriff, as constituting part of the building and Jury fund, the other book according to form B, now produced, and which is adapted for recording all penalties payable to the Receiver General, and also fees of office which are payable to the same officer.

These books will constitute an authentic record of the amount so received from the Judge of the Sessions and which the Clerks of the Peace are bound to remit either to the Sheriff or the Receiver General.

This project, if carried out, will afford as complete a check as could possibly be devised upon, both to the departments of the Police Office and the Clerk of the Peace, and the officers connected therewith.

I desire to add that so long as the controversy between the Judge of the Sessions remained undecided by the Government, it was impossible to inaugurate any new system which could be effectual in so far as fines and fees of office were concerned.

WEDNESDAY, April 22, 1863.
Edward Carter, Esq.—Evidence continued,
I now produce a true copy of the Order in Council of the 8th of May, 1841, marked C, as also a copy of a letter from the Honorable the Provincial Secretary, of the 17th February last, carrying the decision of His Excellency the Governor General in Council marked D.

I desire to call the attention of the Commissioners to another portion of the first mentioned document in which it is stated :—"The Committee see no reason "why these duties, which do not strictly belong to "the Clerk of the Peace, should not be performed by "the Police Magistrate"; as establishing that so far back as 1841, all the duties therein referred to, out of Sessions, were not considered as properly belonging to the Clerk of the Peace, but as legally devolving upon the Police Magistrate. I also desire to call the attention of the Commissioners to Section 81 of chap. 103, Consolidated Statutes of Canada, a provision of law copied from Sir John Jervis' Act, as establishing that in England under the operation of the Imperial Act, as well as in this Province, under the operation of the provision of law above referred to, and which applies to the whole Province and necessarily including Montreal, the parties charged with the responsibility of keeping a true and exact account of all monies received, from whom and when received, and to whom and when paid, and the Clerk of the Special Session, the Clerk of the weekly session, or Clerk of the Justice of the Peace, and the officers so designated are clearly shewn by that provision, to be persons or public officers, other than the Clerk of the Peace for the District, by imposing upon the ordinary Clerk of the Justice, as above mentioned, the additional duty of rendering a fair copy of every such account to the Clerk of the Peace for the District. This provision in so far as it designates who are the proper Clerks to receive and to account for monies in no wise clashes with the provision of Section 85, of the same Act, which only makes the Clerk of the Peace, as public officer, assist the Police Magistrate when he is holding the Sessions and interpreting the two clauses, together, the provision of the 81st Section remains intact in so far as it imposes upon the Clerk or Clerks of the Police Magistrate, employed in his department and in constant attendance upon him, the duty of receiving all monies; keeping a true account of the same; and rendering a fair copy of the said account to the Clerk of the Peace for the District.

I might give as additional reasons in support of the opinion I have expressed upon this point the following, namely :

1stly. That monies are frequently paid over for fines imposed in the Police Office upon persons brought before the Police Magistrate by the Water Police, under the Police ordinance, and these are forthwith disposed of by the Police Magistrate, summarily, and consequently such monies are repeatedly paid to the Police Magistrate's Clerks.

2ndly. If a warrant of distress be issued, in execution of any conviction, it would necessarily be signed by the Police Magistrate and by him delivered to one of his Constables, and if a levy is made the Constable would be bound to pay over the money to the same Clerks who, by Section 81, are bound to receive monies and keep an account, and this in virtue of Section 77 of the same Act, which directs to whom the Constable shall pay such monies levied.

3rdly. All these proceedings are as much matters out of Session as the issuing of summonses or warrants which, by the decisions in Council to which I have adverted, are made the express duty of the Police Magistrate and his Clerks to attend to.

C

Question.--Will you please state what course has been adopted since you have been in office with reference to monies paid into the Peace Office department?

Answer.--All monies were first received by the deputy, Mr. Schiller, and until the period I shall presently mention, were paid over, either weekly or monthly, to my associate, Mr. Brehaut, and when the time arrived for accounting to Government the amount received was remitted; so also, when a warrant from the Government; for the payment of salaries came to hand it was deposited to the credit of Mr. Brehaut, who, thereupon gave me, the Deputy and Clerks, a check for our respective proportions.

Anterior to the 1st January last, considering this system objectionable, from the fact that one of the officers held, exclusively, monies to be accounted for to the Government and which might give rise to difficulties in case of his sudden death, I mentioned to Mr. Brehaut my views upon the subject, and that it would be better to make, every fortnight, a joint deposit in the Bank of all funds which came into our hands, to be withdrawn only upon an official check to be signed by us both.

This Mr. Brehaut agreed to, and this new arrangement has been carried out ever since the 1st of Jan., 1863. When a warrant for the payment of salaries is received from Government it is deposited to the credit of the same joint account, and the salary of each officer paid by separate checks, signed by us both. So also when monies are remitted to the Receiver General, or to the Sheriff, they are withdrawn by means of checks similarly signed.

Q.--Please state your views with reference to the organization of the office of Clerk of the Crown for the District of Montreal, and to make such suggestions as you may consider advisable with regard to the working of that department.

A.--The Clerk of the Crown in no instance is the recipient of any fines or penalties imposed by the Court of Queen's Bench; all such are paid directly into the hands of the Sheriff. The fees which hitherto have been paid to him, in proceedings issuing out of his office, are but very small indeed, so that the quarterly returns of such fees is but for a very insignificant amount. These fees when paid were entered in a small cash book. There has been, properly speaking, no positive authority for charging these fees, as no tariff exists whatever for the Court of Queen's Bench. Long usage and custom have regulated the amount of such fees upon such proceedings and the consequent practice to charge them is the only authority that exists for making them.

Yesterday, however, the authority of the Clerk of the Crown to charge these fees was called in question in a case of a private indictment for forcible entry and detainer, upon the issuing of a writ of restitution.

Not feeling satisfied, in the absence of any tariff, of my strict legal right to demand the fee upon such writ of restitution, which usage had sanctioned, I laid the whole matter before the Judge of the Court of Queen's Bench, as I considered was my duty, being an officer of the Court, and the Honble. Justices Aylwin and Mondelet--the only Judges present--instructed me that until the Government had, either by a law or otherwise, provided a tariff such as would protect me in making such charges, I should deliver this proceeding and every other of a like nature without making any charge. The effect of this decision is that, so long as a tariff is not made, I shall here-

after be unable to make any charge for any proceedings whatever--such as habeas corpus, subpœnas, &c., and shall have no fees of office to remit to Government. The same observations equally apply to the Court of Quarter Sessions, no tariff being in existence for that Court also.

In connection with the organization of the Crown Office as well as the Peace Office, during the sittings of the Queen's Bench and Quarter Sessions, I would refer to a practice which I consider very objectionable, namely--that of making the Deputy perform the duty of a Clerk to the Grand Jury, attending upon them during their sittings and being the person who delivers to them the bills of indictment. This duty of delivering bills to the Grand Jury properly belongs to the Constables who, upon the opening of each Court, are sworn faithfully to discharge that duty and to whom a special form of oath is administered, in accordance with the practice which prevails in England, a copy of which form I now produce, marked E. Notwithstanding they are so sworn to discharge that particular duty, it is performed by the deputy, to whom no oath is administered at all. In making use of the word "Deputy" I mean to designate Mr. Schiller, because it is right I should state that it forms no part of his duty, either as Deputy Clerk of the Crown, Deputy Clerk or the Peace, or Superintendent of Crown witnesses, to attend upon the Grand Jury, or to' deliver to them bills of indictment. It will be obvious to the Commissioners that this officer should not be taken away from his ordinary duty to perform work which should be discharged by Constables sworn for that purpose, apart from the circumstance that it unjustly exposes him to unfounded imputations of partiality, or exercising improper influence with the Grand Jury in the Grand Jury Room.

Grand Jurors are frequently told by the Court, in its opening address, that they can obtain all necessary assistance or information from the Court or the Crown prosecutor, and it would be more consistent with a proper administration of justice, if they sought assistance or information from those quarters than from the person who attends upon them, and who, in my opinion, is not in any way bound to appear before them.

Q.--Since you have been in the office of the Clerk of the Crown have you made a list of recognizances to be estreated under the provision of chap. 99, secs. 120 and 121, of the Consolidated Statutes of Canada, at the close of each term of the Criminal Court, or during the sitting of the said Court.

A.--Prior to the sitting of these Courts, a list is prepared of all persons bound under recognizances to appear before that Court. and on the first day thereof, they are called in open Court. In practice it has not been usual to call parties by proclamation on their recognizances until after the indictment has been returned into Court by the Grand Jury as " a True Bill," and the proceeding then adopted to obtain the estreat of the recognizance is for the Crown officer to make application to the Court that the default of the parties be recorded. In that manner the order of the Court which is mentioned in sec. 121, chap. 99, is observed.

I refer to a more recent law than the one adverted to in the question, namely, sec. 2 of chap. 106 of the Consolidated Statutes for Lower Canada, which introduced material alterations in the law as to the mode of estreating recognizances and the recovery of the penal sums therein mentioned.

This course so precludes, in fact supersedes, the necessity of sending in the list mentioned in sec. 120 of chap. 99, which contemplated a proceeding differing from the one required by the law adverted to by me, and which was introduced by 22 Vic., chap. 23. Anno Di. 1858.

I have shewn that the duty of collecting and accounting for monies is imposed by law upon the Clerk of the Judges of the Sessions of the Peace, but if it were assumed that his Clerks are not bound to receive fees of office upon preliminary proceedings issued by the Judge of the Sessions in the performance of his duties out of Sessions, to assist him in which the Government have lately assigned him two Clerks, it would be impossible that the Clerk of the Peace, who is now left with only one Clerk, if that Clerk required by the last Order in Council, to do duty, as well in the Crown Office as in the Peace Office, to attend to the collection of monies paid into the Police Office, as that duty could not be properly performed unless that party was in constant attendance in the Police Office, I would respectfully suggest to the Commissioners that the organisation of the Crown and the Peace Offices could be materially improved by having two Clerks instead of one, for the performance of the important duties which have to be discharged in those offices. As it is now, the one Clerk we have, besides drawing up the convictions, orders and judgments, copying of letters and various other work, is obliged to keep four important Registers, viz. :--Queen's Bench, Quarter Session, Expropriation Register, and Register of Convictions returned by the Justices in the District, and Register for all summary trials.

THURSDAY, April 23, 1863.

The evidence of Edward Carter, Esq., is resumed and continued as follows, viz. :--

Question.--You have alluded in your examination to the practice which prevails under the new law to which you refer, as to estreating recognizances, please state what course you adopted after the Court has ordered that default be recorded.

Answer.--When the default is on the part of those who have entered into a written recognizance, I make out a certificate of such default, taken from the Register, and annex it to the recognizance and file the same with the Prothonotary of the Superior Court, so that judgment may be entered in favor of the Crown. When the recognizance has been duly entered into in open Court, I make out an extract or certificate from the Register of such recognizance, affixing the Seal of the Court thereto and to which I also annex the certificate of default above mentioned; also depositing the same with the Prothonotary. This I do as soon after the Court is over as conveniently can be done, and in one instance I did it during the sitting of the Court.

The power of estreating recognizances was a discretionary power vested in the Judges and to be exercised according to the circumstances of each case. Hence it was required by sec. 120 and 121 of chap. 99, (Con. Stat.) that a list should be furnished of the the names, &c., of all persons bound under recognizance, but I consider that the effect of secs. 2, 3 and 4 chap. 106 of the Consolidated Statutes of Lower Canada is to remove that discretion and to effect the estreat by simple operation of law upon the default being recorded.

In using the expression "Police Magistrate" in some portions of my deposition, I, of course, intend to refer to the Judge of the Sessions of the Peace, who by a recent law, has acquired this new title, but without, in any way whatever, affecting his responsibility for the proper performance of the duties which attach to the Office of Police Magistrate.

Cross-examined by Mr. A. M. Delisle.

Q.--Is it, in your opinion, a part of the duties of either the Clerk of the Crown or of the Clerk of the Peace, to receive deposits to cover bonds or recognizances for the appearance of parties charged with criminal offences, and will you please state your legal views of the matter, in so far as the Clerk of the Crown or the Clerk of the Peace may be concerned, as also in so far as their Deputy is concerned, assuming the money to have been received by him ?

A.--In answer to the first part of this question I have no hesitation whatever in saying that it in no wise forms any part of the duties of either officer to receive deposits made in lieu of bail, and for this reason that the law in no wise authorises any Justices of the Peace or other public functionary to receive a deposit of money in lieu of bail. The law of England from the earliest times down to the present, has imposed upon Justices the duty of taking bail according to a recognized form, namely, by a recognizance with at least two sureties in some cases, and in other cases four, and these recognizances, together with all information and depositions, they are bound to transmit either to the Clerk of the Crown or to the Clerk of the Peace, as the case may be, and who are no more responsible for the custody of money taken in lieu of bail, than they would be responsible for Jewelry or effects which by an unauthorised act on the part of the Magistrate, he was pleased to receive for the convenience of a criminal, otherwise the offices of the Clerk of the Crown and Clerks of the Peace would be converted into Pawnbrokers Shops. The slightest reflection upon the law, in this respect, will convince any one of the correctness of my observations. In the first place bail is the delivery of the person charged into the custody of his securities, who are called manucaptors, who are, in reality, his gaoler; and thus the law contemplates that in allowing the accused to be enlarged in sufficient bail, it is a mere transfer of the custody from the officers of justice into that of the sureties who are vested by law with the power of seizing upon his person at any time and at any place, even on Sunday, and to carry him before the Justice for the purpose of recommitting him. To accomplish this object, they have also the power to require the assistance of the Sheriff or any of his officers.

This guarantee to prevent a failure of justice is wisely provided by the law in the form of a recognizance, such as I have mentioned ; but it would not exist if that form be departed from by substituting a deposit of money in lieu of bail.

There is, in the latter case, no transfer of the custody of the accused, but, in reality, freedom obtained by purchase, which the accused may avail himself of with impunity.

Another reason can be urged to establish the illegality of receiving such deposits. The provision of law in force, as to estreating recognizances, point out how a forfeit may be made enure to the benefit of the Crown ; but these provisions are totally unapplicable to the security in the form of a money deposit and the absence of any provision to apply to such a case is another proof of the want of authority to receive a deposit. There being no mode of declaring the forfeiture of the money, no Court could have authority to judge the forfeiture, and the proceedings must be regarded as any other unauthorised act, an absolute nullity. For all these reasons I have no hesitation in saying that I would refuse to receive any such deposit, and, if made to my Deputy, I would consider it as if made to an indifferent person and one wholly unconnected with my department.

In so far as the responsibility of the Deputy is concerned, assuming him to have received a money deposit I should say that the only difficulty that might arise would be as to what disposition he should make of the money, there being no provision of law directing whether money so obtained should be accounted for to the Sheriff or the Receiver General.

The only provision having the semblance of an application to such a case is the 21st sec., chap. 109 of the Consolidated Statutes of Lower Canada. But even that clause is made to refer to penalties and the forfeiture of bonds or recognizances ; and regarding the receipt of the deposit as an authorized act, I would consider him liable towards the party from whom he received the money.

Q.—Since you have held the office of Joint Clerk of the Peace, have you had the custody of stolen goods, and please state how many years practice you have had in the Criminal Courts, and whether you conceive it possible or consistent with the administration of Criminal Justice that the Clerk of the Peace should have the custody of such goods ?

A.—Since my appointment to office I have not had any portion of stolen goods, which at the time of my appointment, were in the actual custody of the High Constable, and so remained ever since, in so far as the unclaimed portion of them are concerned.

I am aware, nevertheless, of the existence of the provisions of an old Statute which makes the Clerks of the Peace the legal custodians of such goods ; but during seventeen years practice in the Criminal Courts, and from my experience during one year as an officer of such Courts, I can state that that portion of that law which provides that the custody of the said goods shall be in the Clerk of the Peace, is perfectly impracticable consistently with the due administration of Criminal Justice.

It has been found, in practice, to be absolutely necessary that the High Constable should have the custody of these goods, so that his evidence might be available before the Court to establish from whom he received them, and that they are in the same state as when he received them, so as to complete the link in the chain of evidence connected with the identity of the goods. This necessity is the more apparent in prosecutions at Quarter Sessions, where the Clerks of the Peace are required to conduct the prosecutions on behalf of the Crown. It would be utterly incompatible with the discharge of their duty that they should be at one and the same time a prosecutor and a witness on behalf of the Crown. Hale and other English authors, show that the custody of stolen goods is vested in the Sheriff or Constable. Besides stolen goods, the ends of Justice require the safe custody of articles of clothing, for instance, found on a criminal or on the person slain, and it would be highly inconsistent with the high office of the Clerk of the Peace, that he should be required to become the exhibitor of such articles in a public Court. I have, however, with my associate in office, since I have been in office, endeavoured to carry out that law in so far as it was possible for us to do, by requiring the High Constable to furnish us with a list of all the unclaimed goods in his possession, certified by the High Constable and presenting it to the Court of Queen's Bench (Crown side) during its last sitting, placing before them the provisions of the Act, calling their attention to the fact that they were unclaimed goods in the possession of the High Constable and not in our possession, and giving them the reason I have adverted to, that, in practice, the custody of them should be in the High Constable.

With a full knowledge of these facts the Judges gave the order to the Clerk of the Peace, authorizing them to sell the goods by Public Auction, in the manner required by law, and which sale has since been advertised.

———

SATURDAY, 25th April, 1863.

Charles Jos. Coursol, Esq., Judge of the Sessions of the Peace for the City of Montreal, sworn.

I was appointed to the office which I now hold, as successor to Col. Ermatinger, in February, 1856, as Inspector and Superintendent of Police.

Previous to this time, I had been practicing my profession as an Advocate for several years, during a portion of which time I conducted the business of the Revenue Inspector for the District of Montreal, as his legal adviser.

Having examined the Record of Proceedings in the case of Philip Durnford, R. I., vs. Thos. Drum, defendant ; the conviction in said case bearing date Montreal, 10th November, 1854 ; the writ of summons in this case was issued on the 9th November, 1854, purports to have been served by Wm. Hands, who signed the return of the said summons, as Wm. Hands, Constable. My impression is, that it was the practice to examine the constable who had served the summons when the defendant made default ; but I am not positive as to this point, as there were different Magistrates who sat at different times, and whose practice might not have been uniform. I was the Attorney for the prosecution in the case.

It appears in that case that a warrant of distress was issued on the twenty-third of November, 1854 and signed by Alexis Laframboise, Esq., J.P. ; the return of the said warrant of distress bears the signature of "Wm. Hands, Constable." On the back of this warrant there is a receipt as follows :—"Received, the sum of one pound fourteen shillings currency."

MONTREAL, 5th January, 1855.

C. J. Coursol.—I was Attorney also in the case of Peter Casey, Deputy Revenue Inspector, against Emelie Guilbault, for the prosecutor in which case the conviction was signed by Wm. Ermatinger, Esq., then Inspector and Superintendent of Police, and was made on the 13th November, 1854. There was a warrant of distress issued in the said last-mentioned case, bearing date the 5th December, 1854, and I see that the amount was paid on the 7th December, 1854, by a memorandum on the back thereof, signed, "Wm. Hands, Constable." There is also a receipt thereon, signed by me on the 5th January, 1855, as prosecuting Attorney.

Having examined the proceedings in the case of "The Harbour Commissioners of Montreal against Francois Contant," which took place in the Police Court, for infractions of the By-Laws of the Harbour Commissioners, in November, 1854, in which I was Counsel for the defendant, and the Hon. Mr. Sol.-Gen. Abbott, Counsel for the prosecution, I perceive that the summons and subpœna in that case were served by the said Wm. Hands, and the execution of the same signed by said Hands as Constable. The said Wm. Hands acted as Constable in the service of those papers, unquestionably.

All said cases were disposed of at special sessions of the Police Court. The late Alfred Harvey was a clerk, in the employ of the Clerk of the Peace, and as such performed certain duties in the Police Office, under my supervision.

Q. Had you occasion to complain of the absence of the late Mr. Harvey, who was a clerk in the Peace Office, on the ground that he was absent from said office on other business than that connected with the said office?

A. I did not complain of the absence of Mr. Harvey particularly; but I complained that often in the press of business I did not receive sufficient assistance, the clerks being otherwise occupied in the Peace Office up stairs, especially during the holding of the Criminal Terms of the Court; and I may mention that Mr. Harvey was generally sent to perform duties in the Police Court in the absence of Mr. C. M. Delisle, who was then my clerk, and Mr. René Cotret, who was then a clerk in the Peace Office.

Q. Is it not true that the late Mr. Harvey was very often absent from the said Peace Office on other business than that connected with said office? and if so, state the cause of such absence.

A. As Mr. Harvey was not in my employ, it is impossible for me to say whether his absence was on business connected with the office or otherwise.

Q. Have you any knowledge of said Mr. Harvey having, at any time, or from time to time, during his connection with the said Peace Office, attended to any other business than that pertaining to the Office? —and, if so, state what other business, and for whom it was transacted, during usual office hours.

A. I have no personal knowledge of it.

Q. Will you please favor us with any information you may consider important with reference to the present organization of the department of the Peace and the Crown, and of their relations to your own department as Judge of the Sessions of the Peace.

MONTREAL, 27th April, 1863.

Mr. Coursol's evidence continued:—

A. There exists, since a few days only, a difference of opinion in relation to the performance of certain important duties of office, between the Clerk of the Peace and myself, which requires special mention in the interests of the public and the good administration of the affairs in our department.

The joint Clerks of the Peace contend that the collection and perception of all monies formerly as fees to them, but which presently are paid for certain public uses mentioned in the law, does not devolve upon them, but that such monies, fines, penalties, costs, recognizances, warrants, subpœnas, &c., &c., should be collected, received or paid to the Judge of the Sessions or his clerks. I humbly maintain that, according to law and long-established usage, such a duty devolves on the Clerks of the Peace.

The Clerks of the Peace are commissioned officers of the Crown, directly responsible to the Government for the acts done in pursuance of such commission. In support of the view I have taken, I refer to the 85th Section of Chapter 103 of the Consolidated Statutes of Canada, in which it is said that in all the cities, towns, or other places in Lower Canada where General or Quarter Sessions of the Peace are held, the Clerk or Clerks of the Peace shall act as Clerk or Clerks of the Justices of the Peace and of the Inspectors and Superintendents of Police, as well as at all special as at all weekly Sessions of the Peace therein. As Judge of the Sessions of the Peace, I am possessed of all powers of two or more Justices of the Peace and of the Inspectors and Superintendents of Police in such cities. Therefore the Clerks of the Peace are bound to act as Clerks at all such special or weekly Sessions held by me in the Police Court. By an Act respecting the Registers to be kept by Justices of the Peace, which is to be found at Ch. 98 of said Consolidated Statutes of Lower Canada, every Justice of the Peace in Lower Canada is obliged to keep in a Register true and faithful minutes or memoranda at length of every conviction by him made pursuant to any law or statute in force in Lower Canada; but in the cities of Quebec, Montreal and Three Rivers, such Registers are to be kept by the Clerks of the Peace in the said cities respectively, and who are to account for the fees imposed according to law by the Justices of the Peace in the said cities respectively. They are also obliged to specify in such Register, as well as the day when execution was issued to levy such costs on condemnation, and the day when the fine was paid into the hands of the Clerk pursuant to such condemnation.

In virtue, also, of the 81st Section of the Consolidated Statutes of Canada, Ch. 103, the Clerk of the Special Session, Clerk of the weekly Session, or Clerk of the Justice of the Peace, has to keep a true and exact account of moneys by him received, of whom and when received, and to whom and when paid; and shall, once in every three months, render a fair copy of every such account to the Clerk of the Peace for the District in which such payment has been made. It is evident, in my opinion, that such a clause can only apply to the clerk of the Justice of the Peace in country parts or in places where there is no Clerk of the Peace appointed; but it cannot apply to the Clerk of the Peace for Montreal, as he is, as already shown, Clerk of the Special Session and Clerk of the Weekly Session in such cities, and that the Clerks in the Police Office are not authorised to act as Clerk to the Justices of the Peace or to myself at any of the numerous Special Sessions held daily, nor at any of the Weekly Sessions.

It will be seen by the 77th Section of the same Act, that, on every warrant of distress, the constable to whom the same is directed shall be ordered to pay the amount of the same, to be levied unto the Clerk of the Peace, Clerk of the Special Session, Clerk of the Weekly Session, or Clerk of the Justices of the Peace, "as the case may be," which must apply to the Clerks of the Justices of the Peace for the country parts exclusively, and not to the Clerks in the Police Office, inasmuch as such Clerks are not the Clerks of the Peace, Clerk of the Special Session, or Clerk of the Weekly Sessions. In Lower Canada, as it may be seen by the 74th Section of the same Act; the fees to which any Clerk of the Special Session, or Clerk of the Weekly Session, or Clerk to any Justice or Justices of the Peace out of Session is entitled, are ascertained and regulated by the Justices of the Peace at General or Quarter Sessions for the several districts, and the table of such fees shall be laid before the Secretary of this Province, in order that such Secretary may subscribe a certificate that such fees are proper to be demanded and received by the Clerks of the Special and Weekly Sessions, and the Clerks of the Justices of the Peace throughout Lower Canada.

I beg also to refer the Commissioners to the Chapter 105 of the Consolidated Statutes of Canada, respecting the summary administration of criminal justice. The Inspectors and Superintendents of Police for the cities of Quebec and Montreal, sitting in open Court, may, respectively, in cases of persons charged before them, do all acts by such Act authorised to be done by Recorders ; and all provisions of such Acts, referring to Recorders or Recorder's Court, and the Clerks of the Recorders' Courts, shall be construed as referring to the Inspectors and Superintendents of Police, of the Courts held by them respectively.

Now, by going further and reading the 35th clause, it will be seen that every fine imposed under the authority of such Act, must be paid to the Recorder, Superintendent of Police, Sheriff, Deputy-Sheriff, or Justices of the Peace, as the case may be, who has imposed the same ; or to the Clerk of the Recorder's Court, or Clerk of the Peace, " as the case may be," showing clearly that no power or authority exists in my clerks to receive such fines, and that in the event of their receiving such fines no responsibility could attach to them, inasmuch as they are not accountable to Government.

The power of appointing such clerks is subject, of course, to the approval of His Excellency the Governor-General, is entirely left to me by the Executive Government, and, with the assistance of such clerks, I perform my duties out of Sessions.

I contend that the Clerks of the Peace are the custodians of all the records, convictions, and papers filed or appertaining to any proceeding originating before the Police Court from the time of the opening of the sitting of any Special or Weekly Session ; and that it is their duty, as such custodians and clerks of such Sessions, to prepare all subsequent proceedings which result in any judgment, conviction, discharge, or order emanating from such Court in session, namely, all convictions, warrants of distress, orders for the payment of money, and all commitments in default of payment or satisfaction of the judgments rendered.

I am of opinion, also, that all bills of costs are to be made by the Clerks of the Peace, who may be, in accordance with the 75th Section of Chapter 103, liable to forfeit the sum of $80 if he receives or demands a greater fee than he is authorised by law to exact.

I am aware, also, that the Clerks in the Police Office, at the request and with the sanction of the Clerk of the Peace, have received monies in payment of warrants or other proceedings when such fees are payable ; but it was no part of their duty, and done only to accommodate the Clerks of the Peace.

I have frequently remonstrated against a practice which I considered irregular and productive of confusion, and which might result in the loss of money.

I would also call attention to Chap. 93 of the Con. Statutes L. C., wherein it is stated that until the first January, 1861, all salaries, fees, monies, and pecuniary profits attached to the offices of the Peace should form a special fund called the Officers of Justice Fee Fund ; but that they shall, nevertheless, be demanded and collected by the Clerks of the Peace in their respective districts, and that out of the amount collected in every year of such salary, fees and emoluments, pecuniary profits, the Government might assign an annual fixed salary of two thousand dollars yearly to the office of the Clerk of the Peace, and it cannot be expected that I myself, for my clerks, should be called upon to collect the salaries, fees, and pecuniary emoluments attached to the aforesaid offices. By Chap. III. of the Con. Statutes of L. C., Judges of Sessions have to make an annual report of all prosecutions before them, showing the number of plaints, the number of each offence, the number of convictions, commitments and discharges ; and in cases of summary convictions, punishment awarded, and the number of sentences of each class. No mention whatever is made in the form of the statistical return provided by the Statute, of how the amount of fines and costs imposed at any Session or Sessions held by them, exclusive or inclusive of costs, as the case may be, so as to afford information as to what proportion of those fines were collected. I would add that it would be a matter of great interest to the public if the law should provide that such a return was made by the officers who have been collecting and are by law appointed to collect all monies collected in the department. Under the present practice first referred to, I have no means of showing what are the proceeds of the office under my control.

Cross-examined by Mr. Brehaut :—

Q. Do you consider yourself responsible for the accuracy of all orders, convictions and judgments submitted to you for your signature, and which you may have signed.

A. Undoubtedly.

Cross-examined by Mr. Delisle :—

Q. Had you ever a conversation with Mr. Wm. Hands, late Constable in the Police Office, about two years ago, in which you told him you had been at the seat of Government for about a week, and that you had seen his name in the returns (meaning the returns or pay-lists transmitted by the Clerk of the Peace,) as a clerk, and asked him if he had been such clerk, and if he got any money for being such clerk ?

A. I remember that one day, about two or three years ago, I was in conversation in the office with Chas. M. Delisle, who was telling me that Hands had been charged as a clerk in the office of the Clerk of the Peace ; that he had signed the pay-lists that they were in Quebec, when Hands came into the office, and I asked him, addressing him this way, " Well, Hands, so you have been a clerk in the office up stairs." He replied, " I knew it after my discharge." Then I told him, " I am told that you signed the receipts for your pay, and that the receipts were in Quebec." " Well," said he, " I have not got much for it," or words to that effect. He named a sum he had received ; I cannot say whether it was twenty or thirty dollars. *I never told him that I had seen the pay-lists in Quebec, nor anywhere else ;* and the first time I ever saw them was since this enquiry was commenced.

Q. Will you please state how many years you practiced in the Criminal Courts as an Advocate, and how long you have held the office of Inspector and Superintendent of Police and Judge of Sessions, and state whether you conceive it possible or consistent with the administration of criminal justice, that the Clerk of the Peace should have the custody of stolen goods ?

A. I am aware that by law the Clerks of the Peace are pointed out as the officers who should keep the stolen goods ; but after an experience of nearly twenty years in the Criminal Courts of this city, either as a practicing lawyer, Coroner, or Judge of Sessions, I conceive that it would be impossible for the Clerks of the Peace to perform their duties properly, especially during the holding of the Criminal Courts, if they were obliged to produce in Court, at trials, stolen goods, which must necessarily be deposited in a vault, and which must be sworn to and identified at the trial, in which they themselves are conducting as Crown prosecutors.

When the stolen goods are brought to the Police Court, they are invariably given in charge of the High Constable by me, who produces them when called upon during the preliminary examination, as often as required, and subsequently in Court at the trial of the prisoners, whether at the Queen's Bench or Quarter Sessions. I am aware that the High Constable has kept the key of the vault where the stolen goods are kept. During the said twenty years I am aware that the stolen goods have always been placed in the charge of the High Constable.

TUESDAY, 28th April, 1863.

Mr. Coursol re-examined by the Commissioners:—
It is possible that I had been at Quebec shortly before the conversation I had with the said Wm. Hands.

Joseph Jones, Esq., of Montreal, Coroner, sworn, deposes as follows, viz.:
I was appointed Coroner for the District of Montreal on 9th April, 1838, and have continued to act as Coroner and joint Coroner since that time.

Q. Have you at any time during the inquisition or inquisitions you held as such Coroner in Montreal, consequent upon the Gavazzi Riots, got any stationery, such as paper, pens, ink, subpœnas, warrants and blank forms from any person or persons connected with the Peace or Police Office for the city of Montreal, and for any and what purpose?

A. I have occasionally, for the use of my office of Coroner, procured from the office of the Clerk of the Crown and the Police Office, sheets of paper and blank forms, for which paper and blank forms I never paid any sum or sums of money to the Clerk of the Crown or his Deputy, nor to the Clerks of the Peace, nor to any one whatsoever.

I have not the least doubt that I procured from the office of the Clerk of the Peace, Clerk of the Crown, and Police Office, some stationery for the purpose of my enquiry into the Gavazzi Riot inquest, but for which I did not pay any sum or sums of money; but I did not make any charge against Government for such stationery or blank forms. The enquiry covered a space of 31 days, and my stationery account was only £1 6s. 3d. This was the amount I paid for stationery for said inquest to some stationer in Montreal.

(Signed)   JOSEPH JONES.

Guilliaume Lamothe, of the City of Montreal, Chief of Police for the said city of Montreal, sworn, saith:—
I have been Chief of Police since the month of December, 1861. When I entered into the office, I did not find any stolen goods in the possession of the Police, nor any vault or place set apart for the reception and keeping of such goods.

The only articles I found there were, a breast-pin, two or three studs, two sleeve-links, and a piece of watch-chain, supposed to be gold. These were in the bureau of the late Chief of Police. I enquired whence these articles came, and was informed, at the time, that they had been taken from a prisoner arrested during the visit of the Prince of Wales to Montreal.

When the police under my charge arrest a party in the possession of goods suspected to be stolen, both party and goods are sent to the Police Office before Mr. Coursol, and the goods remain in that office.

Within a few days, however, I notice one or two cases in which the goods have been sent back to the Police Station, and no sale of such goods has taken place since I have been there. About eight months ago I asked the Police Committee if we could not keep the unclaimed stolen goods in our office, and was told in answer that formerly it was the custom to have auction sales of such unclaimed stolen goods, but that within the last seven or eight years there had been no such auctions, owing, I was told, to an order from the Government, or to arrangements between the Police Office and my office. Since I have been in office I have ascertained from Mr. Schiller, for one, and from other persons connected with the Police Office, that I had no right to keep such unclaimed stolen goods. The articles above mentioned as found in the Bureau of the late Chief of Police, remain in my custody subject to order in reference thereto.

Since I have been Chief of Police there has been only one public auction in my office, but it consisted only of old clothing and effects belonging to the Police force, and three or four pairs of boots which had been found in the streets; the proceeds of the sale amounted to about twenty-two dollars. My opinion in the matter is, that all unclaimed stolen goods found or taken by the city police force should be returned to our department and sold for the benefit of the City Police at the expiration of a certain time.

WEDNESDAY, 29th April, 1863.

Mr. Guillaume Lamothe's evidence continued:—
Since my examination yesterday, I have enquired more particularly into the relations heretofore subsisting between the Corporation and the Police Court with reference to the disposition to be made of stolen goods, and have found and now produce a certified copy of an order made by the Police Committee on the 30th September, 1861, by which the Chief of Police was instructed to keep a book for the entry of the stolen articles deposited into his hands, and ordering that all articles found by policemen or coming into their possession in the discharge of their duty, should be placed into the hands of the Chief of Police. Said copy now filed marked A. I have learned, also, on enquiry, from the City Clerk and the City Treasurer, as well as from an examination of the Treasurer's books, that a sale took place in 1855, advertised as unclaimed goods, amounting to £14 14s. 2d. I ascertained, from some of my officers who were in the force at that time, that the said articles sold consisted of an old wagon and old sleigh, and different other rubbish accumulated in our department, and a few unclaimed goods which I was informed had never been taken to the Police Court. The sale now spoken of was the last sale previous to my entering into office as such Chief of Police. I may add that, as a general rule, since I have been in office, stolen goods, unclaimed, are not sent back to our office, with the exception of the few cases I have mentioned above. This order of the Police Committee has never been acted upon, to the best of my knowledge, and I never saw it till last night.

The only unclaimed article suspected to be stolen, which has not been disposed of yet, in my office, is a buffalo robe which was found last winter.

There are articles, now and then, in the possession of the detectives, for the purpose of identification.

I now produce a document headed "Description "and amount of silver ware taken from Thomas "Wyeb, at the time of his arrest, and supposed 'to "have been stolen from persons at the time of the "late disastrous fire at Montreal, and which docu- "ment bears the following receipt: " Received, from Thos. McGrath, Chief of Police, the articles herein enumerated.—Montreal, 5th August, 1852."

"(Signed,)   DELISLE & BREHAUT."

Which document is marked B, fyled, and is now produced by me before the Commissioners, as a docu- ment found in my department of Chief of Police. I also produce, by request of Commissioners, another document, being the Police report, Station A, from 7th to 8th November, 1856, Friday and Saturday, marked C, and which report I looked for in my de- partment, at the request of Mr. Schiller, who spoke to me about the case of a man named Vincenzo Mon- tesi, and by which report it appears that the sum of £9 13s. 2d. was found upon his person, which amount, I was informed by John O'Leary, who arrested the party, was sent before the Police Magistrate with the prisoner.

Cross-examined by A. M. Delisle :

Q. Are you aware that a bag full of unclaimed stolen clothes, connected with the case of the Prang- leys, charged with larceny at the St. Lawrence Hall, was taken from the Police Office to the Police Sta- tion, about two months ago?

A. I am aware that a part of a bag containing coats and wearing apparel was taken back to my of- fice as being goods unclaimed, but belonging to the prisoners themselves, to whom they were restored. At least I was asked by O'Leary whether he should return them to the Prangleys, and I take for granted that he did so.

Q. Was there not a lot of stolen boots delivered to their owner without being brought to the Police Of- fice before the Judge of Sessions, about 3 weeks ago?

A. There were some boots found in a field, under the snow, which were identified by a poor carpenter, who stated that they were his only means of earning a livelihood. I returned them to him, but I believe that the necessary precautions were taken to have hem produced in case they should be required af- terwards.

THURSDAY, 30th April, 1863.

Present :—Messrs. LAFRENAYE and DOHERTY, Com.

A proceeding by " Quo Warranto" having been adopted by Mr. Schiller, Mr. Delisle applied to the Commissioners for permission to put in a written statement explanatory of his position, lest the pro- ceedings under the Commission should be stayed.— The Commissioners told Mr. Delisle that they saw no objection to his filing such a document.

FRIDAY, May 1st, 1863.

Present :—Messrs. LAFRENAYE and DOHERTY.

Mr. Delisle appeared before the Commissioners, and handed in the following statement, after reading it to the Commissioners, and the same was received and fyled :—

Statement made by Alexander Maurice Delisle, Esquire, with reference to the charges preferred against him, before Pierre Richard LaFrenaye and Marcus Doherty, Esquires, Commissioners, named to enquire into certain charges of malversation of office made against him as late Clerk of the Crown and Joint Clerk of the Peace, explanatory of his position, nd of the facts connected with said charges.

When the Act 13 and 14 Vic., chap. 37 was enacted in 1850, funding the fees of the said offices, I made an arrangement with William H. Brehaut, Esquire, Joint Clerk of the Peace with me, as to a division of the labor of the said office between us, to the following effect: I held the office of Clerk of the Crown alone, and I was necessarily bound to perform all the duties of that department individually, and occupied a dif- ferent and distinct office in the Court House from that of the Clerks of the Peace.

I undertook, as my share of the duties of Joint Clerk of the Peace, to take the management of the Court of Quarter Sessions, where I was to act as Crown Prosecutor, and to do all and every the duties connected with that Court, which involved the read- ing and examination of all informations, depositions and examinations in the cases coming before it; the engrossing and preparing of all the bills of indictment to be submitted ; and in a word, to make all the Re- gisters, proceedings and writings connected with that Court. Mr. Brehaut, on the other hand, assumed all the other duties of the office, such as holding the weekly and special Sessions, the superintendence of the clerks; and the receiving of all monies, and ac- counting for them.

When warrants were received quarterly for the pay- ment of the officers and clerks, Mr. Brehaut always paid me by a cheque on the Bank of Montreal, for which I gave my receipt on a pay-list which was pre- sented to me, and which was, subsequently, sent in to the Government. As to Mr. William Hands, who has deposed that, although returned in the pay-lists to Government as a clerk, he never was such, and never received any of the salary represented to have been paid to him, I can only say that after the departure of Mr. Baby in February, 1854, then second clerk in the office, because the salary of fifty pounds he was receiving was not sufficient to maintain him, and wholly inadequate to the duties of a second clerk, Mr. Brehaut spoke to me one day on the subject, and expressed his intention to employ the said William Hands, who was then a constable under the High Constable, alleging, to the best of my recollection, that as an efficient clerk could not possibly be ob- tained for £50 a year, he had the intention of employ- ing the said Hands, (who wrote a good hand,) to fill the vacant office ; and mentioned, also, that he could be used as a messenger, (having no such officer,) which would be very useful. I told Mr. Brehaut, to the best of my memory, that as it was a matter pro- perly connected with his department, as agreed be- tween us, he might do as he pleased, and from that day I supposed that the said Hands had been en- gaged by Mr. Brehaut, for I saw him constantly about the office, and I also saw his name in the pay-lists returned every quarter to Government. As my de- partment was separate and distinct from the office of the peace, I cannot say, particularly at this distance of time how Mr. Hands was employed ; but I frequent- ly employed him myself to do messages for me, and I would have hardly taken that liberty with him if I had not supposed that I could fairly do so, and that I had some control over him. Mr. Brehaut will be bet- ter able to say how he employed Mr. Hands ; but that gentleman informs me that he acted with him, both as a clerk and a messenger, at the time referred to, and that he duly paid him the amount of salary due him, as appears by the receipts he gave, and which were, in due course, transmitted to Government.

As to Mr. Auguste Delisle, he has deposed that he never knew that he was a clerk, and that he does not believe he received more than £70 during the time he was employed, say 9 months. I see that he signed receipts which, together, amount to the sum of £93 15s. 0d. It is somewhat strange that a person of education, such as that gentleman is, should have given receipts, by which he admitted that the money paid him was for the duties he performed as second clerk, without knowing the fact.

Mr. Auguste Delisle is aged, and admitted that his memory was not good, and I can only explain this rather strange pretension from the fact that, indeed, his memory is at fault. I can only say that the most, if not all the work he did, was connected with the branch of duty which I had assumed, and which consisted of making up the registers of the Criminal Courts, and especially of the Court of Quarter Sessions, (the most difficult duty devolving upon a clerk,) and as he performed it under my immediate superintendence, it will, to say the least of it, appear somewhat strange that any doubt could exist that the nature of the duties he was engaged in were not those of a clerk. I am not aware what arrangements Mr. Brehaut had made with Mr. Auguste Delisle, but that he performed the duty of clerk in the office, I most positively affirm.

With reference, therefore, to both Mr. Hands and Mr. Auguste Delisle, I can only say, and most solemnly affirm, that Mr. Brehaut, nor any one else, never directly nor indirectly in any manner, shape, or form whatever, paid me one farthing beyond my legitimate salary, as it was received every quarter from Government, *and that I never received*, in whole or in part, any portion of the salaries alledged to have been paid either to Mr. Hands or Mr. Auguste Delisle, and which those persons deny having received. On the contrary, Mr. Brehaut assures me that he paid both those persons the full amount, for which they gave him their receipts on the pay-lists, transmitted to the Government quarterly with our accounts. I would add, that neither Mr. Hands or Mr. Auguste Delisle ever complained to me on the subject.

As to the stolen goods, the evidence already taken by the Commissioners shows that they never were placed in the charge of the clerks of the Peace, who, by the very nature of their office, which involved the necessity, as I have already said, of their acting as Crown Prosecutors in the Court of Quarter Sessions, could not be made the custodians of them, and the evidence of Mr. Carter and Mr. Coursol, the Judge of Sessions, establish that fact, it appears to me, in the most conclusive and satisfactory manner. As to the sale of unclaimed stolen goods, which, it appears, took place in July, 1858, I can only say that I never had any knowledge of it, nor that Mr. Schiller was in possession of the proceeds of that sale for so long a time. I was, since 1850, frequently sent by the Government in the country parts, to investigate important cases of felony, and, besides, often employed on commissions issued by the Government, which necessitated, frequent, and prolonged absences from my office, between the terms of the Criminal Courts, and I am, necessarily, from that circumstance, not so well acquainted with the details of the department as if I had remained constantly in my office.

As to the sum of £50 said to have been received by Mr. Schiller, under the direction of the Inspector and Superintendent of Police, in August, 1859, in lieu of bail in the case of one John Greene, accused of larceny, I declare that I never had any knowledge of such a deposit; and I would add that, being a proceeding in nowise contemplated by the law, it could not be expected from me, as one of the heads of the department, that I should have contemplated that any such proceeding could possibly arise. I consider, however, that no responsibility whatever can attach to me for such an unusual, and, in my opinion, illegal proceeding. In saying this, however, I wish to be understood not in any manner to impugn the conduct or motives of Mr. Schiller, since the act was done by the direction of the magistrate, and, necessarily, with the knowledge of all the parties concerned.

With reference to my position in this matter, I cannot do better than refer to the evidence of Mr. Carter as establishing that no responsibility can attach to me for an unauthorised act committed by others, and which could not impose upon me the duty of receiving that sum, and accounting for it.

When I have the advantage of adducing evidence in my defence, I shall be enabled, I trust, to establish still more conclusively the points to which I have referred, as explanatory of my position, and, I hope, remove any unfavorable impressions which may exist affecting my character and integrity as a public officer and a citizen, and which a portion of the press of Montreal, for purposes best known to themselves, so freely and unfairly circulated to my prejudice.

(Signed.)   A. M. DELISLE.
Montreal, 1st May, 1863.

Alexander Maurice Delisle, Esq., after being duly sworn upon the Holy Evangilists, doth depose and say that the facts enumerated in the above statement are true and correct in every particular, to the best of his knowledge and belief.

(Signed,)   A. M. DELISLE.
Sworn before me at Montreal,
this 1st day of May, 1863.
(Signed,   W. BADGLEY,
                   J. S. C.

MONDAY, 31st August, 1863,
Received a notice from the Commissioners that they will sit on Wednesday the 2nd September, 1863.

WEDNESDAY, 2nd September, 1863.
Mr. Kerr, Advocate, appeared as Counsel for Mr. Schiller, under reserve, and enquired whether a subpœna had been served upon C. M. Delisle.

The Commissioners informed Mr. Kerr that a subpœna had been served upon C. M. Delisle, of which they held the return of service. By the return it appeared that the service had been made at Ogdensburgh, in the State of New York.

Mr. Kerr asked to be allowed to see the subpœna and the return to it.

The Commissioners intimated to Mr. Kerr that they would give him an answer this afternoon.

Thomas Ireland, of Montreal, Engraver, sworn, saith :

I am and have been an Engraver in the City of Montreal for seventeen or eighteen years past, during which time I remember having been called upon once or twice, to give my evidence in cases of forgery of Bank Notes, as an Engraver; but I never actually did give evidence. I never was paid anything for my attendance at Court.

But I remember a case in which a man was convicted of forgery, and aware that some engraver's tools were in the possession of Mr. Schiller, I asked him what he had done with them, this was three or four years afterwards, and he said if I would come up that I might pick out some of them. I went sometime after to Mr. Schiller, and he took me into a little room and let me pick them out.

I think there were a couple of little eye glasses, two or three small files, made into gravers, and a small piece of copper about the size of my hand, a small hand vice, and a piece of oil stone.

The man so convicted, and to whom those tools belonged, was Nathan Adams. It was about twelve years ago, in the old Court Honse, that the trial took place. I received these tools in the new Court House about four or five years ago. Mr. Schiller and I went into the room adjoining the Police Office, Mr. Benjamin Deslisle, the High Constable, and I believe another gentleman were with us. I think it was Mr. Benjamin Deslisle who opened the door, and we then went into the room. There were lots of things in the room.

Mr. Schiller showed me the tools and I picked them out as I have mentioned. I thought the things would have been of greater value, or I should not have bothered myself about them. That was the only time that I ever went into that room. I would not have given half-a-dollar for the whole lot that I got.

Cross-Examined by Mr. Schiller :

I did not pay Mr. Schiller anything for these tools, I never made him no present for the same. They were given to me openly as I have mentioned.

I had been subpœnad as a witness in this case and was neither taxed or paid for my attendance. I think the gentleman alluded to above was Mr. Charles M. Delisle. I am not quite positive but to the best of my belief it was him. I think it was in the afternoon, on a Saturday. I was not more than five or six minutes in picking them out. I was fully sure from the way in which he acted that Mr. Benjamin Delisle had charge of the things in the room, as he had the key of the vault which he opened. I would not have taken the trouble to come for said articles if I supposed them to be of so little value.

TRANSLATED.

Francois Maurice LePallieur, Bailiff for the District of Montreal, sworn, saith :

I have been acting as Bailiff and Constable in the District of Montreal for eighteen years.

I had occasion of serving subpœnas for each term of Criminal Court held in Montreal since eighteen years, on the different persons who were called before said Court.

I have been in the habit of going to the country to serve such subpœnas.

Mr. Schiller has never been particular in obliging me to make my return on the subpœna; but I made him my reports on a list. It was Mr. Schiller who made up the returns on the subpœnas, and I signed them. I always gave on the list aforesaid the distance from Montreal to the place of such service; but I dont know the reason why the distance was not mentioned in the return; because I never made any remark on that subject. I never thought of putting my fees in my returns, on the subpœnas, I trusted Mr. Schiller for all that. It was he who prepared the returns and I signed them.

It was Mr. Schiller who paid my emoluments. Mr. Schiller gave me the half of my emoluments of such service. On the list that I gave to Mr. Schiller I put so many leagues and so much service, and when each term was over Mr. Schiller exhibited to me the number of copies of such subpœnas, and the distances I had travelled, as well as the original of such copies, and paid me the half of the emoluments due to me. Since eighteen years I have been in the habit of serv-

ing subpœnas for the Criminal Court. I never received more than the half of the emoluments that I had a right to receive, and as so agreed between us. When I begun to work as Constable the condition was that Mr. Schiller should give me the half of the emoluments. This agreement has been observed since eighteen years. I served also subpœnas for the Quarter Sessions; but this had nothing to do with Mr. Schiller. I never kept any account with Mr. Schiller; it is impossible for me, for that reason, to say to how much my emoluments amounted at every term. Mr. Schiller has given me monies in advance, and at the end of the term we settled our accounts.

Sometimes he gave me also money for the poor witnesses who had no means to come to this city. I was ntitled to three shillings per league, and one shilling and three pence for each service. It was not often that another Constable than myself, of the city, was employed to go to the country.

The lists of which I have spoken remained in the possession of Mr. Schiller.

Cross-Examined by Mr. Schiller :

When it was impossible for me to serve all the subpœnas, my son was employed by Mr. Schiller to summon the others. I had but very few subpœnas to serve in the City of Montreal.

I have always been told by Mr. Schiller to bring in the witnesses, so as to have them in Court for the appointed day. He always told me if they were in want of money to pay their travelling expenses, and to advance it to them. At each term, in which it has been the case, that the witnesses were poor, I advanced them money. It often occurred that I brought some witnesses with me in my carriage.

It is to my personal knowledge that in Doctor Paterson's case for murder, Mr. Schiller became responsible for the board of witnesses, and I believe that there were about thirteen or fourteen of them who were poor.

In the said case Mr. Schiller gave me a letter addressed to Mr. Johnson, J.P., at Clarenceville, in which he was desired to pay the expenses of the witnesses who were poor.

The course of Justice has never been delayed by the absence of witnesses.

I was in the habit as soon as I returned from the country, by day or by night, to go to Mr. Schiller, and make my report. When I say night I mean till eleven or twelve o'clock, P.M. Very often I came to Mr. Schiller at ten or eleven o'clock, P.M., to have some subpœnas at the Court House.

It is to my knowledge that in many important cases I travelled by night, which must have cost more than the allowance could give. I might mention the following cases, viz: one in New Glasgow, one in Shefford, one in St. Athanase, one in St. Louis de Gonzague, one in Clarenceville, one at St. Hughes, one in Sorel, one in Bedford, and many others of which I have no remembrance. It happened also that whilst a trial was going on I was sent hastily by night to the country, to have some witnesses by the next morning, and I was obliged to travel all night and have my horses changed two or three times. I have always been satisfied of the payments given to me by Mr. Schiller. I have been liberally paid, and, moreover, sometimes I received more than I expected to have. I have been always ready to work for Mr. Schiller. It was Mr. Schiller who gave me the money to advance to poor witnesses of which I have spoken. He always advanced me money. When I was sent by Mr. Schiller, during a trial, by night, my order was to bring the witness at any cost, and if he was not at his domicile, to go for him at any place where he might be.

I remember once Mr. Schiller told me that he noticed an error to my prejudice in my accounts, in an addition on a settlement, and paid me the amount which was due to me.

Mr. Kerr having appeared the Commissioners gave him communication of the subpœna to C. M. Delisle, but declined to give him a copy of it, or to permit one to be taken.

This subpœna had been issued on the 19th March, 1863. Served at Ogdensburg, State of New York, on the 23rd of the same month, and was returnable at Montreal on the 27th of same month.

William Fraser, of Montreal, Constable, sworn, saith :

I am a Police Constable, and have been so for the ast ten years ; and have acted as Crier the same length of time in the Police Court, and as Messenger in the office of the Clerk of the Crown, and of the Peace.

THURSDAY, 3rd September, 1863.
William Fraser re-appears, and continues his evidence :

As such Messenger my duties were to attend at the Post Office, and to take letters to and from the Post ; deposit money in the Bank, and drawing money therefrom by checks, and generally doing all that was required of me as such Messenger by the heads of the office.

There was and is still one drawer in the Post Office for the Clerk of the Crown, and Joint Clerk of the Peace. With the exception of Sundays and holidays I did the Post Office business for those two departments for the last ten years. On Sundays and holidays Mr. Schiller, I believe, went to the Post Office. He told me he had a key for the Post Office drawer. I brought all the letters I found in the drawer, whether addressed to them in their official capacity or otherwise, or to their families.

On some days there would not be many letters, and on other days there would be a good few.

It has always been the same drawer in the Post Office since I had to do with it. I have no knowledge that Messrs. Delisle, Brehaut, or Schiller, had a separate drawer in the Post Office for their private correspondence, apart from their official drawer.

I believe I paid the postage every three months, being sent for that purpose by Mr. Schiller. I was in the habit of bringing the letters with me to the office in the morning, and went regularly every day at about one o'clock, and on my return home every evening if there were any letters to be mailed I took them with me.

As I always arrived at the office before any of the others had come in, I was in the habit of leaving the letters for Mr. Delisle in his room, and those for Mr. Brehaut in his room. Those addressed officially as Clerk of the Peace, or Clerk of the Crown, I left in Mr. Schiller's room.

I never carried any packages to Mr. Delisle's or Mr. Brehaut's house, excepting in Mr. Delisle's absence from town I sometimes carried a letter for his family. These letters, by the address, appeared to be letters from Mr. Delisle to his family.

I have no knowledge that Mr. Schiller over gave me any package, or stationery, to carry to any place, nor any envelopes.

Some of the letters I took to the Post Office were

franked, or appeared to me to be franked, by Mr. Delisle or Mr. Brehaut.

I have no knowledge of any stationery ever having been taken from the office by any one, except by Mr. Charles Delisle. I have no knowledge, in any shape, of having ever carried, or of seeing any body else carry, any franked envelopes. The letters which I, in a very few instances, carried to Mr. Delisle's house were, if I recollect right, from Mr. Delisle to members of his family, and these letters came through the Post Office drawer of which I have spoken.

Cross-Examined by Mr. Schiller :
If I did bring letters of a private nature to Mr. Schiller they must have been very few. The private letters I brought to Mr. Schiller were from New Orleans, and they bore the American postage stamps. I never carried stationery to Mr. Schiller's house. On two or three occasions I saw Mr. Charles Delisle take stationery away with him, but I dont know what it was for.

On one occasion I saw him take a large parcel of stationery the size of my arm. I remember a part of a water spout which was standing up against the door of the water closet, and one day I heard Mr. Charles M. Delisle and Mr. René Cotret amusing themselves near that place. I heard a noise and I saw them coming out and laughing, and suspected that they had thrown the said spout in the closet. I went in to look and missed the spout, and saw it lying in the bottom of the closet.

I remember seeing two pieces of Canadian Cloth at the Police Office, and observing that one piece appeared to be diminished in size, I examined it and I found it was fresh cut. Shortly afterwards I remember seeing the said Charles M. Delisle wearing a pair of trowsers and vest, which appeared to me to be of the same cloth.

When I said above that I saw said cloth at the Police Office, I meant in a small room opposite the vault where stolen goods are kept. They had been lying there for some time.

I remember Mr. Leslie's storeman coming for a case of Brandy, and he gave a bottle of it to O'Leary and O'Leary gave me a glass of it as he did to several others who were present, and I believe he took the remainder away. I have been attending the Criminal Court of Queen's Bench for the last ten years, except part of a term when I was ill. During that time I have been in the habit of going, at the request of Mr. Schiller, for witnesses and gentlemen of the bar, during the progress of trials. On such occasions I always took a cab, and Mr. Schiller paid for it.

Re-Examined by the Commissioners :
It was sometime after the opening of the new Court House that I saw those pieces of Canadian Cloth lying in a small room above mentioned. It was during the year and about the time that the stolen goods were told ; on some occasions, and about that time, I got the key of that small room from the High Constable so go and get water.

TRANSLATED.
Joseph Rousseau, of Montreal, Constable, sworn saith :

I have given my deposition as a witness in the case of Domina Regina vs Maximin Lemon, in October 1854 in the Court of Quarter Sessions, and have been taxed at seventeen shillings and six pence, and I received all the tax from the Sheriff at that time. I went myself and got that money

I had then my domicile in Montreal.

I have been taxed at two shillings and six pence per day, for seven days. I well remember having given my deposition in the case of Domina Regina vs Napoleon Lepage, in October 1854, in the Court of Queen's Bench, and was then taxed at five shillings per day for eighteen days, which tax was paid to me at the Sheriff's Office.

I am now a Constable of the Water Police on special duty. Previously to that time I was Constable under the High Constable for Montreal. I have been in the Police Department since twenty nine years, with the exception of five years, during which I have been absent from the said Department. For five years I have been Messenger to Colonel Ermatinger, when he was Magistrate in Montreal.

We were only two Messengers in the service of Col. Ermatinger. Our salary was three shillings and nine pence each per day, and we were paid by the Government. When I was not Messenger I was Constable under the High Constable, Mr. Benjamin Delisle.

There was also one Webb, and one Poitras, who were at that time acting as Constables under the High Constable. Mr. Benjamin Delisle paid me one shilling and three pence for the execution of each warrant. His tariff was five shillings, but he never allowed us (the Constables) more than one shilling and three pence. I dont remember on what subject I gave my deposition in the case of Napoleon Lepage, nor do I remember if it was in my quality of Constable that I was called to be a witness in said cases.

In the year 1854 we were four Constables under the High Constable, Mr. Benjamin Delisle. There was one McLaughlin, William Hands, a third one of whom I don't remember the name, and myself.

As such we were employed for the execution of warrants; for conducting prisoners to gaol; for serving subpœnas for the Court of Quarter Sessions, and the Police Court. Mr. Schiller employed me also for serving subpœnas for the Criminal Court in the country. Mr. Schiller paid me the half of the service and the half of the distance.

Sometimes we had to execute half a dozen of warrants a day; some other times more or less. I received seven pence-half-penny to conduct prisoners to the gaol.

I was a Constable when I was called as a witness to give my deposition in the case of which I have spoken above, and think it is in the same full that I entered the service of Col. Ermatinger.

I have been acquainted with the late Mr. Alfred Harvey, who was employed in the Office of the Peace, as writer, for some years. I cannot say if during that time he had some other work to do. I dont know if he was often out of the Office because I seldom went up stairs. Each time I went up stairs I always saw him at his desk. I never carried any where any stationery or envelopes. During the five years of absence of which I have spoken, I was employed the most part of the time on the Champlain and St. Lawrence Railway, and the Champlain and St. Lawrence Railway Company. I was Messenger at the office of the Montreal and Bytown Railway Company, and Conductor on the Champlain and St. Lawrence Railroad.

I am first cousin to Mr. Schiller on my wife's side.

The said William Hands of whom I have spoken above, is the same one who has been heard as a witness before the Commissioners.

I dont remember on what facts I was called to give my depositions in the cases aforesaid. I dont know

if I was called as a witness, in Criminal Court, in some other cases.

FRIDAY, 4th September, 1863.

Joseph Rousseau's evidence continued:

When I entered as Conductor on the St. Lawrence and Champlain Railway, Mr. Alexander M. Delisle was the President of Company.

I continued to act as Conductor in said Company after Mr. Delisle had ceased to be President, and under the subsequent Presidents, John Molson and John Ostell, Esquires.

Mr. A. M. Delisle was the President of the Montreal and Bytown Railway during the time that I was employed there.

The money I got from the Sheriff, as a witness, I kept for myself.

Cross-Examined by Mr. Schiller:

When I have been taxed in the cases of which I have spoken I was not employed by the Government.

Since yesterday I have recollected that I had carried stationery to the Convent of the Congregation, in Notre Dame Street, for the children of Mr. Charles M. Delisle who were at the Convent, and it was Mr. Charles M. Delisle who sent me there. There was a good sized packet of letter paper, foolscap, sealing wax, envelopes, red tape, pencils, half box of steel pens, and handles. I know that Mr. Charles M. Delisle often carried home stationery in the evening.

Mr. Charles M. Delisle was employed by the Government, and he was under the control of Mr. Coursol, the Magistrate of Police. Mr. Charles M. Delisle had a good deal of business, and sent me very often to carry letters for him.

I had a conversation with Mr. Charles M. Delisle in regard to two iron spouts, and he told me that he had thrown them in the closet to annoy his uncle, Mr. Benjamin Delisle, the High Constable, who was the keeper of those things.

I remember that there was a good deal of talk about some Canadian Cloth which disappeared. I saw some of the same piece of Cloth made into clothing, and worn by Mr. Charles M. Delisle, and he told me it was of the same Cloth.

When Mr. Schiller sent me for witnesses and for Advocates, during the progress of a criminal trial, it was always himself who paid the carriage; and this happened frequently, perhaps twice a day, and I know that some others performed the same services.

My services to Mr. Schiller were always very well paid, and I was always desirous of working for Mr. Schiller.

TRANSLATED.

Amable Loiselle, Keeper of the Court House, sworn, deposeth and saith:

Since the year eighteen hundred and forty six I have been Keeper of the Court House, at Montreal. I have been such Keeper as well in the old Court House as in the new one. I always had my rooms in said Court House. There was a vault in the old Court House where the stolen goods were deposited. I saw from time to time boards and deals in the passages of the Court House, which were stolen, as I was told; but I don't know what became of those articles because I never troubled myself about them.

If those matters had concerned the Government and my duty, I should have given them attention; but they concerned the High Constable. I never saw any one carry away goods from the said vault.

SATURDAY, 5th September, 1863.

John O'Leary, of Montreal, Sergeant in the City Police, sworn, saith :

I know the parties hereinbefore mentioned (Delisle, Brehaut and Schiller.) I am and have been for about the last nine years detective and Sergeant in the Police, and during that time they called me to be frequently at the Police Office, and to attend the Sessions of the Criminal Courts. I have seen, from time to time, stolen goods brought in and handed to the High Constable, after the parties had been committed for trial. When the trials were over the parties who had proved their property got it back by an order from Mr. Schiller to the High Constable, in whose custody they were, and the High Constable used to take a receipt on a piece of paper, which I sometimes signed as a witness.

I do not know what was done with the unclaimed stolen goods. I heard that there was sales of them ; but I never was present at them.

I remember the case of the Queen vs Lucas, who was tried in the Queen's Bench for larceny of a number of articles, and among others : a case of Brandy, and drums of Figs. He was committed, and to the best of my recollection, the Brandy was returned to Mr. Leslie's storeman.

I have no knowledge that any stolen goods, or any other property about the Court House, was ever carried away by any one.

I remember a robbery some four or five years ago of a large quantity of silk from Messrs. Benjamin, and a man and a woman were arrested by Constable Richardson for the theft. After they were convicted, the silk was brought over to the Court House by Richardson and myself, and handed over to the High Constable. To the best of my memory there were four or five pieces of silk, of the value of $200 or $300. The accused parties were bailed and never appeared, and I do not know what became of the goods afterwards.

I remember arresting a man of the name of Greene, upon a charge of larceny, some years ago. He was committed for trial at the Quarter Sessions, and was liberated on bail, himself in one hundred pounds, and one William Ennis, a Tavern Keeper, as his surety, in a sum of fifty pounds, which he deposited in the hands of Mr. Schiller, £45 down, and went out to get the other five pounds.

The said Greene never appeared, and last winter Ennis came to my house and enquired if he could take Green back from Toronto, where he said he had heard he was. He said he would like to get back the fifty pounds he had deposited. He asked me if I would go for him. I said I would if I got leave from the Court, and that if he called in the morning we should go and speak to Mr. Schiller on the subject. Accordingly he called in the morning, and we went together to Mr. Schiller. Mr. Schiller said that he might go and get him himself, as it was his business to go for him, and that if he made application to the Government he might get back his money. To the best of my knowledge this may have been about the middle of the last winter.

This happened some time before this Commission sat here. I am positive that it was long before this Commission sat here, but I cannot say in what month in the winter it was.

From the way in which Mr. Schiller spoke I understood that he had still the money in his possession at the time.

I know nothing of any iron spouts : the only iron I know anything of is about twenty tons of iron, stolen from the Grand Trunk, which was returned to them. To the best of my opinion, for the last six or eight months, the goods supposed to be stolen, remaining unclaimed, are kept at the Station House. We, only, at present, carry to the Police Office the goods that are claimed. An auction will take place on Tuesday next, as I am informed, of such unclaimed stolen goods remaining at the Station House.

Before that period of time, no such unclaimed stolen goods were kept at the Station House ; they were all taken to the Police Office, and handed to the High Constable.

MONDAY, 14th September, 1863.

Bernard McAvenue, Assistant Post Master, sworn, saith :

I have been connected with the Post Office Department in this city for over eighteen years, and have been Assistant Post Master for about three years, last, past. I had nothing to do with the accounts then, nor have I now, but about ten years ago I placed letters on the assorting table to be charged, and put in the different drawers of the different parties having accounts with the office. I am familiar with the manner in which they are charged. The Canada Gazette is not subject to postage when sent to any of the Public Officers, or Magistrates. The Departments of the Clerk of the Crown, and Peace, were charged no postage on it. The number of the drawer belonging to the Department of the Clerk of the Peace is No. 32, and I cannot say if the Clerk of the Crown had a separate drawer. I am not aware that the Officers of these Departments, Messrs. Delisle, Brehaut, and Schiller, had a separate drawer or box ; but my impression is that they had not. I cannot say whether communications to these gentlemen themselves were charged to the said box No. 32, but my impression is they would be, because it is the rule of the office, without instructions, from the principals, to the contrary. There is a commission charged to all persons having accounts with the Post Office, which has varied from time to time. Formerly the rates of postage were much higher, the lowest rate being then 4½d, and varying, according to distance, to 2s 3d.

Since the passage of a law to that effect, the rates of postage have been fixed at five cents for pre-paid, and seven cents for un-paid, single rate. It is the invariable custom of all public officers having accounts with the Post Office, to charge all communications, newspapers, and all matters to their drawer. Formerly the postage accounts were paid every three months, but now, I believe, they are paid monthly.

Accounts might run for over three months, and frequently did, and then, as a matter of course, they were made for six months, as appears to have been the case by the several receipts now shewn to me. From the book now before me, kept by the Post Master, and which is a kind of Journal of the daily transactions, I see that newspapers were charged to said box No. 32, but I cannot say, positively, what these newspapers were.

This Book, or Journal, commences first November 1857, and ends thirty first January, 1860.

Accounts of the same kind are still kept, but this is by private arrangement between the Post Master and the parties. I would wish to add that Post Office accounts with the Montreal Educational Office are not chargeable with any commission.

I am under the impression that some years ago Mr.

Schiller used the right of franking, and if letters came addressed to him they would be charged to the drawer.

Cross-Examined by Mr. Delisle :

I have looked over the charges for newspapers for five consecutive months, and I find the average per month to have been about one shilling and nine pence.

(Translated.)

Ludger Pagé, Chief of Police of the town of St. Hyacinthe :—

I am Chief of Police of St. Hyacinthe since eight years. Previous to that I was a moulder, and was working in foundries. Many times I have been called to appear as witness before the Criminal Court of Montreal. I had occasion to give my testimony, as well before the Grand Jurors as before the Petit Jurors. Since seven or eight years past, I came almost at each term either before the Criminal Court, or before Quarter Sessions, to give my testimony in different cases, and I have discontinued to come since a Court of criminal jurisdiction has been established in the District of St. Hyacinthe, about one year ago.

Whenever I had given my testimony I was taxed as witness for my travelling expenses, and five shillings above per day, and sometimes Mr. Schiller allowed me two shillings and six pence more per day. This happened, to the best of my knowledge, three or four times. Once Mr. Schiller told me that he could not grant me more than five shillings per day, because there was a law or a tariff which fixed the allowance to the witnesses at only one dollar per day. I understood by the word tariff that it was a law passed by the Government, or by the Sheriff, which fixed the tax to one dollar per day. It was Mr. Schiller who made my accounts as a witness.

It was the Sheriff of the District of Montreal who paid me ; sometimes Mr. Schiller has paid me. When Mr. Schiller made our accounts as witnesses, we were obliged to give him twenty-five cents, each witness. In making my accounts Mr. Schiller asked me how much I had paid in the cars ; how much I had paid for my carters for going and returning. I told him how much I had paid, and after I was taxed at five shillings per day, and sometimes at seven shillings and six pence per day, for the time I was in Montreal, in attendance to give my testimony. Afterwards he swore us as to the truth of our accounts, and asked us twenty-five cents, and gave us our accounts. At almost every term of the Criminal Court I had some subpœnas to serve in the vicinity, or in the locality of St. Hyacinthe.

Those subpœnas were coming from Mr. Schiller, and sometimes from Mr. Benjamin Delisle, High Constable, and generally Mr. Schiller wrote me a letter in which he told me to send him back the return of service of such subpœnas ; that he would pay me on my coming to Montreal. On my coming to town Mr. Schiller made up my account and paid it.

Sometimes I put on my returns the distance travelled, and my emoluments.

The reason why I did not put constantly on my returns the distance travelled and the amount of my emoluments, was because sometimes my accounts were reduced ; and that was the reason why I left it to Mr. Schiller's generosity, saying to Mr. Schiller "there are my returns," and he then said to me "I will pay you before your departure." He made my accounts, I signed them, and he paid me for the subpœnas that I had served. I dont know if he paid me according to the distance I had travelled, and for the services I had made. I know that the allowance was one shilling and three pence for the service of a subpœna, and as to the travel some one told me that it was three shillings per league, and some others two shillings and six pence. I served above sixty subpœnas in the case of Domina Regina vs Beauregard, for murder, and for the service of these subpœnas I went into the following parishes, viz : in the town of St. Hyacinthe ; in the village of St. Joseph ; in the parish of St. Hyacinthe and Contrecœur ; Les Soixantes ; La Baie des Soixantes ; in the parish of la Presentation ; in le Grand Rang ; in St. Charles ; la Presentation, and St. Barnabé. That is all to my knowledge. Those subpœnas were served by me for the Crown. I do not recollect to have served any for the defence. No one told me not to put on my returns my emoluments, nor the distance because it was Mr. Schiller who made my accounts. Mr. Schiller made my accounts on a piece of paper, and I dont know now where those accounts may be found. I signed them and he paid me. He would tell me, "You have done so much, and I give you so much." He told me, "Pagé, we give you work, and we encourage you." Mr. Schiller was speaking to me as if he took the interest of the Government ; that we should be reasonable and not charge too much. The reason why I said that I served more than sixty subpœnas in Beauregard's case, is because Mr. Schiller had given me orders to notify some witnesses not to come on the day fixed by their bail bond until they would be subpœnaed. I see by the subpœnas now exhibited that I have served only forty-seven, and I believe that I have received from Mr. Schiller twenty-three or twenty-four dollars, for the services of those subpœnas. It was not more than twenty-three or twenty-four dollars that I received for my emoluments. I dont know the rule Mr. Schiller was observing to pay me in the other cases, as well as in those for the service of subpœnas. Mr. Schiller appeared always to be a good friend to me. It is for that reason I always took what he gave me.

Mr. Schiller in making my account for services of subpœnas would say, "You made ten, twelve, or fifteen dollars ; does that pay you ?" and paid me, after making out a receipt, which I signed. It was impossible to do otherwise. When the subpœnas were sent to me, by mail, they were filled up.

I dont recollect if I gave to Mr. Schiller the distances travelled, or if it was Mr. Schiller who put them in himself in the account.

Charles Vidal, of the City of St. Hyacinthe, Constable, sworn:

Since 1835 I have been employed by Mr. Schiller and the High Constable, Benjamin Delisle, Esq., to serve subpœnas to witnesses who were summoned to appear before the different Criminal Courts held in Montreal; generally Mr. Schiller sent me, by mail, at St. Hyacinthe, these subpœnas. Once he gave me some in Montreal, telling me that he would not pay me the distance travelled. I was then in Montreal as a witness. He gave me then, to the best of my knowledge, six dollars. I had been to Acton serving those subpœnas to different witnesses, a distance of nineteen leagues from Montreal, Mr. Schiller said to me that he would pay me only the distance from St. Hyacinthe to Upton, and my expenses for travelling; the distance from St. Hyacinthe to Upton is four leagues. In the case of Domina Regina vs Brodeur, for larceny, I have served subpœnas on witnesses residing at St. Dominique, a distance of seventeen leagues from Montreal, I reecived, in all, four dollars from Benjamin Delisle, High Con. I very often gave my evidence before the Criminal Courts in Montreal, and Mr. Schiller made out my account, and I never asked less than seven shillings and six pence, except in tho case of Beauregard, when I received only one dollar to the best of my knowledge, and I never got less, and I paid to Mr. Schiller one shilling and three pence to make up my account.

Cross-examined by Mr. Schiller:—

When I worked for Mr. Schiller I was always well paid and satisfied. I have always been paid on demand.

15th September, 1863.

Ludger Pagé's evidence continued.

Cross-examined by Mr. Schiller:—

I think when Mr. Schiller allowed me seven shillings and six pence per day, it was because I was Chief of Police, and that the board was higher than it is now. Mr. Schiller paid my accounts, on some occasions, after they had been taxed, himself in order that I might not lose the cars to return home. I was always perfectly satisfied with Mr. Schiller when he paid my accounts for services of subpœnas. To the best of my memory when Mr. Schiller taxed my accounts at $1 a-day, he ceased from that time to charge anything for making them.

(Translation.)

Pierre Guernon, of the City of St. Hyacinthe, Constable, sworn, saith:—

Four subpœnas, issued in the case of Domina Regina vs. Beauregard, for murder, in the term of September, 1859, being now exhibited to me as being served by me to the witnesses therein named, I declare that, to the best of my knowledge, it is not me who signed the returns on those subpœnas, but perhaps it was another with my permission; as

to the one addressed to Ls. Fontaine, of the Parish of St. Hyacinthe, laborer, I do not recollect to have served it. I did not go to the Parish of St. Dominique to serve this subpoena on the said Ls. Fontaine. I cannot read nor write, but I sign my name. During the trial of the said Beauregard I was in Montreal; I never left Montreal nor St. Hyacinthe to serve an order or subpoena to the said Ls. Fontaine. I do not recollect to have ever served any subpoenas on him. I believe that I served a subpoena on P. E. Leclere, of St. Hyacinthe; and to the best of my knowledge, I think that it was in Montreal that I served this subpoena to Mr. Leclere, in the case of Beauregard.

I served two or three subpoenas in the case of Beauregard in the city of Montreal. I am constable in St. Hyacinthe since fourteen years, and I do not recollect that I served any other subpoenas in criminal cases. I think that I was paid before the trial of Beauregard, for the assistance I was called upon to give during the preliminary inquest held in St. Hyacinthe. I never was paid by Mr. Schiller for the service of subpoenas of which I have spoken. I might have been paid by Mr. Pagé. I believe that Mr. Pagé paid me eighteen or twenty dollars for work that I had done for him. I kept the prisoner Beauregard in custody. I assisted at the inquest at St. Hyacinthe, and I believe that he gave me subpoenas to serve at St. Hyacinthe. I believe that it is Mr. Schiller who gave me the subpoenas which I served in Montreal, and of which I have spoken above. When I have been called as witness before the Criminal Courts in Montreal, Mr. Schiller made up my accounts, and I paid him one shilling and three pence, except during the last years.

Cross-examined by Mr. Schiller :—

I recollect to have seen the said Fontaine in Montreal during the trial of Beauregard. I recollect to have served two Subpœnas on the two Misses Beauregard, to Mr. Leclere, to Onesime Genereux, and to Victor Cote. It is probable that I authorised Mr. Pagé to sign my name on the return of the Subpœnas of which I have spoken.

[Translated.]

Louis Turcotte, of the town of St. Hyacinthe, sawyer, sworn, saith:—

I appeared as witness before the Criminal Court held in Montreal, six years ago, and I received a dollar per day. Mr. Schiller made up my account as witness; he asked me one shilling and three-pence, and having no money on me, Pagé lent me *trente-sous*, which I gave to Mr. Schiller for having made my account. I have been employed by Mr. Pagé, during the preliminary inquests held in St. Hyacinthe in the case of Beauregard, to search for the dead body of Anseleme Charron, and I was paid five shillings per day by Mr. Page. He paid me three dollars for three days, and he told me it was by order of Mr. Delisle, who assisted at the inquest at St. Hyacinthe. I was immediately paid before the trial of Beauregard.

SEPTEMBER, 19, 1863.

Eleazar Clark, of the town of Sherbrooke, High 'Constable, sworn, said :

As such Constable I served at Sherbrooke on the eleventh of March, 1853, a subpoena, in the case of 'the Queen vs. Erastus Ranson, accused of having feloniously having in his possession forged Bank notes, and I now see my return of said service on the back of said subpœna, shown to me. I presume that this subpoena came to me by mail from Montreal to Sherbrooke. I suppose it was sent by Mr. Schiller. I served it at the "Magog House" at the town of Sherbrooke ; my charge would have been two shillings if served for our Court there, which fees I did not endorse upon said subpoena, because I served subpoenas for Mr. Schiller there in exchange for like services performed by him for me in the City of Montreal ; we were not in the habit of charging one another for the performing of these services.

I served also two subpoenas, both returnable on the 14th of March, 1853, in the case of the Queen vs. John Coly, and the Queen vs. Pierre Guilbault alias Lavoie ; the former charged with larceny, and the latter for felony ; these came to my hands also by mail at Sherbrooke, and were served by me, upon the understanding aforesaid, and without making any charges therefor. This interchange of civilities between Mr. Schiller and myself has been existing for about the last fifteen years. The principal services which I made for him were in forgery cases, and they were frequent up to within the last four and five years, when we succeeded in breaking up the gang of forgers and counterfeiters who infested the country.

Having examined Mr. Schiller's account, entitled "Province of Canada, District of Montreal—Court of Queen's Bench, Crown side, March term, 1853. Dr. The Civil Government of Canada, to Charles Edward Schiller, Statement of subpoenas served on behalf of the Crown in the following cases, namely :"

I perceive by said account, that in the said case of John Coly, for larceny, the Government is charged with thirty leagues of mileage, and the sum of four pound eleven shillings and threepence service of said subpoena, while the actual mileage was merely from the Post-office to the Hotel, the next building, in Sherbrooke. I see also by the said account, that in the case of Ranson, also above spoken of, thirty leagues mileage was charged by said account, and the like fees of four pounds eleven shillings and threepence for service of one subpoena, that is of the subpoena which I served as aforesaid, which service involves no mileage, nor was any charge therefor made by me, the same is also true in the case of Guilbault, above mentioned. The facts just stated, are also true with the reference to mileage service and charges. I perceive also in the case of the Queen vs. Margaret Molloy, for larceny, I served the subpoena in Sherbrooke for the March term, in the Court of Queen's Bench at Montreal, 1853. Under the same circumstances as above stated, and for which I

see charged four pounds eleven shillings and threepence. I charged nothing for the service. Had I made the travel to serve the subpoena, I would have charged one shilling per mile, and two shillings for service, which is the sum allowed in the District of St. Francis.

For the October and November term of the Queen's Bench, at Montreal, 1853. I see, by return, upon three subpoenas written now, shown to me in the cases, the Queen vs. Robert Darah, for forgery, and J. C. A. Jackman for larceny, that said Subpoenas were served in Sherbrooke on the 12th of October, 1853, by Charles Taylor, a constable at that time acting for me, in which cases no charges for mileage and services were made and by said account against the Government for said term, I perceive that the four pounds eleven shillings and three pence was charged for each said service ; all the Subpoenas that I served or have served at Sherbrooke for the Court of Queen's Bench at Montreal, came to me at Sherbrooke by mail. In regard to the stolen goods in the District of St. Francis, they are placed in a vault in the Court House at Sherbrooke, of which vault the Clerk of the Peace keeps the key, so that when I require to have access to the vault, I am obliged to obtain the key from him. In all cases where I myself have executed the precept and secured the stolen goods, I take them to that vault, and when such duties are performed by constables, they are received and placed in said vault by the Clerk of the Peace.

Cross-examined by Mr. Schiller :—

The subpoenas that have been sent to Montreal by me for service by Mr. Schiller, I would charge for the same as if I had come myself, that is the mileage—it was paid by the Government ; it is a general rule in the District of St. Francis to send subpoenas by mail and charge Government, every term. I came into Montreal during those years prosecuting against the counterfeiters, to confer with the Crown officer in getting up the case, and to see to the issue of subpoenas. I had in my employ, as Constables, James Fuller. William Reid, Charles Taylor, one Chamberlain, and John Heath of Stanstead. When Mr. Schiller sent me subpoenas they were served by myself or by some one of my constables. From the year 1852 up to 1861, Mr. Schiller was employed and assisted me as detective against the counterfeiters. I have already, on a great many occasions, met Mr. Schiller in the evening on detective business. I ought to have, stated during the time of these prosecutions, through Mr. Schiller important services were rendered which enabled me to reach the guilty parties, and it was to him I sent my detectives to give information, and received information during the period of four years; we succeeded in ridding the country of the counterfeiters. Mr. Schiller has never made any charges against me for his services. The detective, to obtain information, must pay out money. I know that in my service I was obliged to pay out money. I recollect the case of Joel Butterfield ; he was detected by Mr. Schiller, and by a man that I sent him, and he was brought to consideration. I know that M Schiller took the leading part in Montreal in this matter, and I had no assistance except through him. I am responsible for all subpoenas placed in my hands, whether by me, or by others employed by me in the country parts. And if an oath was necessary to have an attachment against the witness, I would be obliged to bring the party I employed for such service, at my own expense, before the Court. I get my subpoenas served as cheaply as I can. It has been repeatedly the case that services of subpoenas have cost me more than I was allowed by Government. In some instances, during the sitting of the Criminal Court, the attendance of a witness from a great distance is so required for the next day, and I am obliged to bring them up at my own expense, which heavy expenses cannot be avoided, and we look upon this as a set-off for other cases where a profit is made.

I have always been obliged to advance money to constables and to poor witnesses, There is a great deal of responsibility attached to the office of having the subpoenas served. It is to my knowledge that Crown witnesses have been discharged from their attendance at Court with the greatest expedition. Had witnesses been detained unnecessarily, it would have been a source of expense to the Government.

[TRANSLATED.]

Leon Malard, of the City of Montreal, Clerk at the Post Office, sworn :

For nine years past I have been employed in the Post Office of Montreal, to make the general delivery of letters and newspapers, and to assort the newspapers for the city. The general delivery of letters and newspapers includes also the duty of placing them in the boxes and in the drawers of each person. There is in the Post Office of Montreal a drawer bearing the number 32, in which are put the letters and newspapers addressed to the Office of the Clerk of the Peace, and to the Crown Office of Montreal. Since two or three years ago I had occasion to place in that drawer the letters and the newspapers. Some were addressed to Mr. A. M. Delisle, Mr. Brehaut, and Mr. Schiller, also to the brother of Mr. Schiller who is called William, I think, and kept a grocery ; and also to the sisters of Mr. Schiller, because when there were some letters addressed to Mr. Schiller's family, Mrs. Schiller would not receive them at the house, saying that there was a drawer in the Post Office to receive them. The reason why I remarked that the letters addressed to the brother of Mr. Schiller were put in the drawer, is because the carrier of the letters brought them back as being refused at Mr. Schiller's house, so that I put back the letters in the drawer, No. 32, and they passed by that drawer. Even when the letters had been paid by the brother of Mr. Schiller there remained yet two cents, for the carrier, who had a right to two cents for each letter, so that in putting the letter in the drawer No. 32, the one for whom the letter was addressed saved the fee due to the carrier. We yet put in the drawer No. 32, all the letters and documents addressed to the Office of the Peace, and to the Crown Office at Montreal. All documents, letters, and correspondences which passed through the drawer No. 32, were charged to the Government if they were not pre-paid. When I saw some letters addressed to Messrs. Delisle, Brehaut, and Schiller, I placed them in the drawer No. 32, because I knew of no other than that one, and if there was any other box or drawer for any of them I would have known it.

Cross-Examined by Mr. Brehaut :

In saying that the letters placed in drawer No. 32, were paid by the Government I mean to say that the account of the Offices of the Crown and of the Peace, at the Post Office was made in the same manner as was done for all the other public departments who have boxes at the Post Office. The Prothonotary's Office at Montreal is the only one where letters are paid as they are received.

Cross-Examined by Mr. Schiller :

I have no personal knowledge that Madame Schiller refused letters from the carrier except from what the carrier told me. That carrier is named Arthur Auger, formerly carrier for the St. Lawrence Suburb, who, on several occasions, brought back letters to the address of Mr. Schiller's family, telling me not to give them to him in future because they were refused, for the reason that there was a drawer where they should be put. It is the reason why I say that letters were refused by Madame Schiller at her house. The correspondence to the address of that family was not numerous, but there was some at different times in the year. I cannot say from whence those letters came for Mr. Schiller's family, for we have not time to examine the different letters. I can say that I saw some letters for Mr. Schiller which were not paid. Much more attention is paid in sorting letters to those that are unpaid, than to those that are paid ; because the unpaid letters must be charged. Mr. Schiller's correspondence was very small.

MONDAY, 21st September, 1863.

Maurice Murphy, of Montreal, Clerk in the Montreal Post Office, sworn, saith : aged 52 years. I have been engaged in the Post Office at Montreal for about 17 years last past, and am now an assorter of mails for Montreal delivery, and have been such for about 4 or 5 years past. Mr. Simpson, junior, acted in that capacity before I did. My duties as assorter was to arrange the letters and other documents in the drawers to which they were destined.

In assorting the mails, I throw all unpaid letters on one side. After we have done sorting the mails, I return, sometimes, to the said unpaid letters, and charge them to their respective drawers. Generally this duty is performed by other clerks, but I do it sometimes. The Drawer No. 32 in the Post Office, belongs to the Departments of the Clerk of the Peace and Clerk of the Crown.

All communications and matters addressed to Mr. Delisle, Mr. Brehaut, or Mr. Schiller, were placed in this drawer, and when not pre-paid were charged to this drawer, whether addressed to them in their official capacity or otherwise, or members of their families, or to their care. I remember letters addressed to Mr. Schiller's sisters being put in said box. To my knowledge these gentlemen had no other drawer or box except No. 32. I cannot say what the extent of the correspondence was which was carried on through such drawer, nor have I any means of determining the proportion of matter and correspondence of a private nature with that received on public business.

I remember letters addressed to Mr. Harvey being

D

placed in Drawer No. 32. I understood that Mr. Harvey was then a clerk in the Peace Office.

Cross-examined by Mr. Delisle :

I cannot say whether the private letters I have alluded to were pre-paid or not ; in either case they would have been put in the drawer in the same way. Generally the majority of letters are now pre-paid, whether private or otherwise. All accounts at the Post Office with public officers under the Provincial Government were kept in the same manner as those of the Clerk of the Peace and Clerk of the Crown. There was no difference in the manner of keeping the accounts from those of other public departments.-- The joint Prothonotary of Montreal is, to the best of my knowledge, the only public department which does not keep any account.

In saying that the accounts of other public departments are kept in the same way, I mean to say that all letters and matters addressed to them individually, or to their care, or to members of their family, are passed through the drawers belonging to such department, in the same manner as those of the Clerk of the Peace and Clerk of the Crown.

Robert McCormack, of Montreal, Bailiff, sworn, saith : Aged 60 years. I was a constable under the Head Constable, M. Benjamin Delisle, for about 10 or 12 years, and ceased to be so about 12 years ago.-- During this time I served Subpœnas for Mr. Schiller, My memory has failed, but to the best of my recollection when I used to go to the country to serve Subpœnas, Mr. Schiller used to settle with me by allowing me 7½d. for every service, and paying my expenses when I went to the country, to wit, the carter's expenses. I served some Subpœnas for Mr. Schiller in Montreal, but most that I served were for the High Constable in the city of Montreal, for which I was paid 7½d. on each service. I got a quarter of a dollar, 1s. 3d., for the execution of a Warrant. I do not remember, during my connection with the said office, that any goods were carried away by any one, nor did I ever carry away any myself for any one, nor do I know of any one else having carried away any goods.

Cross-examined by Mr. Schiller :

Mr. Schiller sent me out in the country to serve Subpœnas ; he always paid my expenses for cartage and for boarding. I was paid liberally, and never was out of pocket. I always felt well satisfied with what Mr. Schiller paid me.

TUESDAY, 22d September, 1863.

Thomas Storr Judah, of Montreal, Esquire, Advocate, sworn : Aged 57 years. I have been practicing as an Advocate in Montreal since 1836. For the first twelve or fifteen years of my practice, I daily had occasion to be employed in business connected with the Police Department,--that is to say, in the department of the Clerk of the Peace ; but since that time I have only occasionally visited that office. I know nothing whatever connected with any practice that may have obtained in that office in relation to the franking of letters.

I have no knowledge that it was ever done in any case whatever.

Mr. Schiller never did, on any occasion, frank any letter for me, nor any other document, nor have I any knowledge that he ever did so for anybody else.

Cross-examined by Mr. Delisle :--

I practiced during these 12 or 15 years both in the Quarter Sessions and in the Criminal Court of Queen's Bench. The practice that universally prevailed with regard to the custody of stolen goods, as far as it came under my observation, was that so soon as the affidavit establishing the theft was made and sworn to, immediately the High Constable was called into the Police Office, and took possession of the stolen goods, and subsequently produced them on trial. On the trial he was examined invariably as a witness, to establish the identity of the goods produced by him in Court, on which occasions he used to declare, under oath, that the goods had been kept by him, under lock and key, in his possession, since the arrest of the prisoner. I know of no exception, in the course of my practice, to this rule. The High Constable was so particular in this respect, that if it were possible, --that is, if they were not too heavy for him to carry alone, he always carried them himself from the place he had them deposited, into Court.

The Clerk of the Peace, during these years, acted as Crown Prosecutor in the Quarter Sessions, and I do not conceive it possible for him to have discharged the two offices of Public Prosecutor, which was a very important office, and keeper of stolen goods, a totally different duty.

Re-examined by the Commissioners.

With regard to the incompatibility of the Crown prosecutor and keeper of stolen goods, being at one and the same time keeper of stolen goods, applies only where the Clerk of the Peace consists of a single individual. If there were three gentlemen in the department, I can see no difficulty in one of the other two producing and identifying the stolen goods at the trial.

Cross-examined by Mr. Delisle.

I am aware that Mr. Delisle was sole Clerk of the Peace for about three or four years.

During my practice there was a daily Court held in the Police Office for the trial of cases of a particular class. Sometimes this Court would sit all day, sometimes a part of the day, sometimes several times in a day. It was usual to take the evidence before that Court in writing, and Mr. Brehaut attended to that department. As far as I could see this was an arrangement between the two Clerks of the Peace.

Mr. Schiller was usually occupied, I may say continually occupied, from morning to night attending to the duties of the office which required his attendance continually, except during the Quarter Sessions and the sitting of the Court of Queen's Bench, Criminal Jurisdiction, when he was employed attending to the public prosecutor, by marshalling the witnesses on the different Bills of Indictment, taking care that they were ready to come into Court to give their evidence as well as to give their evidence before the Grand Jury, and attending to the Grand Jury, who were continually in the habit of sending for him. I consider, under these circumstances, that it was utterly impossible for either Mr. Delisle, Mr. Brehaut, or Mr. Schiller to have discharged efficiently, the important office of keeper of stolen goods ; because in all Criminal cases the conviction of the prisoner depended on the evidence given in Court as to the identity of the articles.

Frederick Gerikin, of Montreal, Saloon-keeper, at the St. Lawrence Hall, sworn saith--aged 33 years. I never carried any stolen goods from the Police Office to any one or to any part of the city by order of any one. I never was a Policeman or a Constable. I do not know of any one having carried such goods. I never told any one or made any boast that I had carried stolen goods from the Court House to any place.

Josephine Moss, widow of the late Alfred Charles Harvey, Esq., Advocate, saith--I am aged 45 years. My late husband, Alfred Charles Harvey was for about two years, prior to his decease, a Clerk in the Peace Office of Montreal. The amount of his salary was £125 per annum. During the two years he was in the habit of collecting rents for Mr. A. M. Deslile in the city of Montreal. I do not know what the rents he collected amounted to. My son, Alfred Harvey, succeeded his father in the Peace Office as a Clerk. He was also paid £125 per annum. I used to come every month to the Peace Office and draw the salary of my son from Mr. Schiller, and I began to do so 11 months after my husband's death, during which 11 months my son had himself drawn the salary. I received every month from Mr. Schillier £10 8s. 4d. I heard that my husband was indebted to Mr. Delisle at his death for rents collected ; but Mr. Delisle never claimed or received anything from me of that debt.

My son got the situation as Clerk in the Peace Office the day after the burial of my husband. When I commenced drawing my son's salary, after the 11 months, as I have mentioned, it was because Mr. Delisle had sent for me and enquired whether my son gave me the whole amount of his salary as he drew it, and having informed that gentleman that he did not, but only gave me a part of it, Mr. Delisle called my son, in my presence, and told him that in future I should draw his salary myself, and I continued to do so till my son lost his situation.

My husband told me that he was allowed £25 a year by Mr. Delisle for the collection of his rents. My son, Alfred Charles, told me that Mr. Delisle gave him the same allowance of £25 for the collection of his rents. This was continued for about a year, and the amount was placed to the credit of my late husband's debt. My son has left the city about three weeks ago. I do not know in what amount my husband was indebted to Mr. Delisle.

Cross-examined by Mr. Delisle.

My husband told me that his instructions were to collect such rents, either before or after office hours, and I am aware that sometimes he used to leave immediately after breakfast for that purpose, and on several occasions I have accompanied him after dinner in the evening to go and collect such rents.

[TRANSLATION.

Louis Lacroix, Constable, of the city of Montreal, sworn.--I am 47 years of age. I have been a Constable during six or seven years in Montreal. I ceased to be so last autumn. I was under the orders of the High Constable, Mr. Benjamin Delisle, who employed me as such to execute warrants, serve subpoenas, summon witnesses, and conduct prisoners to the Jail. He sent me sometimes into the country to summon witnesses or to arrest prisoners.

Mr. Schiller whenever he sent me to the country paid the Carters and furnished me with money to pay my board and other expenses, such as Turnpikes and Ferries ; and when the Criminal Court terminated, he paid me sixpence for the serving of each subpoena in Montreal, and for the serving of the same in the country, he used to give me the half of my mileage, and the half of the fee for significations, and he afterwards further recompensed me by giving me some additional money, when I served summonses for the Quarter Sessions, held in Montreal. I was paid in the same manner by Mr. Benjamin Delisle, as I have already stated in regard to Mr. Schiller, but for the service of subpoenas in the City of Montreal, I only received fivepence for each service.

I have sometimes given my evidence before the Criminal Courts of Montreal, during the time I acted as constable, and I was taxed and paid a dollar a day.

There were two of us as constables under the orders of the High Constable, Mr. Benjamin Delisle of the City of Montreal, a man named William Hands and myself, the latter had been in the situation a long time before me. Hands was absent in Upper Canada for three or four months or thereabout, on his return Mr. Benjamin Delisle took him back, and reinstated him as Constable, it was the only time he ever absented himself to my knowledge. I have occasionally been placed in charge of the Grand Jurymen, and sometimes in charge of the petty Jurymen.

Having examined the paper now shown me by the Commissioners, marked " A," I declare that the signature " William Hands," written and affixed to the document in question, is the signature of the said William Hands ; and that the document sets forth that he was placed in charge of the petty jury during the Quarter Sessions at Montreal, on the night of the 11th, and day of the 12th August, 1855. As far as I can remember, William Hands appeared once or twice as a witness before the Criminal Court of Montreal. It was I that acted as crier to the auction that took place on the 9th July, 1858, for the sale of stolen and unclaimed goods. The said auction took place in the Court House of the City of Montreal, and I think it was held in a room adjoining the office of the High Constable.

I have no knowledge that any of the said articles were ever missing or taken away. They were made up in lots. I have never heard such an occurrence talked of, as goods being taken away. I was a long time connected with Hands as a constable, for about four years at one time and another. He received for country notices the same sum that I did from Mr. Schiller, and from Mr. Benjamin Delisle.

Cross-examined by Mr. Schiller.

When I was employed by Mr. Schiller he always paid me handsomely ; and when I went into the country to serve subpoenas, Mr. Schiller always advanced me the money I required on these occasions. Very often during the term of the Criminal Courts Mr. Schiller has sent me to bring up witnesses and Advocates during the progress of a trial ; and it was always Mr. Schiller who paid for the cabs and carters, telling me to make haste. This often happened three or four times in the day.

WEDNESDAY, 23rd September, 1863.

Charles Coallier, of the City of Montreal, Detective Police Officer, sworn, saith :--I am 32 years of age ; I have been a detective police officer for about 2 years; and for about six years before that I was a sergeant in the Police force. I have been in the habit of bringing, sometimes, stolen goods to the Police Office in Montreal, which were always delivered to the High Constable. Sometimes I have delivered a considerable quantity, and at other times less.

A few years ago a man of the name of White, from the United States, and his wife were robbed of a sum of money, and we arrested the parties who robbed him, four women. There were two other constables with me at the time of making the arrest, one of whom was Dissonette, and the other, I think, was Hands, but I am not sure. We delivered the money we found upon those persons to the High Constable, and I believe the amount was $61. Two of the four women pleaded guilty, and were sent to the Penitentiary. Their names were Falvin. When Mr. White was leaving for the States, he told me he would not appear, because he was ashamed to appear before these women. I told him he would lose his money if he did not appear. I am not aware whether any of his relatives, or any one else, ever claimed this money. Mr. Bissonette was then a Sergeant of Police. This occurred in the Winter time. I do not remember any other case similar to the one above referred to.

Mr. Adolphe Bissonette, Joint High Constable, appeared, and declared that he had in his possession the $61 mentioned in the affidavit of the last witness, which he exhibited.

Thursday, 24th September, 1863.

Henry Driscoll, Esq., Queen's Counsel of Montreal, sworn, saith :--I am 71 years, 2 months, and some days of age. My commission as Queen's Counsel dates on the 31st March, 1838. In the interval between that time and the present, I conducted the Crown prosecutions in the Court of Queen's Bench, at a rough guess, from the year 1845 until the year 1858, with two or three exceptions. I represented the Attorney General when I so prosecuted.

Having now seen and examined Mr. Schiller's account as Superintendent of Crown Witnesses against the Government, for the October term of 1852, of which the following is the heading, viz. :--

Province of Canada, }
District of Montreal. }

COURT OF QUEEN'S BENCH.
Crown Side.
October Term, 1852.
Dr. The Civil Government of Canada.
Charles Edward Schiller.

Statement of subpœnas served on behalf of the Crown in the following cases, viz. --I see that I certified the said account as being correct, and that the services therein enumerated were necessary, and that I certified the same as Queen's Counsel, having conducted the business of the said term. My opinion is, that before giving the certificate, I did not examine the subpœnas, for the service of which charges are therein made. I was so convinced of Mr. Schiller's honor, that I trusted implicitly to it; even if I had examined the original subpœnas, I was unacquainted with most of the distances which, in the returns of the subpœnas, would have been stated to have been travelled, and therefore would have been unable to judge whether or not those distances were correct.

In looking at a similar account of March term, 1853, of Mr. Schiller's, for that term by Mr. Schiller, I perceive that I also certified that account; and whenever I acted as Crown Prosecutor, I certified similar accounts for Mr. Schiller.

I was acquainted with the fact that Mr. Schiller was in the habit of employing constables in the country to serve subpœnas, and that he charged the Government in his own bill for such services. I knew that this must be the case, because some of those witnesses were summoned when Mr. Schiller was engaged in Montreal in the performance of his duties. I recollect that a bailiff of the name of Millor, I think from Laprairie, made that a subject of complaint to the Government. The Government referred the complaint to me, and ordered me to report on it. I did

report on it in a letter, copy of which is now presented to me, which is dated 26th July, 1849.

Mr. Delisle, and, I think, the then Solicitor General Mr. Drummond, was referred to also, and reported. I understood that Mr. Schiller's having caused subpœnas to be served in that manner was not disapproved of by the Government of the day; indeed I heard that he was specifically authorised to continue it, that is, to have the subpœnas served by the bailiff in the country, and to charge for them in his bill. But I must observe that I am not aware that there was any authority given to charge for the services of subpœnas, as if the bailiffs had been sent from Montreal. On this point I am ignorant, nor am I aware that Mr. Schiller ever charged mileage from Montreal in cases where he sent the subpœnas by mail or private hand to constables in the country.

Q.--What mode of procedure would you suggest with reference to the service of subpœnas for the Courts of Criminal Jurisdiction, in order to obviate, as far as possible, the possibility of overcharging the Government for such services ?

A.--To answer that question in the manner that it ought to be answered, would require calm reflection and a clear recollection of circumstances which I do not clearly recollect at this very moment, having long ceased those duties, and, in fact, being somewhat flurried; but in my reports as commissioner for enquiring into the expenses of the administration of justice, I have, to the best of my recollection, suggested such a plan. However, one thing appears plain at this moment, that every functionary whose emoluments are variable and dependent on the services he renders, should subjoin to his account an affidavit, drawn with great amplitude and precision, swearing to those particulars in which fraud might be practised. According as I understand this question, further ideas suggest themselves to me : I think that country constables to whom subpœnas are sent for service, should each send in his account to the Clerk of the Crown, sworn to by himself, and the distances to be attested by a magistrate ; and that Mr. Schiller should receive a reasonable remuneration for his very valuable services in selecting the names of witnesses in the various depositions, entering them in a book, making out the subpœnas, and having them served ; as also for making out further subpœnas to serve other witnesses whose attendance new information might show to be necessary. And likewise for causing enquiries to be made and witnesses to be sought on points where the prosecuting Crown officer considers the evidence to be defective. Nothing further occurs to me at the moment. I think it but justice to Mr. Schiller to say that these duties were wonderfully well performed by Mr. Schiller, so much so that to this moment I am surprised how he was able to perform them so well.

Robert MacKay, Esquire, Advocate, sworn, saith : I am 46 years of age. In March, 1856, I, on behalf of the Crown, conducted the prosecutions in the Criminal Term of Queen's Bench at Montreal, for the Term above mentioned. Being now shown Mr. Schiller's account as Superintendent of Crown Witnesses at Montreal, and being asked whether it was ever presented to me for sanction, or certificate of correctness, I say that I believe that I never saw that paper before. I may or may not have made certificates that would bear upon portions of this document, at this distance of time, I really do not know what I certified in respect of any business done that term.

This particular account has not been certified by me, as my signature does not appear upon it. I do not remember whether I was asked to sign it or not, my impression is that I was not.

I would add that during the term, Mr. Schiller and Mr. Delisle would put before me sometimes, papers partly printed and partly written, which they asked me to sign, and which I would sign. These papers, as far as I can remember, were signed first by Mr. Delisle, late Clerk of the Crown, and I would prefer that my certificates should be referred to for information on these points, as I have not retained in my memory all the facts.

FRIDAY, 25th Sept. 1863.
Charles Hibbard of St. Johns, Bailiff, aged 50 years, sworn:

I have been Bailiff of the Superior Court for the District of Montreal and Iberville for the last 15 years or thereabouts, during which time I have made a few services of subpœnas for Mr. Schiller, superintendent of Crown witnesses.

I see that in the case of the Queen vs. Jas. Darling, for uttering a forged foreign Bank note. I served one copy of subpœna on Casimil Ouimet, at St. Athanase about six miles from St. John's.

I lived at St. John's at the time. The return of service is signed by me, and, I believe, was written by my brother, but I am not positive, but I think it is the handwriting of my brother. I did not charge the mileage or service upon the said subpœna, that is,I did not enter the charge on the back thereof. and I cannot now say why I did not.

If my memory serves me right, this subpœna was given to me in Montreal, and in that case my charge would have been 35s. This witness Ouimet was ascertained to be a principal witness, after the other witnesses had to come to Montreal to give their evidence before the Court then sitting. Mr. Schiller has sometimes sent subpœnas to me by Mail to be served in the country. When I was not obliged to come to Montreal with the returns; I charged mileage on the distance I had travelled, and when I came to Montreal with the returns, I charged the subpœnas from Montreal.

I came to town several times and made my charges accordingly. Mr. Schiller always paid me the full amount due for such services.

I have generally been in the habit of putting my fees on the back of subpœnas, and I cannot remember why I did not do so in this case.

I was called as a witness before the Criminal Courts at Montreal, and I was taxed for my attendance.

Mr. Schiller used to make my accounts as a witness, but never charged me anything for them.

SATURDAY, September 26, 1863.
Mr. A. M. Delisle, late Clerk of the Crown, and Mr. Charles Schiller, as his Deputy Clerk of the Crown, being called upon to explain why no fees were received in Term or out of Term, from the 10th September, 1850, when the Act 13 and 14 Vic., chap. 37 was enacted, funding the fees of the said office, up to the 1st April, 1856, as appears by the books kept in that office, entered in a memorandum of books produced before the Commissioners, on the 14th March, 1863. Account Current Book with the Provincial Government, from 10th September, 1850, to 31st December, 1861.

1stly. For writs of Habeas Corpus.
2ndly. Recognizances.
3rdly; For Subpœnas.
4rthly. Copies of Papers.
5thly. For Certiorari.

Mr. Delisle's answer.--"Considering that this question of the Commissioners is predicated upon the assumption that fees were received and not accounted for to Government, virtually embodies a charge of embezzlement, I desire to record my solemn protest against the course pursued by the Commissioners in interrogating me in relation thereto, but as I feel that my character has been most unjustly and injuriously assailed, I waive all formality and will give the fullest information in my power."

"Speaking on my own behalf, I beg to say that, at the period referred to, and subsequently, so long as I continued to hold the Office of Clerk of the Crown, Mr. Charles E. Schiller acted as my Deputy, and in that capacity collected all fees and monies received in the department, and this duty he invariably performed.

"I paid over to the Government everything Mr. Schiller accounted to me for, and having every confidence in his honesty and integrity, I never had any reason to doubt for one moment, that his accounts were not faithful and correct.

"If in any case no fees were collected on any such proceedings, Mr. Schiller is in a position, I have no doubt, to give a satisfactory explanation of it, for instance that the Judges had sanctioned it by a verbal order given to him to that effect on several occasions.

"Having under the law, the power of naming a Deputy the Commissioners will readily understand that the minor details of the Department, such as collecting the fees, would form a part of the duty of such Deputy, as well in cases of Habeas Corpus, where he always attended upon the Judges, as in the less important matters of recognizances, subpœnas, &c., &c., and the Commissioners will not therefore, I hope, consider it evidence of any intention on my part to withhold information if I refer them for more ample explanations to Mr. Schiller himself, whose personal knowledge of these matters will enable him to speak with greater precision in relation to them."

Mr. Schiller's answer to the interrogatories proposed by the Commissioners on the 23rd instant.

"I desire, most respectfully to record my protest against the course pursued by the Commissioners of submitting questions to me, which in reality, import an accusation of embezzlement, The Commissioners having no authority so to do, and moreover it being contrary to all principles of law, that a party accused should be so interrogated. But as I feel conscious of my own innocence of having committed any crime, I make the following explanations.

"During the period referred to, I acted as Deputy Clerk of the Crown, and Mr. Delisle confided to me, as part of my duty as such Deputy, the collection of fees and monies paid into the Department. This was attended to exclusively by me, and when the time arrived for accounting to Government I would furnish a statement to Mr. Delisle, and all the monies included in such statement were transmitted by Mr. Delisle to Government. No fees, whatever, were ever improperly detained by me, and although it may appear that some writs of Habeas

" Corpus were issued, it is necessary I should state
" no fees were collected, and therefore not accounted
" for, arising from various causes and amongst others,
" for example, I could mention the following :--

" 1st. In cases of Habeas Corpus, the Judge would
".sometimes give me a verbal order not to charge fees
".from some circumstances in the case which seemed
" to him proper that he should so order.

" 2nd. In cases of Habeas Corpus the proceedings
" would be prompted by pure motives of charity, and
" it not unfrequently happened that where parties
" were unjustly incarcerated, Mr. McGinn, to whom
" the prisoners' case and circumstances were known
" would solicit some Counsel to apply for the writ,
" foregoing his own fees on the return ; the Counsel
" also acting from the same motive of charity to ac-
" complish the release from gaol of a person unjustly
" and illegally committed and too poor to pay the ex-
" pense of obtaining his release. These facts I am
" in a position to establish if necessary. At this dis-
" tance of time it is impossible to speak from me-
" mory of the several proceedings adverted to, but I
" may add to the above, that there existed no tariff to
" justify me in exacting fees.

" Signed,   C. E. SHILLER."

[TRANSLATION.]

Charles Valiquette, Bailiff, of the Parish of St.
Jerome, District of Terrebonne, being sworn, saith--
I am 33 years of age. To the best of my belief it is 14
years since I have been a Bailiff at St. Jerome aforesaid. I have several times served summonses to witnesses who were to appear at the Criminal Courts in
Montreal. I served four copies of subpœnas in the
cause of Dom. Reg vs. J. Beaudry, for the Court of
Queen's Bench.

It was not I that filled up the returns on the back
of the subpœnas, and I am unacquainted with the
handwriting of whoever filled them up. I have signed them when they have been filled up. Whenever
I came to Montreal to be paid I brought the said subpœnas with me and gave them to Mr. Schiller and
sometimes to Mr. Benjamin Delisle. Sometimes I
came 15 days and sometimes 8 days and sometimes
later after the service had been made. I sometimes
sent my subpœnas by the Post or by an opportunity
that offered, and I did not sign my returns ; but when
I came to town to be paid Mr. Schiller or Mr. Benjamin Delisle filled up my returns and I signed them.
I received these subpœnas from Mr. Schiller by Post,
and I never received but one in Montreal, as far as
I remember. As it was not I that filled up the returns, and that Mr. Schiller or Mr. Benjamin Delisle
gave me the pen and told me to sign the returns, I did
not, in consequence, put down the mileage for the
distance I had travelled because I was paid at once.

They paid me according to the distance I had travelled from St. Jerome to the place where I had notified the witnesses.

I reside in the Village of St. Jerome. The witnesses
in the cause above mentioned, live outside the Village, and the one that resides at the greatest distance
is about four leagues from the Village. In this case
I should receive 3s a league and 1s 3d for each service.

In the case of the Queen vs. Seraphin Chaurette,
I served four copies of subpœnas to witnesses that resided in the Parish of St. Jerome. One of them lived
in the Village and the others one or two leagues beyond. As far as I can remember, it was Mr. Schiller
that filled up my returns. I do not recollect what
was paid me, but I ought to have received from Mr.

Schiller 3s the league and 1s 3d for each service, reck-
oning from the Village of St. Jerome to the greatest
distance I travelled to serve the subpœnas.

The distance from Montreal to the Village of St.
Jerome is 12 leagues. I served four subpœnas in the
cause of H. M. the Queen vs. Augustin Taillefer, on
witnesses who had to appear before the above mentioned Criminal Court, in October, 1853. Of these four
copies, one was addressed to me. I do not remember
if I was called on as witness in the said case. Mr.
Schiller gave me the subpœnas, addressed to Mr.
and Mrs. Grindon, at Montreal, and I served them
on these two persons at Montreal, in the case of the
said Taillefer, in October, 1853. Not understanding
English, it may be stated in my returns, that I had
served the two subpœnas on Mr. and Mrs. Grindon,
at St. Jerome, for it was not I that wrote that return
on the subpœnas in English. As well as I can recollect, my father, Emilien Valiquette, Bailiff, was a
witness with me in Montreal. For having served the
subpœnas in the said case of Taillefer, I should have
received from Mr. Schiller the sum of 1s 3d on each
service and 1s mileage.

I know the signature of my father, Emilien Valiquette, Bailiff, of the Village of St. Jerome, and I see
his name on the back of the two subpœnas, issued in
the case of H. M. the Queen vs. Margaret Molloy, to
summon John Herbert, Bailiff, of St. Jerome, as a
witness before the above mentioned Criminal Court,
at Montreal, in March, 1853. This Mr. Herbert must
have resided at that period in the Village of St.
Jerome. The return was numbered 60 in the aforesaid case last issued on the 4th March, 1853, and
was returnable on the 14th of the same month, and
addressed to John Herbert, is in the handwriting of
Mr. Melchior Prevost, Notary, at St. Jerome, and the
figures, 2s 6d, at the end is in the handwriting of my
father. His expences on the service of said
subpœna to Mr. Herbert, in the Village of St.
Jerome, would amount to 1s 3d for the service, and 1s
for mileage. The distance from the Village of St.
Jerome, to the Village of St. Sauveur, is 4 leagues,
and from the extreme end of the Parish of St. Sauveur, it is six or perhaps seven leagues.

The distance of the Village of St. Jerome to the extreme end of the Cote St. Marie, is six leagues. There
is no Parish of Ste. Marie, but the place is so called
The distance from the Village of St. Jerome to the
Village of the Parish of St. Martin is seven leagues,
and to the Village of Ste. Rose 5 leagues, and to the
Village of St. Janvier de Blainville two leagues.

In 1856 Messrs. Melchior Prevost, Andre Lavalle,
and Hilaire Choall, Wm. Scott, Jean Baptiste Patrie,
Emelien Valiquette, Honore Marior, Jos. Johannet,
Medard Grignon, Francois Vilbon dit Locas, resided
in the Village of St. Jerome.

The subpœnas that I served from time to time on
other parties, for the Criminal Court of Montreal, I
received by Post, except once, when I received
them in Montreal, and on another occasion in the
case of Johannet, when J. B. Patrie brought them to
me.

[TRANSLATION.]

TUESDAY, 29th September, 1863.

Emillen Valiquette, bailiff, of the Parish of St.
Jerome, sworn, and saith :-- I am 56 years of age. I
know Mr. Delisle, Mr. Brehaut, and Mr. Schiller. I
am a bailiff since 1838. I have frequently served
subpœnas on witnesses who had to appear and give
evidence before the Criminal Court of Montreal.

These subpœnas were forwarded to me by the post to St. Jerome, where I have always resided since I became a bailiff, and unless I had business that called me to Montreal, I sent my returns there through the Post Office. Sometimes I caused my returns to be written out by my son, sometimes by Mr. Melchior Prevost, and sometimes by Mr. Schiller, when I happened to be in Montreal attending the Court.

The returns were generally in English, and I do not understand English. When Mr. Schiller sent me subpœnas,--and I had occasion to go to Montreal,--he paid me in his office, and sometimes he sent me what was due to me by the post,

When Mr. Schiller forwarded me subpœnas by post, he paid me according to the distance I had travelled from my own house to the residences the farthest off of the witnesses I had notified. The distance from the Village of St. Jerome to the Village of the Petite Nation is from 22 to 23 leagues, perhaps more or less.

The distance from the Village of St. Adelle is six leagues, and to the Village of St. Scholastique 4 leagues and one mile. At the Criminal Court Mr. Schiller gave me 1s. a mile, and 1s. 3d. each signification. Many of my returns were written by Mr. Schiller, and in signing them I did not remark whether my fees were marked on the returns, for I had my account in my pocket, and gave them to Mr. Schiller, who retained it. I sometimes served subpœnas at Montreal on witnesses when I had to appear myself as a witness before the Criminal Court at Montreal.

I was taxed and paid as a witness, and usually received $1 a day. In former years 1s. 3d. was paid to Mr. Schiller for each account that he made out; but of late years Mr. Schiller has ceased receiving the same.

In the case of H. M. the Queen vs. Margaret Molloy, I had my return made out by Mr. Prevost. It is dated at St. Jerome, and I had my fees, which amounted to 2s. 6d., noted thereon. The summons was directed to John Herbert, constable, who resided in the Parish of St. Jerome at the *Cote Double*, and about 2 leagues from the village.

When my name was inscribed on one of these subpœnas that was sent to me by the post, I held myself duly notified, and proceeded to Montreal accordingly as a witness, and was taxed and paid as a witness for coming to Montreal, and I brought with me my return when I came to town. I have never paid for the bond I gave in the case of H. M. the Queen vs. Denis Herbert *et al*, in March term, 1857, at the Criminal Court, Montreal, nor for that I gave in October, 1857. They never asked me for anything.

Cross-examined by Mr. Schiller.

When I was employed by Mr. Schiller, I have always been well paid, and was quite satisfied. It has occurred very often that during the sitting of the Criminal Court, and during the progress of a case, that Mr. Schiller would send me in great haste late in the evening to serve summonses for witnesses in the country; and on those occasions Mr. Schiller recompensed me over and above what my fees entitled me to, as I had to travel by night over very bad roads. My instructions were, on these occasions, to bring back the witnesses myself, who were required to give evidence the next day.

Edward Carter, Esquire, of Montreal, Queen's Counsel, sworn, saith :--I have frequently made applications during the course of my practice at the bar, exte [...] [...] 17 years, to obtain the discharge o prisoners, or their liberation on bail by means of Habeas Corpus. In many instances I was successful.

In many cases either myself or my client would pay for the writ, and in other cases nothing was paid. When anything was paid, it was paid to the Deputy Clerk of the Crown, Mr. Schiller. I think it was 11s. 8d. for the writ, and the return was paid to the gaoler, and I think it was 12s. 6d. I have frequently seen the fee paid over to him when he brought up the prisoner. When the party was admitted to bail in cases of misdemeanor, the total amount of fees paid was £1 9s. 2d., to the best of my knowledge. I think there was something paid to the constable for the service of the writ upon the gaoler. I have examined the several records placed before me, in the several cases of Clement Chagnon ; Levi P. Denmore Lindsay, Little *et al* ; Jos. Neil, Robert Ross, Michael Dunn, J. B. Deschambault, and Jos. Neil, the latter of 2nd July, 1859 ; and I declare that I find that the petitions for writs of Habeas Corpus in those cases, were either prepared in my own hand-writing or signed by me as the Attorney for the applicant. And being asked whether I am aware that any fees were paid in those cases, and to whom, I declare that at this distance of time it is impossible for me to state from memory whether any fees were paid in those cases or not. I never in practice kept any record in my office in the shape of a cash-book of Criminal proceedings, and for this reason that I acted upon the rule, as far as possible, of being paid before-hand, and, therefore, kept no account with parties incarcerated ; or when not paid, I acted gratuitously in obtaining the liberation of the parties, which sometimes happened, owing to the indigent circumstances of the parties known to me, or acting upon the suggestion of others, who, from motives of charity, were desirous of obtaining the liberation of parties incarcerated. In such cases no fees were exacted at all.'

Being asked whether I am aware that a fee of 5s. for recognizance given in open Court during the course of my practice, I answer that I have sometimes seen 5s. paid for a recognizance taken in open Court in cases of misdemeanor. I am not aware that such fees were paid in cases of felony. On the contrary, I frequently observed parties giving recognizances in cases of felony, without paying any fees. These fees were paid to the Deputy, Mr. Schiller, Deputy Clerk of the Crown.

WEDNESDAY, 30th September, 1863.

John Kennedy Elliott, Esq., Advocate, sworn, saith: I have been in practice since the 1st March, 1859, since which time I have had occasion to make application for Habeas Corpus in the case of the Queen vs. Samuel Butterworth, and the Queen vs. Archibald Young, who was then imprisoned for assault, with intent to murder ; and Butterworth for selling liquors without a licence. Both parties were discharged on my application. There were fees paid in these cases to the Deputy Clerk of the Crown either by me or my client. One case was in 1859, and the other in 1860. The said money was paid in the Court House. I do not recollect what was the amount I paid, but I know there was something paid in each case. Young had been committed for a felony, but was afterwards indicted for a misdemeanor only.

I may have paid for the said bond along with other fees for Habeas Corpus, but I paid no separate fee for bail.

Cross-examined by Mr. Schiller.

I know that Mr. Schiller was in the habit of collecting the Gaoler's and Constable's fees in cases of Habeas Corpus, but in the case of Young, above referred to, I am positive that Mr. Schiller was paid fees for the Habeas Corpus, from the fact that he remarked there was a difference in the fees for Habeas Corpus, in a case of misdemeanour, to that in a case of felony. He stated that the fee was higher in a case of misdemeanour than in a case of felony.

[TRANSLATION.]

Louis Bellanger, Esq., Advocate, of the City of Montreal, sworn, saith--It will be eleven years on the 8th of October next, that I have practised as an Advocate in the City of Montreal. I am 38 years of age. I presented a petition on the 15th November, 1861, to obtain a writ of Habeas Corpus on the part of Joseph Chartrand, farmer, of the Parish of Ste. Marthe, who was incarcerated in the common gaol, in the City of Montreal, who was accused in the warrant for his arrest, as follows:--"Of having hid, or received about nine or ten bushels of Wheat, belonging to L. Adam, Esq., Notary Public, of the Parish of St. Ignace du Coteau du Lac, valued at about $9 to $10, in the said Parish of Ste. Marthe, in the said County, in the said District, on or about the 12th of March last, past." And this petition having been granted, the writ of Habeas Corpus was issued, and the said Joseph Chartrand was discharged on bail.

The brother of the said Joseph Chartrand, who was one of his securities, furnished the money, and in my presence, paid it over to Mr. Schiller, but I cannot recollect the amount so paid to that gentleman.

I did not make any entry in my books of what was paid at the time, as I made no entry in my books as I made my client pay the amount.

Mr. Schiller informed me of the amount that had to be paid, but I cannot recollect how much the amount was. It was there and then that Mr. Schiller, received the money in presence of the said Joseph Chartrand and his securities.

Cross-examined by Mr. Schiller.

The amount thus paid should have included all fees due to the Gaoler and Constable, and to all other persons concerned in the execution of the writ, but I cannot say whether the money so paid included the writ of Habeas Corpus. I did not ask Mr. Schiller how that money was to be distributed nor to whom it should be paid.

[TRANSLATION.]

Joseph Maxime Loranger, Esq., Advocate, of the City of Montreal, sworn, saith--I am 29 years of age. I have practised as an Advocate in Montreal since 1854. Two applications for writs of Habeas Corpus are now shewn me, in the cases of H. M. the Queen vs. Sophie St. Marie et al, and Joseph Savard et al, and I perceive that these applications were made by Messrs. Loranger & Brothers, Advocates, of which I was an associate. It is L. Onesime Loranger, one of my partners, who is at present indisposed, who presented these applications, which were granted.

I have referred to my books of accounts, and I perceive that on the 12th of December, 1859, there was in the cash book two entries, the first as follows:--"Received from Savard, on account of writ of Habeas Corpus £3; paid and expended for Habeas Corpus, £2 9s 9d," without its being stated to whom or wherefore.

I have very frequently made applications for a writ of Habeas Corpus, and I recollect well that money was paid in the Office of the Clerk of the Crown, to Mr. Schiller, but I cannot say how much I was in the habit of paying.

I have referred to our cash book as regards the affair of Ste. Marie, on the said 13th Feb., 1861. I see that the two following entries are in my brother's handwriting:--"Received for Habeas Corpus, from Madam Dubé £1 15s; paid for Habeas Corpus in the same case £1 15s. I see by these that Sophie Ste. Marie is inscribed, wife of Ambroise Dubé. I have no personal knowledge of such application. I was in Europe at the time.

Thomas Patton, of the City of Montreal, Merchant, sworn, saith--I am 40 years of age. I have lived in Montreal for about 17 years. In the month of Nov., 1853, being accused of having participated in a riot and assault, I went to the Court House, at Montreal, where I was ordered to furnish bail to stand my trial for said offence. The Court was in Session, and I then and there gave bail in open Court, and remember that I paid something to Mr. Schiller for said bail. I do not remember whether it was 5s or 10s that I paid. Edward Hanly and Daniel Kerny, were my bail upon said occasion. This was in the case of the Queen vs. Garret Barry, et al. I only gave bail once to my knowledge as above stated. I was acquitted on the charge.

Adolphe Bissonette, Joint High Constable for the District of Montreal, having appeared this day before the Commissioners, in obedience to a subpœna, Duces-Tecum, served upon him and Benjamin Delisle, Esq., Joint High Constable for the said District, declares as follows:--

1st. That he cannot produce a list of cases of all misdemeanours out of Session, charged against the Government for the years 1847, '48, '49, '50, '51, '52, '53, '54, '55, and '56, not being then Joint High Constable. I never charged anything to Government, and the said papers in my Office, and the books in which Mr. Benjamin Delisle made such charges were private books, and were taken away from the office about 15 days ago by Mr. Henry Delisle, who is a Clerk in our Office, I did not oppose it because I had no claim upon them as I considered.

I have no original subpœnas issued before the Court of Quarter Sessions in Montreal, during the years 1851, '52, '53, '54, '55, '56, '57, '58, and '59. Mr. Benjamin Delisle has all the papers. I have none of them. They are not in the Head Constable's Office, having been taken away by Mr. Henry Delisle, by his father's orders, Mr. Benjamin Delisle, ten or twelve days ago, for the purpose, as he told me, of putting them in order.

I did not oppose the removal of those subpœnas because it was in the Court time, and I had no time to look over those papers to put them in order. I cannot produce the original receipts relating to a certain quantity of stolen silks, taken from the Store of Messrs. Benjamin Brothers, in 1858, in the case of the "Queen vs. Emily Philer and Joseph Mondle," but he can produce a receipt which has been given a few days ago to Mr. Henry Delisle, a Clerk in our Office, by a Mr. Fish. I cannot say that a receipt for such stolen Silks was in our Office before, for I never saw it. That he has already exhibited stolen monies from a man named White in the case of the Queen vs. Falvin, Bridget Price, et al. I got that money from Mr. Benjamin Delisle, on the 23rd or 24th January last, when we took stock in the Vault of stolen goods. The same identical money was handed by me in

1860, when I was Sub-Chief of Police to Mr. Benjamin Delisle, High Constable.

THURSDAY, 1st October, 1863.

Godfroy Laflamme, Esq., Advocate of Montreal, saith :—I am 32 years of age. I have been practising as an Advocate since 1852, I believe.

I remember only one application for Habeas Corpus, which was made in our own office, that is, the office of Messrs. R. and G. Laflamme, Advocates at Montreal, on the part of one Maurice Boisvert, mentioned in the said writ of Habeas Corpus as being of the Parish of St. Louis, in the County of Terrebonne, on the charge of neglecting his duty as overseer of roads and bridges, and in not having the front roads under his jurisdiction kept in proper repair, for which he was convicted to pay a penalty, and in default of payment, was imprisoned in the common Gaol of the district of Montreal.

The application was presented by my brother and partner, Rodolphe Laflamme, Esq., and was granted, and the said Maurice Boisvert liberated and discharged, the committment having been declared insufficient in law, as appears by the order of the Judge of 2nd March, 1855.

I did not pay anything myself for this w rit of Habeas Corpus. There is an entry in our books, by which it appears that the sum of £1 10s. 0d. is charged to the said Maurice Boisvert, as having been paid to obtain the writ in question. After the said Maurice Boisvert was liberated, we took an action of damages against John Hale, Esq., J.P., who had committed said Maurice Boisvert to gaol. In order to prove the disbursements made by us in obtaining the suit, Mr. Schiller was examined as a witness in the suit for damages, and his deposition was taken down in writing.

In that deposition Mr. Schiller stated that it was Boisvert or his lawyer who had paid the fees on the said Habeas Corpus, which he made up at £1 6s. 8d., as having been paid. The said sum being made up by him in his said deposition as follows :—11s. 8d. for writ; 2s. 6d. for service of same ; and 12s. 6d. to the Gaoler for his return. The date of Mr. Schiller's deposition is 1st June, 1859. The date of the second writ of Habeas Corpus is the 2nd March, 1855, and the writ is signed by Mr. Schiller as Deputy Clerk of the Crown.

FRIDAY, 2nd October, 1863.

Alexander Cross, Esq., Advocate, sworn, saith.:— I am 40 years of age. I have been practising as an Attorney in Montreal for about 18 years. The firm of Cross and Bancroft, Advocates, of which I was one of the partners, acted for Thos. R. Johnson when indicted before the Quarter Sessions at Montreal for misdemeanor, in 1856. There was a writ of Certiorari taken out to remove the prosecution to the Court of Queen's Bench, (Crown Side,) Montreal. I could not have recollected that the said writ was returned without reference to the Register of proceedings of the Court of Queen's Bench, Crown Side, at Montreal, page 694. To the best of my recollection, the proceedings were compromised, and the case was dropped. The said writ of Certiorari appears to have been returned on the 14th October, 1856. A recognizance was given by Mr. Johnson before Judge Aylwin at Montreal, on the 25th June, 1856, to appear before the Court of Queen's Bench, and upon the removal of the proceedings before that Court by writ of Certiorari. Mr. Bancroft had the general charge of the disbursements in our office. I believe there was something paid for the writ, recognizance and return. I charged £1 1s. 8d. in our bill of costs as a disbursement for the writ of certiorari, recognizance and return, which writ, recognizance and return are now exhibited to me.

Francis Cassidy, Esq., Advocate, Queen's Counsel of Montreal, sworn, saith :—I am aged about 34 years.

I have been practicing as a Lawyer in Montreal since August, 1845.

During my practicing as such, I have several times presented applications for writs of Habeas Corpus on the part of different individuals confined in the Common Gaol of the District of Montreal. I have presented petitions for Habeas Corpus on the part of one Michel Troye dit Lafranchise, on the 5th December, 1856 ; and of John Ingram, on the 28th July, 1859. In the case of Troye dit Lafranchise, the Writ of Habeas Corpus was granted by Sir L. H. Lafontaine, Baronet, Chief Justice of the Court of Queen's Bench, on the 5th day of December, 1856, and the said Troye dit Lafranchise on giving good and sufficient bail to answer, according to law. The said Lafranchise was well able to pay, and my impression is that either he or I paid the fees, but I do not recollect it. Sometimes I paid the fee myself, and sometimes it was the prisoner when liberated, and it was paid to Mr. Schiller, when paid.

The Writ of Habeas Corpus in this case of John Ingram was granted on the 31st July, 1858, and under the peculiar circumstances of the case, all the proceedings on that Writ were made through charity, on the part of the various officers to whom fees were payable, including my own services. As to Writs of Habeas Corpus, they were not so often granted free of charge as bills of indictment in the Quarter Sessions. During the course of my practice there may have been one or two more cases of Habeas Corpus granted in like manner for charity.

In the case of " the Queen vs. Charles Gendreau the younger, the petition for Habeas Corpus is dated the 10th May, 1854, and is signed by Messrs. Moreau, Leblanc and Cassidy, Advocates. It was Mr. LeBlanc, Advocate, who drew the petition and appeared before the Judge to obtain the granting of the Writ.

The Writ of Habeas Corpus was granted, and the said Gendreau was liberated on bail.

I see in our Books of Accounts on the date 19th May, 1854, which goes on to say that £1 6s. 8d. was paid on that day for a Writ of Habeas Corpus, the entry is made in the hand-writing of Mr. LeBlanc, my partner. I have no personal knowledge of such payment.

In the case of the Queen vs. Felix Labelle, the petition was drawn up by myself and signed Messrs. LeBlanc & Cassidy, and presented to the Judge, and the Writ was granted on the 26th July, 1855, and the prisoner was admitted to bail on the following day. I find nothing in my account books showing that any thing was paid by me in that case for fees.

In the case of the Queen vs. Bernard Gannon, on the 29th August, 1856, a Writ of Habeas Corpus was granted, and I acted as Counsel, and the prisoner was admitted to bail on that day. In this case, also, I do not find any entry in our books showing that any thing was paid for fees ; but, as I stated before, sometimes those fees were paid by the prisoner himself. I never enquired, nor was it ever mentioned by the officer of the Court to me, that there was any distinction between cases of felony and misdemeanor, as to the payment of fees on Writs of Habeas Corpus. There were different instances where the amount was not the same. I find in our Cash Book, under date 23rd July, 1856, two entries in the hand-writing of my partner, Mr. LeBlanc; the first is as follows: "Payé pour Habeas Corpus 17s. 6d." The second "Pour Habeas Corpus Lariviere, £2 6s. 8d. I give this item as I find it in our books, but it must include the Bailiff, the Gaoler, and the Clerk's fees; it may also include the payment of carters, and to go to the Gaol.

I did not always pay cash at the time writs were obtained, but as I had other business in the Court, I used to settle now and then with Mr. Schiller.

Many a time I applied for Bills of Indictment in private prosecutions, and obtained them without charge, as the parties were poor.

I do not recollect ever paying anything for indictments which I presented in the Court of Quarter Sessions.

I remember that I required, in three or four instances, of Mr. Schiller, when he was to be paid for renewing recognizances, he used to mention the amount, but I do not recollect how much it was, nor did I see any money paid.

Bernard Devlin, Esq., Advocate, of Montreal, sworn, saith: I am 39 years of age. I have practiced as an Advocate in Montreal for about 16 years, during which time I have had a good deal to do in the Criminal Court, and frequently made application for Writs of Habeas Corpus, on behalf of parties imprisoned. Having examined the petition of Edward Cleary et al, now shown to me, and purporting to have been filed on the 30th November, 1852, for a Writ of Habeas Corpus, and which I perceive was granted on the same day and the conviction in said case quashed. I see that I acted as Counsel for the prisoner. I have had several Habeas Corpus, on some of which I paid fees, and on others I have not. I mean the Gaoler's fees and Constable's fee, which was, I believe, about 5s. In cases of felony, I know of no case at all where fees were charged or paid except the Gaoler's and Constable's fees. I perceive by the records now shown me that I acted as Counsel upon applications for Habeas Corpus in the following cases, viz.:—"The Queen vs. Patrick McCaffrey; the Queen vs. Francis Burns, in 1853; the Queen vs. Sarah Brown, alias McFarlane; the Queen vs. Thomas O'Neill, in 1854; the Queen vs. James Vaughan, in 1855; the Queen vs. John White, in 1856." Some of which are for charges of felony, and others for misdemeanors, and I have no recollection of having paid in any of these cases more than the Gaoler and the Constable's fees; 12s. 6d., I think, was the fee for the Gaoler, and the Constable's fee was 2s. 6d. These fees were paid to Mr. Schiller for the Gaoler and Constable. When Mr. McGinn was present, I have seen Mr. Schiller hand him over his fee, but sometimes he was not present, and sometimes these fees were not paid at the time of granting the writ. I know of no case in which the prisoner paid.

Q. When you were obtaining Writs of Habeas Corpus in the foregoing and other similar cases, did ou or did you not understand that either you or your client would be called upon to pay something for the Writ itself, over and above the Gaoler and Constable's fees?

I never so understood it, nor was it ever asked of me, nor from any of my clients to my knowledge, but in cases of misdemeanor I think the charge was £1 3s. 4d. That, I think, embraced all the charges except the Constable's fee, which I believe was 2s. 6d. Where I have acted for the private prosecutor in the Court of Quarter Sessions for many years past, I have paid nothing for the Bills of Indictment.

I am aware that in cases of renewing or giving bail in open Court, in cases of misdemeanor, it has been the practice of Mr. Schiller to receive a fee of 5s. for the bail bond, but there are instances in which no fees were charged in case of indigent persons.

In explanation of matters which are not herein spoken of by me with certainty, I would add that I kept no record of my disbursements in criminal cases, inasmuch as I had no partner in this branch of my practice.

MONDAY, 5th October, 1863.

Bernard Devlin, Esq., Advocate, re-appears and continues his evidence:

Witness being asked whether he has any suggestion to make respecting the organization of the offices of the Clerks of the Crown and of the Peace, states as follows, viz.:

It is my opinion, founded upon several years' experience, that the Police Department should be detached altogether from the office of the Clerk of the Peace, and that the Police Magistrate should confine his attention exclusively to the duties of that department; and also that the monies received therein should be accounted for to the proper authorities directly from that department. As I understand its management now and for years past, monies are received by the Clerks in that establishment,—that is, in the Police department—and subsequently paid over to the Clerks of the Peace, thereby affording that officer no certain guarantee, from personal observation, of the correctness of the receipts of the office, presented to him by the various Clerks in that office.

My opinion, also, is that stolen property should remain in the custody of the High Constable, from the time of its reception up to the time of its delivery to the owner, or until disposed of by judicial authority. With respect to the office of the Clerk of the Peace, my opinion is that the duties of the office will be better performed by entrusting them to a single individual than to two persons as joint Clerks, as is now the case. My reason for this opinion is, that the amount of business done does not, according to my views, require the time and attention of two Clerks of the Peace; and for this further reason, that if in former years, when the criminal business of the District of Montreal embraced all the new Districts into which it has been subdivided, two persons were capable of performing the duties of the office, it is manifest that now, when it is reduced by such a subdivision, one officer, with a competent deputy, ought to perform all the duties appertaining to such office.

I desire further to add, that I have known Mr. Schiller for about sixteen years intimately; that I have had several pecuniary transactions with him, arising from my practice before the Courts, in which he received monies for me, and I confidently declare that I have never known him to have erred in any single instance in his dealings with me in those matters.

I have always found him scrupulously exact and honest, and I believe I express the opinion of every member of the profession, when I say that he has ever been most efficient, remarkably so, in the discharge of his duties, and at the same time extremely courteous to those with whom he was brought in contact in the management of his office.

Cross-examined by Mr. Brehaut:—My opinion is, as I have already stated, that one Clerk of the Peace and a Deputy is amply sufficient to discharge efficiently all the duties which now devolve on that officer, circumscribed as it is by the numerous Districts of recent creation.

THURSDAY, 8th October, 1863.

Mr. Lafrenaye intimated that the Commissioners had nothing further to examine, and desired that we should appoint such a day as would suit us to enter on our defence. After some conversation, it was agreed that we should enter on our defence on Thursday, the 15th instant, at eleven o'clock A.M., to which time the Commissioners adjourned.

Mr. Brehaut applied to be informed by the Commissioners as to the points or charges on which the Commissioners expected evidence to be adduced.— The Commissioners declined to give the information.

THURSDAY, 15th October, 1863.

Mr. Delisle requests to be furnished Subpœnas for the following witnesses :—

The Honble. Charles Mondelet,
The Honble. Wm. Badgley,
The Honble. Samuel Cornwallis Monk,
Francis G. Johnson, Esq.,
Chs. Joseph Coursol, Esq.,
Henry Judah, Esq.,
The Honble. Thos. Cushing Aylwin.

The Honble. Charles Mondelet, Assistant Justice of the Court of Queen's Bench, M.L.C., of Montreal, sworn.—61 years.

Produced by Mr. Delisle.

Would you have the kindness to state for how many years you have been engaged in the practice and administration of criminal justice in this Province as an Advocate, Judge of the Circuit Court, and Judge of the Court of Queen's Bench ?

A. I have practiced at the Bar 19 years, from the commencement of 1823 to the end of 1841, and from the commencement of 1842 to the end of 1843. I administered justice as District Judge in the Districts of Terrebonne, L'Assomption and Berthier ; and from the commencement of 1844, or latter part of 1843, to the end of 1849, as Circuit Judge for the Lower Province, and specially in the District of Montreal ; and from the end of 1849 to the month of June, 1859, I administered justice in the Superior Court for Lower Canada in the District of Montreal. In June, 1859, I took my seat in the Court of Queen's Bench as Assistant Judge thereof, and am still administering justice in that capacity.

Whilst at the Bar, I was engaged in a considerable practice in the different Criminal Courts.

During the six years of my tenure of the office of Circuit Judge, and since my apppointment to the Court of Queen's Bench, I have been considerably engaged in presiding both over the Court of Quarter Sessions and Queen's Bench in Criminal Sessions and Terms respectively.

Q. In your experience, will you please state whether you consider it feasible or practicable that the Clerk of the Peace should be the custodian of stolen goods, and at the same time entrusted with the

prosecution of offenders before the Court of Quarter Sessions ; and whether in practice it is not necessary that the custody of such goods should be vested in the High Constable, as being the proper officer to produce such goods in Court whenever required ?

A.—It would not only be indecorous in the Clerk of the Peace, acting both in the keeping and the producing in Court of the stolen goods, it would also be impracticable, at least in such a District as Montreal, where there is so much Criminal business. I believe it to have been the constant practice for the Clerk of the Peace to conduct the Criminal business before the Court of Quarter Sessions, and it will at once be suggested to any one's sense af propriety and knowledge of regular and safe administration of Criminal Justice, that that functionary neither could nor should be transformed into a witness, go for, or cause to be brought into Court stolen goods, which he should not allow to go out of his possession, and then stand in the witness box and be interrogated as such, touching the coming into his possession, his safe keeping thereof, and his producing into Court the stolen goods, and all that upon self-examination of himself, by himself· I presume that this impracticable course, which would have to be resorted to in the given case, may account for the fact of the Provincial Statute 6, William 4, Chapter 5, not having been carried out in the Criminal Courts, in the District of Montreal, for years, so far as known.

The above specially applies to the Court of Quarter Sessions. In the Court of Queen's Bench the above remarks would apply more forcibly in one respect, so far as propriety is concerned, where the Clerk of the Crown, is also Clerk of the Peace, subjected to the indecorous, and, I may say, improper course which I have referred to in the foregoing part of my deposition.

Q.—In practice, has not the custody of the stolen goods always been vested in the High Constable, and has not his production of them before the Court's of Queen's Bench and Quarter Sessions, met with the approval of the Judge's of those Courts ?

A.—I cannot positively say as to other Judges, but as far as my own experience goes I can state that I have never known of any difficulty about it, and I believe it to have been the constant practice, both in the Queen's Bench and the Court of Quarter Sessions·

Q.—Did you ever hear of any complaint that such goods were withheld from their owners ?

A.—No, I never did to my recollection.

Q.—Would you have the kindness to state your opinion as to the general management of the Criminal business of this District, by Mr. Delisle, during his tenure of office as Clerk of the Crown, and Clerk of the Peace ?

A.—In the Court of Quarter Sessions, when I was at the bar, and when I was a Circuit Judge, Mr. Delisle conducted the Criminal business of the Court with remarkable intelligence, energy, zeal, and success ; and I have no hesitation in adding that, from my personal knowledge, it is my opinion that Mr. Delisle was better qualified for, and more efficiently conducted the business for the Crown, than some Attornies General we have had the misfortune to have in this country, and others who may have assumed the responsible duty of doing what they never were brought up to, or had any qualification to perform.

The witness is cross-examined by the Commissioners :

Q.—When you have stated above that the Provincial Statute 6, William 4, Chap. 5, had not been carried out in the Criminal Courts, in the District of Montreal, for years, so far as you know, are you understood to say that the 6, Wil. 4, Chap. 5, does not oblige the Clerk of the Peace to keep a record of the stolen goods, as therein provided for, and to be the responsible person towards the Court, when orders are given, by the Courts, for the restitution of such goods to their respective owners, or for the sale of the unclaimed stolen goods, at the different periods indicated by that law, without reference to the party who should produce them, in open Court, at trials?

A.--I have not expressed, nor should I express, any extra judicial opinion on the above mentioned Statute, which speaks for itself. I have, as I should, confined myself to what I have stated would be an indecorous, improper, and impracticable course, and what had been done for years, so far as my own personal experience goes.

Q.--Are we to understand that your observations only apply to the production of such goods at trials?

A.--My observations, as a matter of course, extend no further, nor should be construed to apply to any other circumstances or transactions, but those which have come to, and are within the range of my own personal knowledge and experience.

Q.--To whom, in practice, were the orders of the Courts given for the restitution of stolen goods to their owners?

A.--In the Court of Quarter Sessions, over which I presided, in my turn, during my tenure of the Circuit Judgeship, I cannot call to my recollection that I was ever applied to, or that I ever gave any. Since I have been in the Court of Queen's Bench I am not aware that I ever gave any formal order touching the matter enquired of me.

Examined by Mr. Schiller :

Q.--Would you have the kindness to state from your own personal observation, your opinion of the manner in which Mr. Schiller discharged his duties as Deputy Clerk of the Crown, Deputy Clerk of the Peace, and Superintendent of Crown Witnesses?

A.--I can only speak as to what came under my own eye and personal observation in Court, having had no opportunity of observing the manner in which Mr. Schiller discharged his duties in the office. With respect to his conduct of such business in Court, and in immediate connection with the business of the Court, both in the Quarter Sessions, and in the Queen's Bench, it has appeared to me that the intelligence, zeal, and efficiency with which he discharged the duties pertaining to the Offices of Deputy Clerk of the Crown, Deputy Clerk of the Peace, and Superintendent of Crown Witnesses, could not be surpassed by any one ; and my reason for unequivocally expressing that opinion is, that in those Departments, as well as in others of a similar nature, the full and satisfactory discharge of such duties requires long training and experience.

Examined by Mr. Delisle :

The Honorable Samuel Cornwallis Monk, Assistant Judge of the Superior Court, Montreal, sworn.--Aged 49:

Q.--Would you have the kindness to state for how many years you have been engaged in the practice and administration of Criminal Justice in the District of Montreal, as an Advocate, Queen's Counsel, and Assistant Judge of the Superior Court?

A.--I prosecuted on the part of the Crown at Montreal between two and three years in the Court of Queen's Bench.

Q.--In your experience will you please state whether you consider it practicable that the Clerk of the Peace, who is entrusted with the prosecution of offenders in the Court of Quarter Sessions, should be the custodian of stolen goods, and whether, in practice, that duty has not always been performed by the High Constable, and if you consider that officer the proper person upon whom that duty should devolve?

A.--I do not think it either practicable or expedient that he should be the custodian of stolen goods, and this applies as well to goods having this character coming before the Quarter Sessions or the Queen's Bench. The Clerk of the Peace prosecuting in the Quarter Sessions, on the behalf of the Crown, it would not be at all practicable that he should produce stolen articles and identify them before the tribunal where he prosecutes.

It is obvious that such a practice could not be carried out. Although this practice would not be equally difficult in the Queen's Bench, yet acting as Clerk of the Court, it would be in the highest degree inconvenient that he should be called upon to produce and identify stolen articles during the progress of a trial as is always the case.

So far as my experience extends I can say positively that the High Constable has, always had the charge of property stolen, or supposed to be stolen, I have invariably called upon him as the person in possession of this description of goods to produce and identify the same before the Court, which he has invariably done, when in his possession.

I am also aware as a general rule, to which I know no exception, that these goods were on all occasions delivered to the High Constable, for safe keeping, I believe that such goods were always given to the High Constable by the seizing officer, or by the party who produced them.

I have in many instances given orders to the High Constable to deliver these goods after trial to owners. I am clearly of opinion that the High Constable is the proper officer to have charge of these goods, though under the Statute which in this particular may be considered as having fallen into disuetude, in the District of Montreal, the Clerks of the Peace are declared to be the legal custodian of such goods.

Q.--You have said that the practice was for the High Constable to produce stolen goods at trials before the Court, was this course not, in fact, practically approved of and sanctioned by the Courts?

A.--All I can say of this is that I entirely sanctioned it as representing the Attorney General, and from my knowledge of the fact that such had been the practice, previous to my representing the Attorney General for a number of years, I am of the opinion that it had received the sanction of the Courts.

Q.--Did you ever hear any complaint that such goods had not been returned to their owners?

A.--I cannot recollect any case where parties have complained of not receiving their property, except in this way. Parties prosecuting have called upon me representing that they could not get their property from the High Constable, upon which complaints I have given orders to the High Constable, and have heard no more about it. I presume that the goods were delivered upon my order.

Q.--Would you have the kindness to state your opinion as to the general management of the Criminal business by Mr. Delisle?

A.—Mr. Delisle's entire efficiency, as a public officer, was a matter of public notoriety, and I can, from my own experience state my belief that whether in the Queen's Bench, as Clerk of the Crown, or in the Quarter Sessions, prosecuting on the behalf of the Crown, a more able and more efficient officer could not be found. I have always found him attentive to his duty and zealous for the public service.

Q.--Are you aware that Mr. Delisle was frequently sent to the country, by order of the Government, to investigate important cases of felony, such as murder, arson, and other crimes, and if such services did not occupy a good deal of his time ?

A.--I, on several occasions, acting for the Attorney General, and under his express authority, directed Mr. Delisle to make investigations in country parts into capital felonies, such as those mentioned. These investigations extended, in some instances, over a considerable length of time and caused, necessarily, absence of some duration from his office. I may add that these investigations almost invariably led to important results, either in obtaining the conviction of the parties accused or in collecting a large mass of evidence which, in all probability would not have been obtained. I can, from my own experience, testify to the ability, tact and the fidelity in which these investigations were made.

Examined by Mr. Schiller:

Q.--Would you have the kindness to state your opinion of the manner in which Mr. Schiller discharged his duties as Deputy Clerk of the Crown, and Superintendent of Crown Witnesses.

A.--As Crown Prosecutor during the terms of the Criminal Court, and immediately previous, my official relations with Mr. Schiller were constant, and I can say that I never met with a more efficient, if so efficient, a public officer.

I can safely state that the activity, industry, and faithful discharge of his duties generally, contributed greatly to the proper administration of Criminal Justice. I base this statement upon the fact of the regularity with which the papers for prosecution were brought before me ; his minute knowledge and recollection of each case; his assistance to the Crown Prosecutor, always readily given; his attention in procuring the attendance and marshalling witnesses before the Grand Jury, and at the trials, and his ability and devotion to his duty as Deputy Clerk of the Crown and Superintendent of Crown Witnesses.

FRIDAY, 16th October, 1863.
Mr. Schiller's examination of the Honorable Mr. Justice Monk continued :

Q.--Would you have the kindness to state your opinion as to whether, in consequence of the zeal, activity, and efficiency of Mr. Schiller as Deputy Clerk of the Crown and Superintendent of Crown Witnesses, of which you have spoken, he did not contribute materially to accelerate the business before the Criminal Courts, and consequently to lessen their duration, and thus to economize time and money, in the payment of the Jurors, Witnesses, and Constables, who were paid so much per day for their attendance ?

A.--I am decidedly of opinion that owing to the vigilance and assiduity of Mr. Schiller, in the performance of his duties as Superintendent of Crown Witnesses, the business before the Court was greatly accelerated. I recollect but few, if any, instances where cases were postponed in consequence of the absence of material witnesses. Not only were the necessary Witnesses in attendance, but in consequence of Mr. Schiller's attention to each case, these Wit-

nesses were produced at all times when required, and in order to facilitate the progress of the trial. He seemed to have directed his attention to each case brought on for trial, and the witnesses were brought forward in a manner to cause no confusion or delay in the progress of the case. So far as my experience extends this course secured a great economy of time. There can be no doubt whatever that upon the business of the term there was thus effected a great saving in time, but there must also have been a considerable economy in the expense, owing to the distance from which witnesses were brought, the necessity for conducting the proceedings in two languages generally, and the vast amount of business before the Court. During the time I was Crown Prosecutor, I had to rely much on the co-operation of Mr. Schiller, and I can state, without hesitation, that I never had occasion to find him slack, or at fault, in the performance of his duty, but the reverse.

Q.--Did it not frequently occur during the terms that Mr. Schiller had to wait upon you with the Crown Witnesses, both before the opening and after adjournment of Courts?

A.--He did, and here, as in other particulars, he was alike assiduous and discriminating in the discharge of his duty.

Q.--Would you please state your opinion of the manner in which Mr. Schiller caused the Witnesses for the Crown to be taxed and discharged after their attendance was no longer required ?

A.--When the attendance of Witnesses was no longer required, it was Mr. Schiller's practice personally, and at once to attend to this duty, occasionally working to a late hour after Court, before the Witnesses were all disposed of. Not only was there no time lost, but it is a fact to my knowledge that Mr. Schiller exercised great care and discrimination in the taxation of these Witnesses. In cases where he had doubts, referring to me, and calling my attention, frequently, to the claims of Witnesses to be taxed whose taxation he had refused, and in some cases receiving directions from me to allow the taxation to be made. I speak now of what came to my personal knowledge.

The Honorable Thomas Cushing Aylwin, Justice of the Court of Queen's Bench, a witness summoned on the behalf of Mr. Delisle appeared. On the oath being tendered him he declined to be examined, and made the following statement :

"I decline to be sworn upon the ground that the Commission under which you are acting is illegal, and it is my bounden duty to resist, as one of Her Majesty's Judges of the Court of Queen's Bench, for Lower Canada. It may be advisable to state the reasons why I refuse. This proceeding is supposed to be governed by the 13th Chapter of the Consolidated Statutes of Canada, by which it is enacted, that whenever the Governor in Council deems it expedient to cause enquiry to be made into and concerning any matter connected with the good government of this Province, or the conduct of any part of the public business thereof, the administration of Justice therein, and such enquiry is not regulated by any special law, &c. Now the enquiry is stated to be into certain charges of malversation of office, which have been made against the late Joint Clerk of the Peace and Clerk of the Crown, at Montreal, Messrs. Delisle and Brehaut, and their Deputy also, Charles Schiller. Now malversation of office in a Clerk of the Crown is a matter which is perfectly well regulated by a special law, and, therefore, the present Commission does not come within the province of the 13th Chapter. The matter to be examined into is properly before my own Court, and, therefore, not to be taken at all into consideration by the Commissioners. If this Commission be allowed, I may to-morrow, upon a charge of malversation of office, be treated the same way, contrary to the law which gives immunity to me in my particular office of of a Judge of the Court of Queen's Bench.

By Mr. Doherty.--Allow me to state that the Commission empowers us also to enquire into the organization of the office.

By Judge Aylwin.--In that way there might be a most abominable injustice done by the Government. Recollect that I am entrusted with the administration of the law, and it is my duty to see that no man be imperilled by an abuse of the law.

SATURDAY, October 17, 1863.

Motion made by Mr. Delisle for a Rule against the Honble. Mr. Justice Aylwin, as follows, viz. :--

Motion by the undersigned that inasmuch as the Commissioners, on Thursday, the eight day of October, instant, appointed Thursday, the fifteenth day of October, instant, for the examination by the undersigned of such witnesses as he might have to adduce on his behalf, and that two witnesses have already been examineed, and inasmuch as the Honorable Thomas Cushing Aylwin, of the City of Montreal, one of Her Majesty's Justices of the Court of Queen's Bench was duly summoned by a subpœna, signed by the said Commissioners, and has appeared before them in obedience to the said subpœna, but declined to be sworn before the said Commissioners and to give his evidence as required by the said subpœna, although the oath was duly tendered to him by the said Commissioners ; that the said Honorable Thomas Cushing Aylwin be held and adjudged, in contempt of the said Commissioners, and for such contempt, committed to the Common Gaol of this District, until he shall have purged himself of the said contempt, or for such time and subject to such conditions as the said Commissioners may direct, or be otherwise dealt with according to law, for such contempt, unless cause to contrary be shewn on Tuesday next, the 20th day of October instant, at the hour of eleven o'clock in the forenoon, at the Court House, in the City of Montreal.

Signed, A. M. DELISLE.

Montreal, 17th Oct., 1863.

Mr. Delisle was heard on the said motion. Taken en delibere.

Jean Louis Beaudry, Esq., Mayor of Montreal, sworn, saith--I am 54 years of age.

This witness produced on behalf of Mr. Schiller.

I have been one of Her Majesty's Justices of the Peace in Montreal for about twenty-one years past. As such Justice of the Peace I have sat in the Court of Quarter Sessions, special and weekly Sessions frequently.

While I had so occasion as J. P. to sit in the Quarter Sessions as well as the weekly Sessions, and also in the Police Court, at all of which Courts I sat during many years, I have always found Mr. Charles Schiller in the discharge of his official duties to be very attentive and obliging to all parties that I have seen coming in contact with him.

I was Foreman of the Grand Jury once in the Quarter Sessions and twice in the Court of Queen's Bench, when Mr. Schiller on those occasions acted as Superintendent of Crown witnesses. I had occasion to consult him on matters coming before the Grand Jury, and I always found Mr. Schiller well informed as to his duties, and to my knowledge, fulfilling them faithfully and effectively. I always found Mr. Schiller to put all the business before the Grand Jury in a very lucid and intelligent manner, and in such a manner as to accelerate the business before the Grand Jury, and to bring the business to a close as quickly as possible.

On three occasions I had been robbed of goods from my Store, on two of which there were many articles of various kinds, the goods were deposited with the High Constable, and after the trials returned to me as they had been received. On many occasions in which it came to my knowledge that the services of Mr. Schiller were required by day or by night, he was ever ready to discharge them. So far as I have known either by myself or from what I heard from others Mr. Schiller conducted his business honestly and to the satisfaction of those who spoke to me of Mr. Schiller, and when I took the oath of office as J. P. I was informed by Mr. A. M. Delisle that I might place confidence in any document presented to me for signature by Mr. Schiller, or any information I might require of him in the discharge of my duties as J. P., and I have much pleasure in saying that I have never had cause to regret the confidence I placed in him.

Cross-examined by the Commissioners.

Q.--You said just now that you always found Mr. Schiller to put the business before the Grand Jury in a lucid and intelligent form, so as to accelerate the business before the Grand Jury, would you please state how, and in what manner that business was accelerated by the intervention of Mr. Schiller ?

A.--My reason for saying so in my examination-in-chief is, that after the swearing in of the Grand Jury and taking them to the Room provided for them, Mr. Schiller generally made his appearance, and informed the Grand Jurywhat business would come before them, and Mr. Schiller very soon afterwards would place the Bills of Indictment for investigation before them, always observing the rules of presenting to the Grand Jury the Bills on which witnesses were in readiness to be heard. Mr. Schiller generally used to indicate that such a witness could prove such a thing, and such another witness such another thing, whenever a difference of opinion arose amongst the Grand Jurors. Whenever Mr. Schiller was consulted I always found him ready, to give such information as would satisfy the Grand Jurors, and even to point out the law as to the point in question whenever required.

Francis Godschall Johnson, Esq., Q.C., of Montreal sworn, saith--I am 45 years of age. Having been sworn without making any objection to the power of the Commissioners to administer the oath, it might appear to imply disrespect for the authority of the eminent Judge who has given so decided an opinion on this subject, if I proceeded to give my evidence without stating my reasons for so doing.

Summoned here as a witness I know nothing of the terms of the Commission. I hold no office requiring interference on my part ; I find a Commission constituted and sitting de facto, and I am ready to answer any question which may be put to me.

This witness is produced on behalf of Mr. A. M. Delisle.

Q.--Would you please state for how many years you have been engaged in the practice of Criminal Law in the District of Montreal, as an Advocate, Queen's Counsel, and if in the latter capacity you have acted for and on behalf of H. M. Attorney General as Crown prosecutor for several years?

A.--I have been practising for twenty-three years and upwards. I have been a Queen's Counsel for thirteen years, and have represented different Attorney Generals for Lower Canada, in the conduct of the Criminal business of this District for nearly five years.

Q.--Do you consider it practicable for the Clerk of the Peace, who prosecutes on the part of the Crown, in the Court of Quarter Sessions, to be the custodian of stolen property, and whether, in practice, that duty has not always been performed by the High Constable, with the sanction of the Courts, and whether you consider that officer the proper person to discharge that duty?

A.--Statutory Law is clear upon this subject; but in my time it has been invariably disused with the express sanction of every Criminal Judge with whom I have been acqainted on the Bench. Its disuse, I take it, arose from its obvious impractibility, and the Clerk of the Peace has never, since I have practised, had personal custody, or been called upon to identify stolen things, these duties having invariably been practised by the Head Constable.

If I am called upon for the first time to say who is the proper person to perform these duties, I should, of course, say the person named in the Statute; but as I have said before, those duties have been expressly delegated by the invariable practice to the High Constable.

Q.--Did you ever hear any complaint that stolen property was not returned to its owners?

A.--I never did.

Q.--Would you have the kindness to express your opinion of the manner in which Mr. Delisle discharged his duties as Clerk of the Crown and Clerk of the Peace?

A.--I think it is impossible to speak too highly of the efficiency of Mr. Delisle as a public officer. I have never heard any other opinion upon that subject.

Q.--Are you aware whether Mr. Delisle was frequently sent to the country by Government to investigate important cases of felony, such as murder, arson, &c., and if much of his time was not thus employed by him in that manner, and how he discharged those duties?

A.--I am aware that such is the case. Some of those duties necessarily consumed much of his time, and in several instances that I could mention of the most important description, his zeal and ability were the means of securing justice to the public. He always evinced the greatest energy and judgment in such matters.

Q.--Is it to your knowledge that as Clerk of the Crown, Mr. Delisle always occupied seperate Rooms from those used by the Clerk of the Peace?

A.--It was the case, as far as my recollection serves me, in all the Court Houses which have been in my time.

Q.--Would you please state how you certified Mr. Schiller's accounts as Superintendent of Crown witnesses, with Mr. Delisle as Clerk of the Crown, for the service of subpœnas?

A.--Mr. Schiller's accounts, when presented to me, were signed by me with the most implicit and necessary reliance upon his perfect integrity,--a reliance which has never abated, and without which it would have been utterly impossible for Mr. Delisle or myself to conduct our departments for the public service.

MONDAY, October 19, 1863.

The Commissioners reject the motion for a Rule against Judge Aylwin.

The evidence of Mr. Johnson resumed. Examined by Mr. Schiller.

Q.--Would you have the kindness to state your opinion of the manner in which Mr. Schiller discharged his duties as Deputy Clerk of the Crown, Deputy Clerk of the Peace, and Superintendent of Crown witnesses.

A.--In each of those offices, Mr. Schiller's ability, energy and knowledge of duty have been conspicuously remarked by every one whom I ever heard mention the subject, from the Judges of the land down to the witnesses whose attendance and remuneration he looked after.

Q.--Would you have the kindness to state your opinion as to whether, in consequence of the zeal, activity, and efficiency of Mr. Schiller as Deputy Clerk of the Crown, Deputy Clerk of the Peace, and Superintendent of Crown Witnesses, of which you have spoken, he did not contribute materially to accelerate the business before the Criminal Courts, and consequently to lessen their duration, and thus economize time and money, in the payment of Jurors, Witnesses, and Constables, who were paid so much per day for their attendance?

A.--I have no doubt whatever, that in consequence of Mr. Schiller's aptitude and efficiency, Justice was accelerated in its administration, and secured in its results in a manner that nobody with whom I am acquainted could have effected as well as Mr. Schiller did. From his complete knowledge of his duties, combined with his long practice of them, the administration of Criminal Justice was worked out, as I sincerely believe, as economically and efficiently as is possible under our difficult and imperfect system. By his mode of marshalling the Witnesses, whose attendance he contrived should never be wanted, the right Witnesses were always forthcoming at the right moment, and during an experience of upwards of twenty years in prosecuting and defending in the Criminal Courts, I have never known a single instance of dereliction or omission of duty on his part.

Q.--Did it not frequently occur during the terms of the Court of Queen's Bench that Mr. Schiller had to wait upon you with the Crown Witnesses, both before the opening, and after the adjournment of the Courts?

A.--It frequently did so occur. The arduous duties of Crown Prosecutor, in cases of life and death, of which no man feels the weight who has not experienced them, frequently require by night and on Sundays the most anxious appreciation of the exact nature of evidence to be adduced, for this object Mr. Schiller's services were, at all hours, freely and zealously rendered, and in the general run of cases, also both before the hour of the meeting of the Court, and after its close a great deal of labor had often to be bestowed on such matters, which without Mr. Schiller's able assistance, would have been impracticable.

Q.--Would you please state your opinion of the manner in which Mr. Schiller caused the Witnesses to be taxed and discharged, after their attendance was no longer required?

A.--The systematic and discriminating manner in which Mr. Schiller invariably performed this part of his duty cannot be too highly spoken of. He has often press'd me to continue a trial until a late hour at night, by my applying to the Court for that purpose for the sole object of discharging the Witnesses that evening, and so avoiding another day's expense. I was often struck by this and other expedients, such as discharging at once, without examination, witnesses who had nothing material to say, with a view of avoiding useless expense, which would have arisen in some instances for their increased taxation, and in others prolonging the trial, and locking up, and paying the expenses of Jurors.

Q.--Did it not frequently occur during the progress of important trials that Mr. Schiller was directed to send to the country by night, at considerable distances, for witnesses, whose evidence was necessary to secure the ends of justice, and to procure their attendance or the following morning, and must not, in your opinion, such services have compelled Mr. Schiller to expend more money to procure their attendance, than the ordinary allowances would yield him?

A.--Such is undoubtedly the case, I could mention numerous instances, if required where apparent impossibilities were surmounted, and the witness's attendance secured next morning.

Cross-Examined by the Commissioners:

Q.--Please state what you meant to convey by the expression, "our difficult and imperfect system," which you have spoken of?

A.--The difficulties and imperfections which were uppermost in my mind when I answered as above, arose principally from the imperfect information and evidence sent him from the country by unpaid and illiterate Magistrates, rendering it extremely difficult, without great experience and discrimination, to separate material from useless testimony, a duty in which I received the greatest assistance from Mr. Schiller. The general defects of our system I do not wish to enlarge upon unless required.

TUESDAY 20th October. 1863.

The Honorable William Badgley, of Montreal, Assistant Judge of the Court of Queen's Bench, sworn. I am 62 years of age.

Q.--Would you please state for how many years you were engaged in the practice and administration of Criminal Justice as Attorney General, and Judge of the Circuit Court, and the Court of Queen's Bench?

A.--I acted as Attorney General in the conduct of Criminal business for two or three terms, in 1847 and 1848. I had previously presided at the Court of Quarter Sessions as Circuit Judge, for two or three years, from 1844 to 1847, and I have, during the last term of the Queen's Bench held in this city, acted in that Court as Assistant Judge.

Q.--Will you please state whether in your experience you consider it practicable that the Clerk of the Peace, who prosecutes criminals in the Court of Quarter Sessions, should be the custodian of stolen property; and whether, in practice, that duty has not always been performed by the High Constable, with the sanction of the Courts, and whether you consider that that officer is the proper person to discharge that duty?

A.--I can say nothing personally, except that in the Courts in which I acted the High Constable, for the time being, has always produced before the Court the stolen articles required, and as being the custodian of them. I think he is the only fit person to have charge of them, as in many cases it would be manifestly inconvenient for the Clerk of the Peace to be prosecutor and witness, as would be the case in the Quarter Sessions.

Q.--Did you ever hear of any complaints that stolen property was not returned to its owners, after the trials of parties accused were over?

A.--No.

Q.--Would you have the kindness to express your opinion of the management of the criminal business by Mr. Delisle, as Clerk of the Peace and Clerk of the Crown, and, generally, how he discharged his duties?

A.--Very efficiently, as far as I could see.

Examined by Mr. Schiller:

Q.--Would you please also to state your opinion of the manner in which Mr. Schiller discharged his duties as Deputy Clerk of the Crown, Deputy Clerk of the Peace, and Superintendent of Crown Witnesses?

A.--He appeared to discharge them in the most efficient manner.

Henry Judah, Esq., Q. C., of Montreal, sworn, saith --I am aged 53.

Produced by Mr. Delisle.

Q.--Would you please state for how long you have practised law in the Criminal Courts as an Advocate and Queen's Counsel, and if in the latter capacity you have acted on behalf of the Crown in Criminal cases, in the Court of Queen's Bench?

A.--I have practised the law for 32 years, and have been employed in conducting Criminal cases on the part of the Crown.

Q.--Do you, from your experience, consider it practicable for the Clerk of the Peace to be the custodian of stolen goods, acting, as does that officer, in prosecuting criminals in the Court of Quarter Sessions.

A.--I have had considerable experience in this matter, having discharged the duties of Assistant Clerk of the Crown for six years in the District of Three Rivers. Those goods were invariably in the possession of the High Constable, who produced them on trial as the articles found in the possession of the prisoners. This course is manifestly the only course by which goods could be identified. I do not consider the Clerk of the Peace to be the proper person, because the goods in most cases first come into the possession of the High Constable, and it is important that he should retain the possession for the purpose of identification.

Q.--Would you have the kindness to express your opinion of the manner in which Mr. Delisle always discharged his duties as Clerk of the Crown and Clerk of the Peace?

A.--I believe there is no doubt of the very able manner in which Mr. Delisle always discharged the duties of his office.

Q.--Are you aware that Mr. Delisle was frequently sent to the country by Government to investigate important Criminal cases and on Government Commissions, and was therefore, necessarily often absent from his office.

A.--I am aware that Mr. Delisle was frequently employed in investigating Criminal cases in all of the three Districts. I may instance the Corrigan case in Quebec; the troubles resulting from the burning of School Houses in the District of Three Rivers, which occupied six months; also in charges made by the Returning Officers in the District of Montreal, which lasted over two years; besides many other important cases of felony committed in the country.

Q.--What is the custom with reference to certifying the accounts for the service of subpoenas in the Criminal Courts, and what responsibility do you consider attaches to the officers certifying such accounts?

A.--I certified similar accounts during six year

and manifestly could only be responsible for the issuing of the subpœnas and the attendance of the witnesses ; but not for either the distance or the disbursements made for the service. The latter charge resting with the officer who makes the charge. For instance, a witness residing in the Parish of Lachine, at the nearest point from Montreal might be represented by the Bailiff, as living at the extremity of the Parish, which would make a difference of ten miles, and, of course, be to a much larger extent in a larger Parish, and more remote from the city. The officer certifying is manifestly only answerable for that which comes within his knowledge or which he may by enquiry ascertain.

Examined by Mr. Schiller.

Q.--Are you aware how charges are made for the service of subpœnas by Constables or Bailiffs, and in the Criminal Courts ?

A.--The system alluded to in this question existed, to my knowledge, in the District of Three Rivers for thirty years. The duties performed, for which the charges alluded to are made, were performed by the High Constable, who invariably obtained the subpœnas from the Crown Office and caused the service to be made by Bailiffs or Constables at a remuneration agreed upon between them, charging the Government with the full distance. In 1849 I was selected by the then Attorney General, Sir L. H. LaFontaine, Bart, Chief Justice, to conduct the business of the Crown, in the District of Three Rivers, and to report particularly on the charges made by the High Constable for the service of subpœnas, Accordingly, after the close of the Term, when called upon to give my certificate of the correctness of the charges for the service of subpœnas made by the High Constable, I ascertained from him that the services had been made by different parties and paid for in sums less than these charged. I thereupon granted the usual certificate, and on my return to Montreal, reported the fact to the Government. It is, to my knowledge, that the system existed for many years before, and it is undoubtedly true that it has continued to the present day. However objectionable it may appear to persons not conversant with Criminal proceedings in the absence of any officer, whose special duty it is to attend to these matters, that this is an improper mode of remunerating the officer ; but in fact it is only a fair way of indemnifying them for labor performed, and as the fact was known to all Governments for the last thirty years, it is but fair to presume that they have sanctioned it.

Cross-examined by the Commissioners.

Q.--Did the High Constable at Three Rivers receive an extra allowance during the Sessions of the Courts in which he served ?

A.--I am not aware.

Q.--Did you make a written report to Government concerning the charges made by the High Constable at Three Rivers for the service of subpœnas ?

A.--The reference to me being verbal, I made a verbal report.

William Workman, Esq., President of the City Bank, of Montreal, sworn, (produced by Mr. Schiller) saith--I am 55 years of age.

Q.--Would you please state if, on several occasions you acted as Foreman of the Grand Jury in the Court of Queen's Bench, and expre s your opinion of the manner in which Mr. Schiller discharged his duty as Superintendent of Crown witnesses, and Deputy Clerk of the Crown ?

A.--On several occasions I acted as Foreman of the Grand Jury in the Court of Queen's Bench, and was always very much pleased with the efficient manner in which Mr. Schiller discharged his duties. As Superintendent of Crown witnesses, owing to 'the great efficiency which he showed on these occasions, a very great saving of time and of public money also was effected. The last Court in which I acted as Foreman of the Grand Jury, I think we investigated one hundred and thirty and odd Bills of Indictment in the space of about ten days, visiting during that time the Montreal Gaol and the Reformatory Prison at St. Vincent de Paul.

Q.--Did you ever find that time was lost, owing to the non-production of witnesses, or did it seem to you that he discharged his duty with dispatch and economy to the public ?

A.--Owing to his quickness and attention to his duty, a very great saving of time was effected, and this was frequently remarked by some of my brother jurors and myself, during the progress of our labor. In fact I think I never saw a more efficient officer.

WILLIAM ENNIS, hotel-keeper, of the City of Montreal, sworn, saith :--Aged 45 years. It is now about thirty two years since I first settled in Montreal. I deposited, in the month of August, 1859, to the best of my recollection, in the hands of Mr. Schiller, by direction of the Acting Magistrate, (it was either Mr. Louis Beaudry, or the Police Magistrate Mr. Coursol,) the sum of £50 0s. 0d., in lieu of bail for the appearance of one John Greene, then arrested on a charge of stealing a gold ring, the property of Mr. Townsend the jeweller.

The said Greene entered into recognizances to appear at the Court of Queen's Bench then following, and being a stranger in the city and known to me, having worked with him in the United States, I deposited, as above mentioned, the said sum of money, firstly £45, and two or three days afterwards the balance of £5 0s. 0d., into the hands of Mr. Charles Edward Schiller.

The said Greene did not appear at the following term, and his recognizance was forfeited. Four or five months afterwards Mr. Schiller saw me, and told me that I ought to make an application to Government to get back my money, or get an order from justice, saying that he did not consider it right to give up the money to Government ; that he still had it in his possession, and that if I could get an order from Government or from Justice, he would give me up the money.

WEDNESDAY, 21st October, 1863.
[TRANSLATED.]

Sir Louis Hypolite LaFontaine, Baronet, Chief Justice of the City of Montreal, sworn,--a witness produced by Mr. Delisle.

Q.--Would you have the kindness to state if it was not the case when you were Attorney General for Lower Canada, that the Government frequently sent me to the country, and even to the district of Three Rivers, to investigate criminal cases of felony, and whether these investigations did not necessarily cause my absence from the city and my office for more or less time, according to circumstances ?

A.--Yes ; but as to the precise nature of the offences I have no recollection.

Q.--Will you be good enough to express your opinion of the manner in which I have always discharged my duties as a public officer ?

A.--To my knowledge always extremely well.

E

Examined by Mr. Schiller.

Q.--Would you be good enough to express your opinion of the manner in which I have acquitted myself of my duties as Deputy Clerk of the Crown and Superintendent of Crown Witnesses?

A.--To my knowledge always very well; in fact one could not wish to have a more efficient Clerk of the Crown than Mr. Delisle, or a more efficient Deputy Clerk than Mr. Schiller.

The Hon. Louis Simeon Morin, of the City of Montreal, Esquire, Advocate, Q.C., sworn, aged 31 years. Witness produced by Mr. Delisle.

Q.--Would you please state whether when you held the office of Solicitor General for Lower Canada, you did not frequently give me written instructions on the part of the Government to go to the country to investigate important cases of felony, such as murder and arson; and if besides I did not also receive similar instructions from the Government, through other official channels, to perform the same duty when you held the said office, and if such duties did not necessarily involve frequent and long absences from my office?

A.--Since my appointment to the office of Solicitor General for Lower Canada, on the 19th January, 1860, I thought it proper to give orders to Mr. Delisle, on many occasions, to go and investigate in the country parts, cases of murder and arson, more particularly before the establishment of Courts holding criminal jurisdiction in those parts of the country formerly embraced in the District of Montreal. The Government had observed that there was a failure of justice, on account of the incapacity or unfitness of the magistrates in the country to investigate such cases, and it was thought advisable to send men of experience to investigate such cases, and the Government designated Mr. Delisle as one of its officers best qualified to perform that duty. to secure the ends of justice. The result afterwards was, as the Government expected, on that account. In the absence of the Attorney or Solicitor General from Montreal, Mr. Johnson, Queen's Counsel, had instructions to exercise his discretion in causing the same services to be performed by Mr. Delisle; it is to my own knowledge that in the cases in which I gave the instructions myself, he was obliged to remain for many days, and sometimes for weeks, absent from his office.

Q.--Would you have the kindness to express your opinion as to the manner in which I always discharged the various duties devolving on me as a public officer.

A.--Since 1853, the date of my admission to the profession of the law, I have had occasion to plead before the Courts of Queen's Bench and Quarter Sessions, at nearly all their sittings, up to the year 1860, at which time I was appointed Solicitor General, and I ceased to practice before those Courts for the time being, except the Court of Queen's Bench, where I occasionally appeared, I have always looked upon Mr. Delisle as a most efficient officer in his capacity of Clerk of the Crown, and of the Peace.

From what I know he gave general satisfaction both to the Bench and the Bar, and in his office, to which I had frequently to go, I always observed that the records and papers were kept in perfect order. I speak of all the papers and records to which the public had access. We were afforded great dispatch in the communication of all such papers and records.

Examined by Mr. Schiller :--

Q.--Would you have the kindness to state your opinion of the manner in which Mr. Schiller discharged his duties as Deputy Clerk of t Crown, Deputy Clerk of the Peace, and Superintendent of Crown witnesses?

A.--Since I have belonged to the profession I have known Mr. Schiller; I do not think that any one could have discharged his various duties of Deputy Clerk of Crown, Deputy Clerk of the Peace, and Superintendent of Crown Witnesses, in a more efficient manner than Mr. Schiller did. I never had any reason to complain of him, nor did I ever hear any complaints from any other person of him in the performance of his various duties.

Q.--Are you aware that by an order from Government the Clerk of the Crown, or his Deputy, before accounts of Bailiffs or Constables, for the arrest of parties, were paid, had to examine and certify such accounts before an order for their payment was made, and if Mr. Schiller did not frequently make considerable reductions from them?

A.--I am aware of the order in question, and it is to my personal knowledge that in very many cases Mr. Schiller made such reductions as are mentioned in this question.

Q.--Are you aware if Mr. Schiller has been very punctual and assiduous in his attendance to his duties and office?

A.--I know that Mr. Schiller has been very punctual in his attendance, and he is the most diligent officer I know. I have seen him frequently in his office from half-past eight in the morning till six o'clock in the afternoon.

Mr. William Benjamin, of Montreal, merchant, sworn :--

Saith, aged 47--I remember that in the summer of 1858, my brothers Goodman and Samuel Benjamin, now absent from Canada, were robbed of a quantity of silks, satins and other goods, and that two persons by the name of Emily Phila and Henry Mendal were arrested for that robbery. To the best of my belief these parties did not appear, but forfeited their recognizances.

I have no personal knowledge that the goods in question were returned to my brothers; but I should think my brothers, as men of business, would not have allowed the goods to have been kept over by the Court, and to the best of my belief the goods were returned to my brothers. I know that the goods of which I am now speaking are not the same as those for which I see copy of a receipt to Mr. Benjamin Delisle. dated 19th October, 1859. Signed on behalf of Messrs. Benjamin Brothers by S. B. Fish.

I was robbed myself, about a year after the time first referred to, of a quantity of goods which were, after the trial, restored to me by the High Constable, but I cannot recollect whether I gave a receipt for them or not. Being shown two receipts now exhibited by the High Constable, Mr. Bissonette, one of them being all in my own hand-writing, and the other under the signature of Thomas Leslie, one of my clerks at the time,—that is, in 1859,--I now perceive that I did, with my clerk, give receipts for the goods that had been stolen from my premises.

THURSDAY, 22nd October, 1863.

Charles Joseph Coursol, Esq., of Montreal, Judge of Sessions, a witness produced by Mr. Delisle, sworn.

Q. Have you practiced as an Advocate in criminal matters in the Courts of Queen's Bench, Quarter Sessions, and also the Weekly and Special Sessions and the Police Court, and be pleased to say how long.

A. I have practiced in all these Courts as Advocate, from 1842 till 4th February, 1856, when I was appointed Inspector and Superintendent of Police for the city of Montreal, and I continued to discharge the duties of that office under that name until changed, by an Act of the Legislature, to that of Judge of the Sessions of the Peace, which office I still hold.

Q. By which of the Clerks of the Peace, during the whole of the time you refer to, were the Courts of Quarter, Weekly and Special Sessions respectively held?

A. I always saw, with very few exceptions, Mr. Delisle act as Crown Prosecutor in the Court of Quarter Sessions. Mr. Brehaut often acted as Clerk of the Weekly and Special Session, and also prosecuted before the Police Court, under the Summary Jurisdiction Act; but in general, the Deputy Clerk of the Peace, Mr. Schiller, acted as Clerk of those Courts.

Q. Do you know if any arrangement existed between Mr. Delisle and Mr. Brehaut as to a division of their labors as Clerks of the Peace?

A. I have no personal knowledge of any arrangement between those two gentlemen; but judging from what I daily saw, it appeared as if Mr. Delisle had the management of the Court of Quarter Sessions and Crown business, and Mr. Brehaut of the other branches of the department connected with the Clerk of the Peace office.

Q. Did Mr. Delisle not always occupy separate apartments, as Clerk of the Crown, from those of the Clerk of the Peace; and is it not a fact that you rarely saw him in the latter office?

A. Yes. Mr. Delisle occupied the same apartments as are now occupied by the Clerk of the Crown, Mr. Carter, which are separate and distinct from those occupied by the Clerk of the Peace; and often when I wished to communicate with Mr. Delisle, I had to go or send to the office of the Clerk of the Crown.

Q. Are you aware that Mr. Delisle was frequently sent to the country parts, by order of Government, to investigate important cases of felony, such as murder and arson, and other grave crimes; and if that business did not necessarily cause his absence from his office, and on some occasions for a considerable time?

A. To my personal knowledge, Mr. Delisle, for many years past, was very often sent on such missions into the country, and this, of course, involved absence, and sometimes prolonged ones, from his office. And I might add, that upon several occasions I received instructions myself to go to the country also to investigate different cases of felony, and Mr. Delisle accompanied me by the direction of Government.

Q. How did Mr. Delisle acquit himself of his duty on such occasions, and how did he discharge his duty as Crown Prosecutor in the Court of Quarter Sessions?

A. To the entire satisfaction of all the Judges presiding at the different Courts, the Grand Jurors, and, I have no doubt, to the entire satisfaction of the public.

Examined by Mr. Schiller:

Q. Would you have the kindness to state your opinion of the manner in which Mr. Schiller discharged his duties as Deputy Clerk of the Crown, Deputy Clerk of the Peace, and Superintendent of Crown witnesses?

A. Mr. Schiller discharged those duties in the most intelligent, business-like, and indefatigable manner, working, to my own knowledge, during the Term, so late as ten and eleven o'clock at night, and resuming his duties every day during the Term at or about 8 o'clock A.M.

Q. Would you have the kindness to state your opinion as to whether, in consequence of the zeal, activity and efficiency of Mr. Schiller as Deputy Clerk of the Crown, Deputy Clerk of the Peace, and Superintendent of Crown Witnesses, of which you have spoken, he did not contribute materially to accelerate the business before the Courts of Quarter Sessions and Queen's Bench, and consequently to lessen its duration, and thus economise time and money in the payment of jurors, witnesses and constables, who were paid so much per day for their attendance?

A.—I have no doubt that but for the activity displayed by Mr. Schiller, the duration of the Terms would have been much longer, and that time and money spent for the attendance of Constables, Jurors and witnesses, would have been much greater.

Q.—Would you please state your opinion of the manner in which Mr. Schiller caused the witnesses to be taxed and discharged, after their attendance was no longer required.

A.—Mr. Schiller had the bills of the witnesses prepared for taxation in all cases without any loss of time, and the witnesses were discharged forthwith, and were paid their allowances at the Sheriff's Office. Sometimes, when sitting on the Bench, I have been called upon by Mr. Schiller to sign witness accounts presented to me by him, in order that such witnesses might be dispatched by the Steamers and Railways.

FRIDAY, October 23, 1863.

The Honble. Lewis T. Drummond, Queen's Counsel, Montreal, sworn, says—I am aged 50 years.

Produced by Mr. Delisle.

Q.—Would you please state for how many years you have been practising in the Criminal Courts in Lower Canada as an Advocate, Solicitor General and Attorney General.

A.—I have practised in the Criminal Courts for L. C. as an Advocate, from 1836 until sometime in July, 1848; as Solicitor General from the last date until I was appointed Attorney General in October or November, 1851. While I was Attorney General, I occasionally appeared in those Courts. I resigned that latter office in May, 1856, since when I have continued to practice in those Courts as an Advocate and Queen's Counsel.

Q.—Do you consider it practicable for the Clerk of the Peace, who acts as Crown prosecutor in the Courts of Quarter Sessions, to be the custodian of stolen property, and whether, in practice, that duty has not always been performed by the High Constable, under the sanction of the Courts, and whether you consider the High Constable the proper person to discharge that duty?

A.—Although the legal custodian of stolen property, the Clerk of the Peace cannot conveniently take charge of it. So the duty of receiving such property, producing it in Court when required, and restoring it to its rightful owner has (very properly I think) devolved upon the High Constable. Such has been the practice, I believe, in all the Courts of Criminal Jurisdiction in Lower Canada, ever since I was admitted to the profession.

Q.—Did you ever hear any complaints that stolen property had not been returned to its owners.

A.—Never, except in cases where doubts existed as to the person to whom such property rightfully belonged. Whenever such cases occurred, within my experience, the Head Constable invariably applied at once to the prosecuting officer, or to the Court for directions, upon which he immediately acted.

Q.—Would you have the kindness to express your opinion of the manner in which Mr. Delisle discharged the various duties devolving upon him ?

A.—I entertain the highest opinion of the manner in which Mr. Delisle has always managed the Criminal business as Clerk of the Crown and Clerk of the Peace. I have always considered Mr. Delisle as one of the ablest, most efficient, and most zealous public officers in Canada.

Q.—Were you, when Attorney or Solicitor General ever called upon to investigate charges made against Mr. Schiller that he paid less for the services of subpœnas than he charged the Government, and that he sometimes sent subpœnas by mail to country Bailiffs, and subsequently charged the Government mileage from the city, as if a Constable had been sent to the country to serve such subpœnas and what was the result of your investigation ?

A.—I was, while Solicitor General for Lower Canada. The result of my investigation and the opinion I pronounced upon the anonymous complaints then made will be found in a letter addressed by me to the Deputy Inspector General on the 10th of August, 1849, a copy of which was filed before this Commission on the 6th April last.

When I began to conduct the Criminal business in 1848, as Solicitor General, I found that my predecessors had not been in the constant habit of taking the necessary precautions to secure the attendance of witnesses within the Court Room for more than one or two cases on each day. The consequence was, as I had often observed while defending accused parties that the Court was frequently obliged to adjourn at an early hour whenever a case was unexpectedly postponed, owing to the absence of witnesses or any other cause.

To obviate these delays and remedy other defects in the mode of prosecuting Criminal cases, I availed myself of Mr. Schiller's extraordinary intelligence, activity, zeal and experience to organize an entirely new system, not only in this city, but at Quebec, Three Rivers, and Sherbrooke, taking Mr. Schiller with me, or sending him to several places to inaugurate them.

The result of this system under Mr. Schiller's superintendence has been to diminish the cost of the administration of justice, especially at Montreal, to a very material extent.

Since it was inaugurated I remember one instance of the Criminal Court in Montreal having been compelled to adjourn before the usual hour for want of a witness. The instructions received by Mr. Schiller from me in 1848, obliged him to clear a sufficient number of benches in the court-room for the accommodation of the witnesses required, in at least three cases, besides the one that was under trial, and to watch over them constantly, so as to secure their services when required, and this part of his duty he performed in a manner so satisfactory as to secure the result above mentioned.

Notwithstanding the annonymous complaints conveyed to me through the Deputy Inspector General, I did not deem it my duty to enquire whether Mr. Schiller did or did not, in a legitimate way, add a few dollars to his yearly salary as Deputy Clerk of the Crown.

He had then no salary for the distinct and separate office of Superintendent of Crown Witnesses, nor as Clerk of the Grand Jury, before whom he marshalled the witnesses, *in carrying out a system under which thousands of dollars, if not pounds, were annually saved to the Government.* If Mr. Schiller received from Government more than he paid his constables, I take it for granted that he did so under arrangements made with them, and with which they were satisfied, *else the work would not have been done as efficiently as it was.* I held Mr. Schiller personally responsible for the appearance of all Crown witnesses, and their attendance before the Court until duly discharged.

In order to carry out my orders, it doubtless became necessary for Mr. Schiller to secure permanently the services of a certain number of active constables, upon whom he could depend at all times and under all circumstances. If Mr. Schiller paid these constables in some cases less than he received from Government, if his charges against the Government were not beyond the tariff rates, *I can see nothing more reprehensible in his conduct, in that respect, than in the conduct of the Prothonotary or other officer at the head of a department paid by fees, who takes $5 as a fee upon a Writ, the labor of getting up of which does not cost him more than a quarter of a dollar."*

Whether Mr. Schiller has been reprehensible or not in making such charges, (the details of which I know nothing,) it would be unjust to make him the victim of a system which has been acted upon and tolerated, if not approved of, by the Government in this, as well as in other districts in Lower Canada, for at least a quarter of a century.

Q.—What responsibility, in your opinion, attaches to the Clerk of the Crown for certifying accounts for the service of subpœnas ?

A.—In certifying the service of subpœnas, I conceive that the Clerk of the Crown or the Clerk of the Peace can vouch only for the fact that the attendance of the witnesses was requisite, and that the charges made are conformable to the tariff or allowances usually made. He cannot be presumed to certify the precise distance travelled in making every such service.

Q.—Was Mr. Delisle not frequently sent into the country by order of Government to investigate felonies, such as murder, arson, &c., and also execute Government Commissions; and was he not necessarily frequently absent from his office, and sometimes for very long periods ?

A.—Yes, when I assumed the superintendence of all matters connected with the administration of justice in criminal matters in Lower Canada, the Attorney-General of the day being exclusively absorbed in matters connected with public politics and the general Government of the country, I found it necessary to introduce several reforms which have been since carried out, principally through the efficient assistance given to me and my successors in office by the Clerk of the Crown and Peace, and their efficient staff in this city. After an experience of a couple of terms in the prosecution of criminals, added to an experience of upwards of twelve years in defending accused parties, it became evident to me that three-fourths of the persons who escaped punishment, although really guilty, owned their impunity mainly to the defective preliminary enquiry in their cases. Attaching, therefore, the greatest importance to what the French Jurists call " *L'Instruction du Procès,*" I

thought proper to avail myself of Mr. Delisle's ability
and experience to have each *instruction* made by him
whenever information of a series of violations of
the law having been committed in the country parts,
came to my ears. Mr. Delisle was constantly, during
the greater part of the time I was in office, that is to
say, from about July, 1848, until May, 1856, frequently
sent to the country parts, not only in the district of
Montreal, but also in the district of Quebec and
Three Rivers, either to make such enquiries under
written instructions, or under commissions specially
issued for that purpose. I know that after a species
of rebellion against the School Laws had taken place
in the district of Three Rivers, sometime about 1850
or 1851, Mr. Delisle was sent down to St. Gregoire to
act as commissioner with two other gentlemen, and
that he remained there for about six months visiting
the city only occasionally during that time. He was
afterwards sent to St. Sylvestre, where he remained a
considerable time. On another occasion, previous to
the two last mentioned, Mr. Delisle was engaged on a
commission of enquiry into the cause of burning the
Parliament House in this city for several months,
during which, although the commission sat here, it
was quite impossible for him to perform his ordinary
official duties in person. At a later period, before I
withdrew from the Government of the country, I had
caused Mr. Delisle, conjointly with Mr. Mathew
Ryan, (then an officer in the Inspector-General's Department,) to enquire into certain frauds alelged to
have been committed by Returning Officers in Lower
Canada. I cannot say how long Mr. Delisle was engaged upon this task. I could not, without some reflection, remember all occasions upon which Mr. Delisle's services were required by me away from his
office. It was a matter of frequent occurrence for me
to request his services at some distant point, frequently allowing less than an hour for his preparations.

Whenever I employed Mr. Delisle in this manner
he never received more, in addition to his salary, than
a liberal allowance for his travelling expenses, except
when a special Commission was issued.

Examined by Mr. Schiller :

Q.--Would you have the kindness to state your
opinion of the manner in which Mr. Schiller discharged
his duties as Deputy Clerk of the Crown, Deputy
Clerk of the Peace, and Superintendent of Witnesses?

A.--I have already expressed my opinion as to the
highly satisfactory and I should have said admirable
manner in which Mr. Schiller performed his duty as
Superintendent of Crown Witnesses. He was equally
efficient as Deputy Clerk of the Crown and of the
Peace, as also in the arduous duties performed by him
before the Grand Jury, where he usually relieves the
Prosecuting Crown Officer from all trouble, and thereby enables the latter to continue his attendance in
Court without interruption. From Mr. Schiller's prodigious memory, from his admirable talent for organization, extraordinary powers of endurance, and his
experience about the Criminal Courts since he was a
mere child, I came to the conclusion, at a time when
from seventy-five to one hundred and twenty-five Indictments were brought up before the Criminal Courts
here, that no other person in the country could fill his
place, and it would at least require two other men to
perform the work he was in the habit of going through.

Q.--How did Mr. Schiller perform his duties in
causing the witnesses to be taxed and discharged after
they were no longer required?

A.--With the greatest celerity, often compelling me
to remain an hour after the Court had adjourned to
sign the Bills.

Cross-Examined by the Commissioners :

Q.--Was that letter by you addressed to the Deputy
Inspector General on the 10th August, 1849, the only
report you made at the time upon such anonymous
complaints?

A.--I have no recollection of having made any other
report, or written any other letter on the subject. I
could almost positively say I did not.

Q.--When you wrote that letter did you examine
and compare the subpœnas with Mr. Schiller's account?

A.--I did not, for the reasons already stated by me,
and because, moreover, I never would in my official
capacity have stooped to investigate an accusation
made by persons who had not courage or honesty sufficient to give their names as vouchers for the truth of
their allegations.

Q.--Did you enquire then whether such witnesses
as were under bonds were subpœned or not?

A.--I did not. When prosecuting criminal cases
personally, I made it a point to have the witnesses
bound over to appear at the next term, in every case
that stood over from one term to another. I never
saw the subpœnas except when it became necessary
for me to look into the returns of service in special
cases.

Q.--Were you aware to what extent the principle
contended for by Mr. Schiller that his accounts did
not represent his disbursements was carried?

A.--I never heard Mr. Schiller contend for that
principle, nor have I any personal knowledge, at this
moment, of the fact that Mr. Schiller ever made any
charge against the Government for monies paid beyond his actual disbursements. I never made any
enquiry into the matter; Mr. Schiller has never dis-
closed any such fact to me; but knowing that this is
one of the accusations preferred against Mr. Schiller,
I have given my opinion as upon an hypothetical case.

Q.--Were you aware that Mr. Schiller, as Superintendent of Crown Witnesses, was receiving from the
Government an extra allowance over and above his
salary, of $4 per day, during the Sessions of the Court
in which he served?

A.--I have recently heard that such an allowance
was made to him, but I was under the impression
that he received no such allowance at the time when
I wrote the letter above alluded to as having been
addressed to me by the Deputy Inspector General. I
have just now learned, however, from Mr. Schiller
himself, that that allowance was made to him by an
order in Council, passed before I went into the Government.

Mr. Delisle declared his evidence closed and so did
Messrs. Schiller and Brehaut.

MONDAY, 26th October, 1863.

Mr. Delisle handed in a statement, sworn to before
Judge Mondelet, after reading it to the Commissioners.

STATEMENT made by ALEXANDER MAURICE DELISLE,
Esquire, and submitted to the Commissioners,
Messrs. LAFRENAYE & DOHERTY.

Having now completed the evidence which I had to
adduce, save and except that of the Hon. Mr. Justice
Aylwin (a very important witness summoned on my
behalf) who declined to give his evidence for the reasons which he gave and which were placed on record.

I can only say that I regret much having been de prived of the testimony of that Honorable gentleman as it must have been, I have no doubt, highly interesting to me : a fact which will be readily understood from that Honorable gentleman's notoriously long and intimate acquaintance with the proceedings of the Criminal Courts in which I was, I may fairly say, almost exclusively engaged during my tenure of office s Clerk of the Crown and Clerk of the Peace.

I am thus compelled to rest my case without having been able to place on record the whole of my defence, and I may thus be exposed to the most serious results without that full hearing which, I conceive, I was entitled to. In saying so I must most distinctly disclaim any intention of reflecting upon the decision of the Commissioners by which I was deprived of Judge Aylwin's evidence; and the Commissioners are too well aware of the difficult situation in which Judge Aylwin's refusal to afford me the advantage of his evidence, placed me not to appreciate my position in that particular.

I see myself again libelled by a correspondent in the Montreal Herald on that very subject, who says : —" Mr. Justice Aylwin not having been compelled " by any known legal process to attend before said " Commissioners, must be held to have gone there at " the request of Mr. Delisle, for the purpose of refus- " ing to be sworn and to give his evidence, and to give " publicity to his opinion," &c., &c.

I can only say that this assertion is a base and calumnious falsehood, intended to operate my ruin, and is of a piece with other newspaper libels which have been so widely and persistently indulged in to my prejudice, and to which I adverted in the statement I placed before the Commissioners on the 1st day of May last. I feel bound most solemnly to affirm that not only I did not know that Judge Aylwin would decline to give evidence before the Commissioners, but, on the contrary, I had every reason to believe that, like all the other Judges examined, I should have the benefit of his testimony.

I had the honor, on the first day of May last, of submitting to the Commissioners a statement in writing, to which I have just referred, duly attested by my oath, explanatory of my position with reference to the evidence so far as it had then been heard, and for allowing me, at that stage of the enquiry and out of the regular order of proceedings, to put in that statement. I now tender to the Commissioners my sincere acknowledgments for, as the enquiry stood then, the Commissioners are aware that the absence of those explanations must have operated seriously to my prejudice had the proceeding adopted by Mr. Schiller by Quo Warranto resulted in arresting the proceedings of the Commissioners at that stage of the investigation. The proceeding on the part of Mr. Schiller was adopted upon his own responsibility and against my express wish to the contrary, for I had no desire of seeing the proceedings of the Commissioners interrupted. On the contrary, I felt highly interested in having the fullest enquiry made.

Having said thus much I shall now proceed to advert generally to all the points involved in the charges and the evidence as it appears to affect me.

The Commissioners, by their notice to me of the 4th March last, intimated that they had been named by Commission to investigate " certain charges of mal- " versation of office recently made against the late " Joint Clerk of the Peace and Clerk of the Crown at " Montreal, Messrs. Delisle and Brehaut, and their De-

" puty, also, Charles Schiller, and to enquire into the " organization of the said offices," &c., and further then and there informed me "that" we will on the 9th day of March "instant at ten o'clock in the forenoon, "in the Grand Jury Room in the Court House, in the " City of Montreal, proceed, &c., &c., "and we notify " you to be there and then present in order to furnish " such information as you may be possessed of to fa- " cilitate the object of the said investigation and en- " quiry, and to answer and explain such charges as " may be there and then and from day to day during " the sitting of the said Commission be preferred " against you, &c., &c." I appeared as desired on the 9th March last, when, after the charges had been read over to me, I answered them on the 14th of the same month by my plea of Not Guilty, then filed of record.

I then called attention to the fact that the notice served upon me embodied more than I considered the Commissioners had a right to do under their Commission, inasmuch as the notice referred to charges which might "from day to day" be made, whereas the Commission limited the enquiry to charges actually brought, and not to such as might thereafter be made.

The Commissioners then remarked that the words might be erased from the notice, and on being told that it was not intended to convey the meaning I attached to them, the notice was not altered.

No other charges than those above mentioned, having been made or brought against me during the investigation which I was called upon to explain or answer, save the explanation demanded on the 23rd Sept. in reference to the non-reception of fees by the Clerk of the Crown between September 1850 and April 1856, which I answered on the 26th of the same month, I take it for granted that the Commissioners can only expect me to do so with reference to the charges, twelve in number, to which I have already alluded and to none other.

Although the Commissioners, in many instances, extended their enquiry to matters foreign to the charges communicated to me, yet, as nothing, in my opinion, was elicited which appears to me to require any explanation at my hands I shall refrain from saying anything in reference to them.

The Commissioners having made an elaborate enquiry into the accounts of Mr. Schiller, as Superintendent of Crown Witnesses,—a subject which, I conceive, can in nowise affect me.—still, having certified his accounts, it may be fitting that I should say something upon that point.

The system followed in the service of Subpœnas has prevailed for many years past, and in July, 1849, it would appear that the Government received some complaint (anonymous, I believe), to the effect that Mr. Schiller charged the Government more than he paid for such services, and the question was then referred by Government to the Hon. Mr. Drummond, then Solicitor-General, Mr. Driscoll, Q.C., and my-self, as Clerk of the Crown, for our report on the matter. These three reports are now in the hands of the Commissioners, and I would refer particularly to my own, where I discussed the subject matter under enquiry.

After these reports were sent in to Government, Mr. Schiller's accounts were paid, and I necessarily believed that the practice followed by Mr. Schiller was sanctioned by Government, who have continued to pay his accounts up to the present time.

These accounts have almost invariably been certified by the Queen's Counsel, who represented the Attorney-General in the Courts of Queen's Bench (Crown Side), the Solicitor-General, and myself as Clerk of the Crown; and it could hardly be made a subject of reproach to the Attorney-General, his representative or myself, that we certified those accounts when acting upon a custom which, to me at least, appeared to have been recognized by Government.

It is quite impossible for public officers, certifying such accounts, to investigate them as to distances travelled, and as to how or by whom the services were performed. For instance, as mentioned in the evidence taken, a witness appears in the account to be of the Parish of Lachine. Now, the Parish of Lachine, at its nearest point from the city, may be about four miles, and at its most distant about eleven or twelve miles; and how can it be possible, in certifying such accounts, to know in what part of the Parish the witness may reside.

It must be evident, therefore, that the honor and integrity of the officer making the charges must be relied upon as stated by Mr. Driscoll, Q.C., Mr. Johnson, Q.C., and the Hon. Mr. Drummond, in their evidence, and that the only responsibility that can possibly attach to the officers certifying such accounts, is as to the necessity for and the number of Subpœnas issued, and that the charges are conformable to tariff or usage.

I shall now proceed to consider each charge separately :

The first was, I think, fully explained, and in such a manner as to relieve me from responsibility, by the statement I had the honor of submitting to the Commissioners on the first day of May last.

The second is also answered by the explanations I have made in the statement just referred to.

The third was, I consider, fully disproved by the evidence of the Post Office clerks who were examined.

The fourth. The evidence taken by the Commissioners fully disproves this charge and I refer particularly to the evidence of Mr. Coroner Jones as evidencing that fact.

The fifth was particularly directed against Mr. Schiller, my Deputy, and has not been substantiated in any particular.

The sixth. This charge was not proved.

The seventh. This charge has reference to Mr. Auguste Delisle, when he was a Clerk in the Office of the Peace, and the statement I made on the first day of May last, of which I have already spoken, fully, I trust, explains my position with reference to it.

The eighth, ninth, tenth, eleventh and twelfth charges are made against Mr. Schiller, and do not concern me.

As it was proved by the evidence given before the Commissioners, I was employed by Government in the country parts, and thus obliged to be absent from my Office very frequently, and, on some occasions, for long and protracted periods, from the year 1849 until I ceased to be Clerk of the Crown. And I will refer, particularly, to the evidence of the Honble. Sir L. H. LaFontaine, Baronet, Chief Justice, the Honble. Mr. Drummond, the Honble. Mr. Morin, the Honble. Mr. Justice Monk, F. G. Johnson, Esq., Q.C., Henry Judah, Esq., Q.C., and C. J. Coursol, Esq., Judge of the Sessions, as furnishing ample information upon that point, such inquiries having not only extended to the District of Montreal, but to those of Quebec and Three Rivers, where I was engaged for long periods.

I thought it right to place that evidence before the Commissioners because in my statement of the first day of May last, to which I have adverted, I made mention of the fact, that from that cause, I was not necessarily so well acquainted with the details of the Office of Clerk of the Peace as if I had been there uninterruptedly.

Alexander M. Delisle, Esq., of Montreal, being duly sworn doth depose and say that the facts contained in the foregoing statement are true and correct in every particular, to the best of his knowledge and belief.

(Signed) A. M. DELISLE.

Sworn to before me, at Montreal, this 26th October, 1863. (Signed) ___ C. MONDELET, Judge.

MONTREAL, 15th Oct., 1863.
Th Messrs. LAFRENAYE & DOHERTY,
Commissioners.

GENTLEMEN,—The investigation connected with Mr. Charles M. Delisle's complaint being declared closed, I propose to offer some remarks on the evidence which may appear, or at all events is intended to affect me.

On the first day of the sitting of the Commission I entered a formal denegation of the accusations laid to our charge, and have since readily given to the Commissioners such information as was contained in the books and papers of my Department, as from time to time they required ; the reason for a general denial will be appreciated when the nature of the accusations is considered.

The evidence, it appears to me, refers chiefly to three points.

1st. To the unclaimed stolen goods.

2nd. Hand's evidence as to his not receiving the monies referred to in his receipts.

3rd. Mr. Auguste Delisle's evidence as to his salary as second clerk.

As to the first point, it is in evidence, that long previous to my appointment as Joint Clerk of the Peace, the custody of unclaimed stolen goods had always been committed to the exclusive care and keeping of the High Constable, a practice which has constantly been followed ever since, and previous to the appointment of Mr. B. Delisle in 1831. By Chap. 104 Consolidated Statutes of Lower Canada, section first, it is enacted, that " the Clerks of the Peace shall keep a book in which " shall be regularly entered all goods and effects " brought to their respective offices as having been " stolen or suspected to be stolen, &c." ; but if no such goods were ever brought to our office, it is impossible we can be in default. When the goods were produced before the Magistrates they were never on any occasion put into the custody of the Clerk of the Peace ; but into that of the High Constable, an officer appointed by the Government, and in no way under the control of the Clerk of the Peace. They are kept solely by him for the purpose of identification, and are by him produced before the Courts, and taken back by him. Mr. Benjamin Delisle and Mr. Bissonotte, as well as every witness who has undertaken to speak on this subject, has certified most unequivocally to this, nor is there any evidence or pretension that such was not the uniform practice. We have never on any occasion, received, kept, or restored, any of those goods, and on the occasion of the sale of the unclaimed goods referred to in the evidence, the proceeds of the sale did not come into our possession.

This course of proceeding was perfectly well known not only to all Constables and Police officers, but also to the Crown Officers, and the public, and as I believe to the Government. It must be equally well known to yourselves from your professional experience, and indeed no other course could have been pursued, as is clearly stated in the evidence, in order to satisfy the strictness of identification required by law—nor could the Clerk of the Peace, so long as he continues to act as prosecuting officer, properly have the charge of those goods consistently with his duty as prosecutor.

As to the evidence of Hands, or Hans, it is not only utterly at variance with fact, but is inconsistent with itself, and shows him to be unworthy of credit. That he acted in the department as Clerk and Messenger, besides his position as Constable, appears from his own statement and from the evidence of those who saw him acting not only as " Messenger, but filling up blank subpœnas, copy- " ing documents, and performing other official du- " ties when required to do so." His duties appear to have been well understood by him, for he enumerates them without hesitation ; in fact, so strong did he consider his claim, from this temporary employment, that he repeatedly declares that he expected to be continued as permanent Clerk in the Office. As his reason for signing the pay-lists he says : " When Mr. Schiller asked me to sign " such pay-lists I did not like to disoblige him, " and I did not think that there was any bad mo- " tive for so doing ; my impression was that the " Clerk of the Peace was after paying a salary in " advance to a clerk who retired, and that I was " got to sign it for the purpose of getting the " money refunded to the Clerk of the Peace from " the Government. I also thought I was going to " get the situation myself." And previous to this, in another part of his evidence, he says "he " only suspected that Mr. Schiller had advanced " the money to a former clerk, and that he wanted " to draw it back through me."

He at first says he only signed "two pay-lists," but when it appeared likely that the others would be produced, he qualified his statement, and pretended he did not know that the others were pay-lists. Why he should call only two pay-lists and the other four by another name, does not appear.— They were all identical printed pay-lists, signed by us, by him, and the other clerks. Of a similar nature is his denial of the receipt he gave me ; he swears that if it exists it is a forgery, yet when produced he admits his signature.

It is highly improbable, not to say incredible, that a man of intelligence, who had been eighteen years in the Irish Constabulary, Master of the Golden Auxiliary Workhouse, in charge of five hundred boys, and connected with the Criminal Courts here, could have satisfied himself with such an excuse, and that he should remain nine years after his dismissal without complaining to me, whom he knew was in daily attendance at the office, and still more extraordinary that he should never have spoken to Mr. Schiller on the subject, whom he knew to have suggested his name for employment, and who always presented the pay-lists to him for signature.

The fact is, that Mr. Hands was disappointed in some work he did for Mr. Delisle as his agent ; he was to have a house, which he did not get, and he was dismissed from a temporary employment (which he repeatedly declares he expected to get permanently), as he could not make the Registers, and hence his ill-will towards my late colleague and myself, and his readiness to put himself on a footing with Mr. Charles M. Delisle in bringing charges against us.

The evidence of his having been paid, which would be conclusive in a Civil Court to prevent him recovering the amount of his salary, should be sufficient here. This evidence is furnished by six regular and formal pay-lists, sent to Government quarterly, and by a receipt which I retained in my own hands, for my personal protection, which he calls a receipt for a Christmas-box, though given in the month of July. If this evidence is not conclusive, the signature being proved, what is the use of vouchers ? They are the regular guarantee required by the Government, and if they are not held to be sufficient, they become worse than useless. The public officer generally takes no further precaution than this, insisted on by the Government, and if he is not protected thereby, he is liable to be placed in the truly painful and distressing position in which we now find ourselves by the conspiracy of disappointed employees.

Hands informs us that he left the Irish Constabulary because his health rendered him unfit for service, his pension being recommended and granted on the same day ; yet his next employment, immediately upon leaving that force, is as Master of the Golden Auxiliary Workhouse, where he had five hundred boys under his control, which he suddenly leaves for Canada, and on his arrival joins the Montreal Police at Laprairie, and changes his name from "Hans" to "Hands." At first he did not know where Smith O'Brien's trial took place, nor when ; he did not remember whether it was before or after he left the Constabulary, and yet on cross-examination he is compelled to admit that he was one of the force massed at Tipperary for that trial.

Next is the evidence of Mr, Auguste Delisle as to his salary as temporary clerk.

As to the employment of Mr. Auguste Delisle in the office, it is fully admitted by him ; he cannot speak positively about anything. He admits that his memory is defective ; he does not undertake to contradict the receipts he gave in the official pay-lists, and unhesitatingly admits the final receipt he gave, and there is nothing in his evidence not consistent with good faith on his part.

At this distance of time, after a lapse of over nine years, it is impossible for me to remember all that took place amid the daily and hourly occupations of an office; and as I before stated, we can only refer, for positive accuracy, to documentary evidence and receipts, and reason from such evidence with reference to these witnesses, and state that they were paid, from time to time, as the second clerk has always been, in our Department, sometimes in advance, or by small payments at their request, in accordance with their exigencies, sometimes by me personally, or out of the petty cash received daily by Mr. Schiller, our Deputy. For these temporary advances, when made by me, I most probably took temporary receipts, which were destroyed, as a matter of course, when a general receipt was given in the official pay-lists at the end of the quarter; and so soon as the pay-lists were signed, examined by me, and transmitted to the Department of the Inspector-General, the subject was dismissed from my mind, as having been disposed of, in the ordinary course of official routine.

I can see nothing further in the evidence connected with the office of the Clerk of the Peace, but if explanations are required respecting any portion of the evidence, I should be happy to afford them.

As an officer of over twenty years' standing, and hitherto of unimpeached—and, I trust, still unimpeachable—character, I can confidently refer to the Judges, the Bar, and the public, to establish the faithful and daily discharge of my official duties.

Under the circumstances, I feel myself justified in stating that I ought not to have been lightly exposed to the pain and disgrace of unsupported accusations, originating from such a source as Charles M. Delisle, a man destitute of character, and a refugee from justice.

In conclusion, I beg leave to submit, that the present proceeding, under the authority of a Provincial Statute, is of an exceptional character, and one that affects me very painfully and very injuriously. If I am held guilty of the offence imputed by the verbal evidence of Mr. Hands, which his written evidence directly contradicts, I am guilty of an indictable misdemeanor, to the penalties of which no British subject can lawfully be subjected, without the intervention of a jury of his country; and such a tribunal would doubtless give me the full and explicit benefit of the utter incredibility of Hands' verbal evidence, contrasted, as it must be, with his recorded acts. Nor do I permit myself to doubt, for an instant, that those who, in any capacity, are called upon to deal with the honor of a public officer, will fail to apply the inflexible rules of law and justice, applicable to the testimony of persons in the position that

Hands states himself to be. That position, assuming for argument's sake, his statements to be true, is that we systematically defrauded the Government, and that he perseveringly aided in the fraud. Such a statement, from such an accomplice as he describes himself to be, requires, more than in ordinary cases, complete confirmation from other sources,—confirmation which those other sources, however, not only fail to give, but emphatically refute.

Mr. Delisle having made a statement as far back as May last, respecting the management of the office, I may be expected to say something on that subject, and will, therefore, briefly state that Mr. Delisle conducted the prosecutions in the Court of Quarter Sessions, except when absent, or otherwise engaged. I attended to the duties in that Court, and acted as his Deputy in the Court of Queen's Bench. Mr. Schiller and myself, assisted by the clerks, performing all the other duties, which necessitated our daily and constant attendance.

Mr. Schiller, as Deputy, received all monies, whether as fees or fines, which he regularly entered in the official cash-book, which was examined by me, and compared with all proceedings upon which fees or fines were payable. With the Cash Book Mr. Schiller submitted, half-monthly, a memorandum showing the gross amount of fees and fines as entered in the Cash Book, deducting therefrom the sums paid by him as office expenses, advances made to the second clerks on account of their salary, and any monies paid on my account. These several sums being deducted, the balance was paid to me.

Mr. Delisle, Mr. Schiller, and the Senior Clerk, were paid quarterly. At the end of the quarter, or such other times, as directed by law, I paid over and accounted to the respective officers to whom they were payable, the full amount as they appeared in the Cash Book, and transmitted the receipts to the Inspector-General's Department.

In addition to the memorandum submitted by Mr. Carter and myself, on the first of May last, and the suggestions made by Mr. Carter in his deposition before you, I enclose the accompanying form for your approval, to serve as Entry Book and Index for all documents received in the office, and the proceedings had thereon.

I have the honor to be, gentlemen,
Your obdt. servant,

[Signed,]   W. H. BREHAUT.

[Here follows deposition attesting the truth of the foregoing statement.]

MONTREAL, 27th January, 1863.

To W. H. Brehaut, Esq.,
    Joint Clerk of the Peace:

SIR,—With reference to the explanations you request me to make with regard to the sale of unclaimed stolen goods, which took place in July, 1853, I beg to enclose a copy of the account sales, the nett proceeds of which amount to £20 14s. 2½d.

I also received from the High Constable, in September, 1859, unclaimed monies amounting to £27 5s. 7½d. Both these amounts I have retained in my possession ever since, and the amount has stood to my credit in the Bank of Montreal, with a larger amount of my own monies. The reason why these two amounts were not accounted for were these:—after the sale of unclaimed stolen goods had taken place, there was still a considerable amount of forged and counterfeit Mexican dollars, and you are aware that it was intended to have them destroyed as directed by law, and the metal sold as it was of some value, and the proceeds added to the produce of the unclaimed goods and accounted for to Government simultaneously. I called upon Mr. Robert Hendery, Silversmith, several times and desired him to call and examine this base coin, with a view to its sale, and he did call twice when I happened to be much engaged and prevented from going to the vaults for the intended purpose with him. He promised to return but did not do so.

Although often desired by you to prepare and forward those accounts, I was, from a pressure of business, prevented from doing so, for a sufficiently long time that I at length thought it would be as well to account for the amount in my hands when the next sale of the same kind took place. Having made up my mind to that course the matter was accordingly left in abeyance for the time. An order was accordingly obtained from the Court of Queen's Bench in April last, ordering the sale, as directed by law, of the unclaimed goods then in the custody of the High Constable; but owing to some informality (a list not having been submitted to the Court), the order was not acted upon, the sale did not take place, and the sums above mentioned have remained in my hands and have not been as yet paid in.

These are my reasons for this unintentional neglect on my part.

I am, Sir,
Your obedient servant,
(Signed,)   C. E. SCHILLER,
Dy. Clk. of the Peace.

Memorandum by Charles E. Schiller, Superintendent of Crown Witnesses.

To the Honorable J. J. C. Abbott,
Solicitor General :

In the year 1839, I was appointed Superintendent of Crown witnesses in the Court of Queen's Bench, Montreal, by the Honorable Atty. Gen. Ogden. This duty imposed upon me the responsibility of securing the attendance of all the Crown witnesses before the Court. There was not, nor is there now, any Tariff in the Queen's Bench, Crown Side, but the usual and customary charges made by my predecessor in that office and by the High Constable, and adopted by me, and ever since allowed is 3s. per league and 1s. 3d. for each service.

Having this responsible duty thrown upon me, I adopted the system of employing those in whom I could confide for effecting services at a distance, it being very frequently necessary that I should give to the party I employed, not only funds to cover his own expenses, but also those of the witnesses whose circumstances did not admit of their paying railway and other travelling expenses to give their attendance in Court. In all such cases having to advance to the Bailiffs I employed and to wait myself for repayment by Government, I considered that I had a perfect right to make any bargain I pleased with those I employed, provided the Government were not charged any more than the usual and authorized charges. Then also as to services effected by remitting the Subpœna by mail, to be served in the country, the risk and responsibility rested with me if the witness did not attend (and frequently the Bailiff would have to bring in the witnesses) and pursuing the course adopted by my predecessor and by the High Constable, I charged 3s per league according to the distance but not for actual travel—the Government having to pay no more than it would have paid if the Bailiff had been sent by me from Montreal.

In July 1849, my account for those services during the six months preceding, was under examination in the Inspector-General's Office, and owing to complaints then made similar to the charges now preferred by Mr. C. M. Delisle, the payment of my account was suspended until the reports of the Hon. T. L. Drummond, then Solicitor-General, Henry Driscoll, Esq., Q.C., and A. M. Delisle, Esq. Clerk of the Crown, were obtained thereon.

I refer to these reports, particularly to that of Mr. Drummond, in which the course I adopted was fully sanctioned; and my account containing these charges for distance and not for actual travel was passed and paid.

Ever since that time my accounts have been certified and approved by every Crown prosecutor and allowed and paid by the Government—the accounts themselves being so headed as to show that the charge was not for actual travel, but according to the distance of the place.

I may also refer to the Hon. Mr. Drummond in proof of what I am now about to state, that he himself when Solicitor-General told me that I had a perfect right to charge according to the distance of the place from Montreal where the witness resided, and that I might adopt my own course, either to mail the subpœna or send a Bailiff to serve,—that all the Government required was the attendance of the witness, and that no more was charged than the Government would have had to pay by sending a person from Montreal.

The delay and enormous expense incurred by Government, owing to the absence of witnesses upon criminal trials, led to the adoption of the rule, of making it the especial duty of some person to see that the administration of justice was not retarded by the absence of witnesses.

I may without impropriety, now that my conduct has been called in question, refer to the fact that while I openly and without secresy made the charges in the way I refer to, with the full knowledge of the Government, and thereby derived some advantage and remuneration for the risk and responsibility I assumed, I nevertheless saved very large sums of money to the Government by not summoning all witnesses for the first day of the Court as had been the case, but only for the day they would be actually required, and also that I invariably never detained Crown witnesses one hour more than was necessary; also that no case was ever delayed for want of proper diligence on my part, and no rule was ever taken against any witness for absence.

It must be evident that so to contrive the procurement of witnesses the day they are needed and not before so as to save expense, and to obtain their discharge when no longer required, necessitated the exercise of care and vigilance, which the Government at any rate on the occasion I advert to, thought was fully deserving of any incidental remuneration I might derive by pursuing the course I have adopted.

The duties devolving upon me not only engaged my time during the holding of the Courts, but for a long time before in making the necessary preparations, and even after the Courts; and for the efficient manner in which I discharged them I think I may safely refer to all the Crown Officers under whom I acted.

These explanations will I trust be deemed sufficient to exonerate me from any intention to defraud the Government or to do what was wrong; but should the Government think proper to adopt any other rule than that which has hitherto been openly pursued and sanctioned, I am perfectly willing to be relieved from all further responsibility in that respect.

Respectfully submitted.

[Signed]   C. E. SCHILLER.

Montreal, 28th January, 1863

To Messieurs PIERRE RICHARD LA FRENAYE, and MARCUS DOHERTY, Esquires, Commissioners, &c., &c.

GENTLEMEN,—Your enquiry having been brought to a close, it is now my duty to offer such explanations on the charges brought against me, as I deem it necessary to make.

With regard to the sum of £29 14 2½, the proceeds of a sale of unclaimed goods which took place on the 8th July, 1859, and the further sum of £27 5s 7½d which was handed to me by Mr. Benjamin Delisle, High Constable, as unclaimed monies ; and also with reference to the sum of £50, deposited with me in the case of John Greene, accused of Larceny, in lieu of bail on the 26th August, 1859, I have to say that, if there is any

blame attached to any one, I consider myself alone responsible for those acts ; but I feel it to be my duty to explain the circumstances connected with them.

As to the sale of stolen goods unclaimed, and the proceeds thereof which remained for a long time in my hands, I am, in justice to Mr. Brehaut, bound to state that he frequently desired me to make up the account of it and pay in the proceeds to Government, but I, from various causes, which I must explain, did not do so.

I must premise by stating that when the charges against me were publicly promulgated by Mr. Charles M. Delisle, the matters referred to formed no part of the complaint, and that when the Hon. Mr. Solicitor General Abbott held a preliminary enquiry into said charges, I, of my now free will, stated to him that I held the monies produced by said sale, as well as that which had been handed to me by the High Constable.

That gentleman, I understood, was satisfied with my explanations, and desired me to pay the money on the 1st of April following, at the expiration of the then ensuing quarter, to the Receiver General, which I accordingly did. I was also desired to explain by letter, why I had retained the two first mentioned sums, and I did so. I am aware that my letter is in the hands of the Commissioners, and will form a part of the proceedings. I will only therefore refer to it as containing the explanations I have to offer in connection with these matters,

Referring to the said sum of £50, placed in my hands by one William Ennis, of the City of Montreal, Hotel Keeper, as a deposit in lieu of bail, in the case above mentioned, I have to say that I so received it by the directions of Mr. Coursol, then Inspector and Superintendent of Police, that at the next term of the Court of Queen's Bench, the said Greene failed to appear; but no order of the Court was made, respecting the said deposit of money. The said William Ennis frequently told me that the money was his and I was aware of the fact, and that he was going to petition the Government to have it restored to him, as will be seen by the evidence of the said William Ennis, given before the Commissioners. I urged him frequently to adopt steps to get back his money, and this so late as the month of December last, which will prove that I made no concealment of the fact, and that I wished to get rid of the money. This deposit had come into my custody, as I soon found out irregularly, and that it properly or legally formed no part of the monies, which as Deputy Clerk of the Crown, or Deputy Clerk of the Peace, I had a right to receive. I was somewhat perplexed as to what I should do with it, and told Mr. Ennis that he must act promptly to obtain it. I have that sum still in my hands, and am ready to pay it over to anybody authorized to take it, at a moment's notice.

I would mention with reference to one of the charges, the 5th made against me, of taking two iron spouts or gutters from the Court House, that the Commissioners must have been as astonished as myself to find by the evidence of L. D. Rene Cotret, Esq., first Clerk in the Police Office, and Wm. Fraser, constable, that they were present when Mr. Charles M. Delisle threw them into a privy, and then made this the subject of a charge against me.

The several enquiries made, no doubt, on the representations of Mr. C. M. Delisle, as to a case of brandy, a piece of cloth, a quantity of silk and sixty one dollars in money, as having been abstracted from the Court House, where they were deposited, the Commissioners have seen not only could not be supported ; but in the case of the cloth, its disappearance was clearly traced to the said C. M. Delisle himself, and the brandy, the silk, and the money were satisfactorily accounted for, the former having been delivered to its owner, and the silks and money being still in the possesion of the High Constable, and exhibited to the Commissioners.

Mr. Hands signed all the pay lists, to the number of six, without ever offering the slightest objection or remark, when desired to do so by me, which very naturally led me to suppose that he was perfectly satisfied.

Mr. Brehaut assures me that he always paid Mr. Hands as he did all the other clerks. I personally know nothing of the transactions between Mr. Brehaut and Mr. Hands, but all I can and do say is, that I never received directly or indirectly, one cent except my salary from Mr. Brehaut or any one else.

As to the said William Hands, to say the least of it, he made a mistake in swearing that I hand ed him £5, as coming from Mr. Brehaut as a Christmas box, for I never did such a thing either in the shape of a Christmas box or in any other way.

I can say as regards Mr. Hands that I frequently employed him in the office in making Subpœnas and copies of official documents, at the time he refers to in his evidence, and to do messages.

Mr. Brehaut desired me to place his name as second clerk in the pay-lists, and to take his receipts in the same, which I did.

As regards Mr. Auguste Delisle, I know that he was exclusively employed as a clerk while he worked in the office, and that he frequently used to get money in advance from Mr. Brehaut and myself at Mr. Brehaut's request, but how much I cannot say.

Having already furnished a statement to the late Solicitor General, Mr. Abbott, explaining how and in what manner I caused Subpœnas to be served and how I made my charges for so doing, which I am aware is in the possession of the Commissioners, to form a part of their proceedings, I will refrain from saying anything more on that subject, furthur than calling particular attention to the evidence of the Honorable L. T, Drummond, Q. C.; Henry Judah, Esquire, Q. C., and others

who have been examined on that point, but especially to that of the two gentlemen above named.

With regard to the non-reception of fees between September 1850 and April 1856, in the Office of the Clerk of the Crown, I gave my explanations upon that subject to the Commissioners on the 26th September last, in which I stated that, to the best of my belief I had collected no fees during that period of time. Yet I find by the evidence which is of a secondary and uncertain character, that it is proved that during that period (of nearly six years) I did receive fees in three cases of Habeas Corpus at 11s 8d each, one recognizance 5s and a writ of Certiorari and recognizance £1 1s 8d, making in all £3 1s 8d. I accounted to Govt. for 16s 8d received for the Certiorari and recognizance when the Clerk of the Crown paid in fees to Government in June 1856, and paid the balance of 5s to the constable to whom it was due, so that in point of fact, assuming the evidence to be correct, I did not account for a sum of £2 received during the said period of nearly six years.

That such inaccuracies may have occurred will readily be understood by those who are acquainted with the nature of the duties I was called upon to perform. At this distance of time it is impossible for me to remember the circumstances under which I received those several amounts, if I ever received them at all.

Admitting hypothetically that I did receive the said sum of Two pounds and did not account for it, I can only explain it by the well known fact that the amounts composing it may have been received as they generally are amidst the bustle and confusion prevailing in the several Courts in which it was my business to attend, and, with the flattering testimony given in my behalf by the several judges and witnesses who testified to my character, it will hardly be credited that I did so intentionally.

I would state in addition to the above that I regret that the circumstance of the Hon. Mr. Justice Aylwin refusing to be sworn before the Commissioners, has deprived me of the means of placing before the Commissioners material evidence relating to many points of importance, and, amongst others, that he had frequently given me verbal orders not to charge fees on writs of Habeas Corpus.

Referring again to the question of my charges for the service of Subpœnas, the evidence of Henry Judah, Esquire, Q. C. ; Elzear Clarke, Esquire, High Constable of Sherbrooke; and the Honorable Mr. Drummond, show that the system followed in Montreal by me, has prevailed, and continues to the present time, in the Districts of Quebec, St. Francis and Three Rivers; a fact which is to my personal knowledge, and the testimony of the several bailiffs and constables whom I employed to serve such Subpœnas, establishes clearly that they were all perfectly satisfied with the remuneration they received for their services, and on this point I would refer particularly to the evidence of Francois M. Lepallieur, Bailiff and Constable.

In every term of the Court of Queen's Bench I made disbursements for the service of Subpœnas, which yielded me considerably less than I charged the Government. For instance, during the progress of important trials, where the offence had been committed in the country, it frequently was discovered (generally owing to the inefficiency of the investigating Magistrate,) that essential witnesses were wanting, whose testimony was unavoidably required to establish some important fact, or to connect the chain of evidence ; and on such occasions I had to despatch Constables, by order of the Crown Officer, late in the evening, to distant parts, with injunctions to bring them the following morning, when the case would be resumed; and these services invariably involved me in considerably more expense than I could obtain by making the regular charge, and I never charged anything beyond the regular tariff for such services.

I may remark here that the Terms were held in the latter end of March and October, when the roads are always bad, and when travelling is, in consequence, much more costly than at other seasons.

I was daily obliged to send for gentlemen of the bar and witnesses in the city, who were absent, to oblige both as they could not conveniently lose their time by waiting in Court until required; in all such cases I made disbursements for carriage hire for which I received nothing, and did not charge anything. All these facts are established by the Constables who gave evidence before the Commissioners upon that branch of the enquiry.

I was always allowed 20s a day during the sittings of the Court of Queen's Bench, and that allowance existed when the complaints on the subject of my charges for Subpœnas were investigated, as I have before mentioned, by the Honorable Mr. Drummond, Mr. Driscoll, Q.C., and Mr. Delisle, Clerk of the Crown, in 1849, so that it cannot be contended that I was not known to derive pecuniary advantages for such services beyond my allowance. I always understood that that allowance was made to me for marshalling the witnesses and the evidence before the Grand Jury, a duty totally distinct from that of serving the subpœnas, which properly belonged to the office of constable; and with reference to this point, the evidence of the Honorable Mr. Drummond I beg to call particular attention to, as the system followed was inaugurated by that gentleman, and as he properly remarked, led to the saving of large sums to Government. I would remark that the duties I had to perform in connection with the service of subpœnas, occupied me generally two or three weeks before the terms of either Courts were held, and for this I received no allowance.

In concluding this statement to the Commissioners, I believe they will admit that it is manifest that there was, on my part, no desire to conceal facts from them; that

where blame might possibly attach, I have frankly admitted my responsibility for it ; but at the same time, while making this admission, I most solemnly deny that any intention existed on my part to defraud the Government or do anything that was dishonest. I appeal also to the Commissioners that before they impute to me any improper motives, they will consider the evidence, which in so far as my trustworthiness is concerned is of the highest character, and such as to establish that if any irregularity or neglect on my part has taken place, it cannot be imputed to design or any dishonest motive. Finally I would ask the Commissioners to consider, as an excuse for any such irregularity or neglect, the facts that the routine and financial work of both the departments, that of the Crown and Peace Office, besides the daily Sessions held in the Police Office, and my duties as Superintendent of Crown witnesses, were duties of so numerous and varied a character as to admit of any irregularity or omission occurring, being explained consistently with the honest discharge of my duties.

The whole nevertheless respectfully submitted.

(Signed,) C. E. SCHILLER.

The said Charles E. Schiller being duly sworn before the undersigned doth depose and say that the several matters and things alleged in the foregoing statement are and each of them is true.

[Signed,] W. BADGLEY, Asst. J. Q. B.

CROWN OFFICE, QUEBEC, 27th October, 1863.

MY DEAR SIR,—In answer to your letter of the 26th instant, the receipt of which I have the honor to acknowledge, I have to state that the High Constable for this District, has an allowance of fifteen shillings per day, i. e. six days previous to the Term of the Court of Queen's Bench (Crown side) and the same sum each day during the sitting of the said Court.

I have the honor to be, Sir, Your most obedient humble servant,

(Signed,) P. A. DOUCET, Clerk of the Crown.

C. E. SCHILLER, Esquire, Deputy Clerk of the Crown, Montreal.

PEACE OFFICE, THREE RIVERS, 27th October, 1863.

DEAR SIR,—Your letter of yesterday has just come to hand. In answer, the High Constable tells me that he is paid for his services and attendance at the Court of Queen's Bench, at the following rates, viz.:—Three dollars per diem during the Term, and eight days previous.

Yours truly, (Signed,) L. U. A. GENEST.

CHAS. E. SCHILLER, Esq., &c., &c., Montreal.

MONTREAL, 29th October, 1863.

GENTLEMEN,—I have the honor to enclose the accompanying statement, and two letters, one from P. A. Doucet, Esquire, Clerk of the Crown at Quebec, and the other from L. U. A. Genest, Esquire, Clerk of the Peace at Three Rivers.

I have the honor to be, Gentlemen, Your obt. and humble servant, C. E. SCHILLER.

Messrs. LAFRENAYE & DOHERTY, Commissioners, &c., &c., &c., Montreal.

REMARKS OF MR. A. M. DELISLE

ON

SO MUCH OF THE REPORT OF THE COMMISSIONERS—M.M. LAFRENAYE & DOHERTY—AS HAS APPEARED IN THE MONTREAL HERALD.

It has been my constant determination to abstain from all comment or remark on the subject of my dismissal from office, until I had put the public in a position to judge of the real merits of the case, by reference to the actual text of the evidence taken before the Commissioners. This task I have now completed. But in order not to trouble those, who are desirous of knowing the facts of the case, with unnecessary details, I was also anxious to procure the report of the Commissioners and that of the Attorney General, and the order in Council thereon, by means of which I should be enabled to confine my remarks to those accusations, which they allege to have been proved, and to pass by without notice, the volume of calumnies on which even they have not ventured to insist. These documents would have rendered my defence more precise and clear, or my guilt more apparent. I was willing to run the risk. Indeed, so eager was I to obtain this record of my conviction that on the very day I received the letter of the Assistant Secretary, notifying me of the revocation of my commission, (22nd Dec.,) I wrote requesting that I might be furnished with copies of these documents. By return of mail I received the usual official acknowledgment of the receipt of my letter. On the 2nd of January, not then having seen the article in the *Mercury* of the 31st December, I again wrote urging my claim to be furnished with copies of the reports, and on the 4th I was informed that both my letters had been referred to the Hon. the Attorney General for Lower Canada for his report. So that at least five days after it had been thought fit to communicate to the editor of the *Mercury* the report of the Commissioners, a paper affecting me individually, the Attorney General had not yet reported as to the propriety of communicating it to me!

Not satisfied with one publication of the libel contained in the *Mercury* of the 31st, it was thought necessary to reproduce it in the *Herald*; but so monstrous a proceeding required some apology, and the *Herald*, therefore, proffered the following excuse as well for its ally the *Mercury* as for itself:

"*The Court House Dismissals.*—The Quebec *Mercury, in consequence of the documents communicated to our contemporary of the Gazette,* gives the following as the *reasons* for removing Messrs. Delisle and Brehaut, and requiring e dismissal of Mr. Schiller."

How stupid are the malignant; or rather I should say, how difficult is it to conduct a crooked policy to a successful termination!

I have no means of knowing in what way, or by whom, the *Herald* was invited to publish this excuse; but it is perfectly evident that the apology of the *Mercury* is in reality that of the Government.

Without having had communication of the " reasons " for the removal of Messrs. Delisle and Brehaut, it would have been impossible for the *Mercury* to give them.

I may, therefore, conclude that the Government communicated to the *Mercury*, previous to the 31st of December, the report of the Commissioners, for the purpose of counteracting the effect of the publication of the evidence upon which the report purports to be based!

To the great regret of my persecutors a full and exact transcript of the evidence was in my hands, and its publication could not be prevented; but one means of embarrassing my defence was in their hands, they could withhold the reports and the order in Council—the motives in fact which, it is pretended, justify my dismissal; and that they have carefully done, while the reports are fully communicated to those who are hired to write me down.

The hurried libel of the *Mercury* of the 31st was not, however, considered to be sufficiently ample, or widely enough circulated to effect this laudable object of Her Majesty's Provincial advisers, and recourse was had to the Montreal *Herald*. In four successive numbers of that paper, everything that ingenuity could invent has been done to misrepresent me. Portions of the Commissioners' report in "a somewhat *dislocated* order," I quote the *Herald's* own words, are laid before the public, who are carefully informed that the authors of this atrocity "are not aware that they have—certainly they have not intentionally—omitted anything that makes for the defence." The *Herald* would have it believed, moreover, that the strange dislocation of putting the "concluding remarks" of the report first was done "to show the spirit in which these gentlemen (the Commissioners) acted," and "*to place in the foreground an acknowledgment of the merits, in certain important particulars, of the officers whose conduct has been the subject of inquiry;*" and further on it is said that "it is no necessary part of our duty, at present, to say anything to heighten the effect of the Commissioners' report." Curious to say this sentence is almost the last one of an article containing the concentrated essence of calumny, extracted from so much of the report as was published in the same issue of the paper, and each "batch," (the *Herald's* name for its daily ration of report) was accompanied by a similar epitome. This is what the *Herald* understands by a publication without comment.

After this, am I not justified in saying that I begin the examination of the evidence, with a *prima facie* case already made out in my favor? Are not the appearances of guilt rather with my accusers than with me? Whose conduct is most open to suspicion—the man who is willing to exhibit every fact that can throw light on his conduct, or he who has evidently something to conceal? We have high authority for deciding as to the cause why some "prefer the darkness rather than the light."

If the report of the Commissioners had been so condemnatory, and if its condemnation had been so easily sustained by the evidence, why has it been withheld from me in its entirety? Why has the public been invited to form an opinion on the "somewhat dislocated" version of the *Herald?*

It cannot be pretended that the Government have not had time to prepare copies, for copies for me cannot be longer to write, one would suppose, than those that were furnished to the *Mercury* and the *Herald*. But if my criticism was so much to be feared, without the *Herald's* antidote, as to make it dangerous for my persecutors to give me the advantage of having the first copy, it seems to me that decency required that I should at least have had a copy of the papers I asked for, at the same time they were communicated to the Government apologists.

My adversaries, however, have entirely mistaken the weak point of my character if they suppose that I am to be cast down by their little tricks and subtleties. The suppression of the full text of Messrs. Lafrenaye and Doherty's wisdom, and of the learned conclusions of the law officers of the Crown, may possibly force me to lengthen my remarks, it shall not deter me from making any. Not having the whole of the report, I therefore propose, at present, to comment so much of it, affecting me, as the *Herald* and Mr. Holton, in solemn conclave, have decided it is prudent to print.

But first I would beg my readers to observe, that as I lay claim to no infallibility in treating my own case, so I hope they will not take for granted as true the unsupported allegations of the Commissioners. It is true I am only an advocate, an interested advocate, pleading to maintain my own innocence; but the Commissioners are no more. They, too, are advocates, desperately interested advocates, striving to establish my guilt.

It is vain to say they have no bias. I do not require to hunt up the evidence of its existence, in the malignity of expression, which heightens each deprecatory remark, and pales each alleviating admission. It is natural to suppose that private individuals, taken from a very humble sphere, and consequently but little under the salutary influence of enlightened public opinion, should readily become penetrated with the feelings of those to whom they were indebted for the profits of their temporary employment. It is perhaps hardly fair to expect, and certainly it is hardly possible to believe, that such persons should have the magnanimity to rise above the prejudices of party and association, and have the dignity to repel secret dictation and interference. I have therefore a right to contend that the dicta of Messrs. Lafrenaye and Doherty, contained in their report, should have no greater weight than attaches to the arguments of any other advocate.

In treating the argument of the Commissioners, I shall follow in so far as it is possible, the order in which it is given in the mutilated version of the *Herald*, only reuniting the subjects misplaced by the calculated confusion of the Commissioners, or which have been dislocated by the disingenuous scissors of the *Herald*.

CHAPTER I.

It will scarcely be denied that no ordinary amount of mere carelessness, at all events on a first complaint, would justify a government in the dismissal of officers, the youngest of whom has served for a quarter of a century, and much less a dismissal from an office, in which it is not even pretended any carelessness took place.

In the present instance, however, there can be no question of carelessness. Evidence of the highest authority establishes in a manner not to be questioned, that

"Messrs. Delisle and Schiller discharged their duties as public officers, with energy, ability and efficiency." This evidence, the Commissioners hasten to add, only proves " what the Commissioners *were always will- ing to admit,*" and which they also " deem it just and proper to admit for Mr. Bréhaut, who has produced no evidence."

Of the pertinence of this evidence " to the present investigation," they however insinu- ate a doubt ; and from the sequel, one is dis- posed to conclude that they had no doubt at all, for they have given it no effect what- ever.

As the pertinence of this unquestioned evidence is not apparent to the Commis- sioners, I may be permitted to observe that to my unsophisticated understanding, it seems to overthrow any attempt to justify my dis- missal on the ground of carelessness. It is impossible that I can be at once " able, energetic and efficient," and care- less and incapable.

I have not the vanity to suppose that I have been guilty of no act of omission during the thirty-six years I have been employed in the public service ; but having been put on the trial of my whole life, before those, too, who were determined to find me in the wrong, I am unfeignedly rejoiced to know that I have extorted, even from my enemies, the ad- mission of my ability, energy and efficiency. I may therefore claim that the first point of my defence is made good, by excluding the possibility of any charge of carelessness, by the very evidence of which theCommissioners do not see the pertinence ; an obscurity of mental vision to which I am probably indebted for their ready admission of its truth. It only remains for me then, in the following chapters, to repel those accusations, which if true, would entail moral guilt.

The Commissioners conclude their report with the following remarks :—

"It is to be remarked, in the case of Mr. Delisle, that he was frequently absent, and *for considerable periods of time,* from his office, *by directions of the Government,* upon business per- haps foreign to that of Clerk of the Crown and Joint Clerk of the Peace ; *but how far such absence could exempt that gentleman from the re- sponsibility attaching to the proper performance* ·*of the duties of his office, the Commissioners do not consider themselves authorized to decide.*"

Why the Commissioners should not con- sider themselves authorized to decide as to how far my absence, for considerable periods of time, by directions of the Government, should exempt me from responsibility, it is impossible to conceive, unless it be that their authority was specially limited to what could be turned to my disadvantage, which, I have no doubt, was the case. But since they can- not take upon themselves to decide, I will venture to suggest the decision at which every honest man must naturally arrive. Such absence relieves me of all *moral* responsi- bility attaching to the improper performance

of the duties of my office during such ab- sence, and generally would be a great ex- cuse, if not a complete justification, for errors of omission, if any such had been proved.

I fear that the science of ethics has been slightly neglected in the education of Messrs. Lafrenaye and Doherty.

CHAPTER II.

William Hands.

The first accusation which appears in the version of the Commissioners' Report, as given by the *Herald,* forms the 7th in the series of charges communicated to us at the beginning of the investigation. It is thus expressed :—

" 7th. That they speculated in Government monies, by drawing a sum £125 a year allowed for a clerk, and paying that clerk only £60 a year, and pocketing the balance."

This charge the Commissioners pointedly find proven, at least in part. They say :—

" Whether he (Hands) received the salary affixed to his name on such pay-list or not, *the fact of his not having been a clerk in that office from and for the month of March,* 1854, *to the thirtieth day of June,* 1855, *is undoubted,* and the return of his name as such in accordance with the provisions of the 10th section of the act 13th and 14th Vic. chap. 37, or the pay- ment to him of such salary, was, in the opinion of the undersigned, unwarrantable, *the Commis- sioners finding no evidence whatever of his having acted as such clerk.*"

In this holding the Commissioners estab- lish a distinction which is obvious. They separate the consideration of the charge into the following questions :—

1st. Was Hands paid ?

2nd. Was he employed as clerk and mes- senger ?

With regard to the first of these questions, I can hardly do more than repeat what I have already said under oath, with respect to this matter, in a statement I furnished to the Commissioners on the 1st of May, 1863. It is as follows :—

" I undertook, as my share of the duties of Joint Clerk of the Peace, to take the manage- ment of the Court of Quarter Sessions, where I was to act as Crown prosecutor, and to do all and every the duties connected with that Court, which involved the reading and examination of all informations, depositions and examinations in the cases coming before it ; the engrossing and preparing of all the Bills of Indictment to be submitted, and, in a word, to make all the Registers, proceedings and writings connected with that Court. Mr. Brehaut, on the other hand, assumed all other duties of the office, such as holding the weekly and special Sessions, the superintendence of the Clerks, and the re- ceiving of all monies and accounting for them."

It is, therefore, evident that whether Hands was paid or not, cannot morally affect me, unless it should appear that I was privy to the non-payment, or that I had profited by it. Of this there is not a tittle of evidence worthy of the name ; on the contrary, Hands'

F

testimony is entirely rebutted by the proof of his signature to the six pay-lists, and by the receipt which he gave to Mr. Brehaut, and of which the *Herald* has thought proper only to publish one half. But the question as to whether Hands was paid or not, loses almost all its interest, since it appears that, with all their good will, the Commissioners do not venture to affirm that he was not paid.

The argument of my exemption from all moral responsibility in respect of the acts with which *de facto* I had no concern, the Commissioners combat as follows :—

" The undersigned cannot concur in the opinion that such a division of labor in the performance of the duties of a public office, can be exercised in such an absolute manner as to exonerate from *all responsibility* a public officer, holding a joint office or appointment under the Crown, particularly when taking into account that during the illness or the absence of the other, such joint public officer would be bound to perform the duties of such office, and to certify under oath the accounts of such public office, under section 19 of 13 and 14 Vic. c. 37. The right to make such a severance of office has been denied by the Court of King's Bench for the district of Quebec, in which then sat the Hon. Mr. Justice Kerr, the Hon. Mr. Justice Bowen, and the Hon. Mr. Justice Tachereau, on the 19th April, 1828, with respect to Mr. Sewell, joint Sheriff for that District with Mr Young, although it appeared that Mr. Sewell had not taken the oaths of office under his Commission, and that he had obtained leave of absence from the King's representative."

By omitting the word " moral " before " responsibility," the Commissioners endeavour, either designedly or ignorantly, to confound " moral " and " legal " responsibility. As I have explained in Chapter I, of these remarks, it is only necessary for me to establish my immunity from moral, and not legal, responsibility, and the Commissioners had therefore a point to make against me by overlooking this distinction, which is undeniable. I do not require MM. Lafrenaye and Doherty to tell me that a joint officer is legally liable to a third party for damages arising from the act of his colleague; but, on the other hand, it is an utter absurdity to pretend, that any one man can be morally liable for the acts in which he personally had no part, though done by a colleague or a deputy. This is an elementary principle of criminal law, and one of which it is inexcusable that MM. Lafrenaye and Doherty should be ignorant. In support of their proposition however they cite a case decided in Quebec on the 19th April, 1828, in which they allege that Mr. Sewell, being joint Sheriff with Mr. Young, was held liable for the acts of Mr. Young, and this although Mr. Sewell " had not taken the oaths of office under his commission, and that he had obtained leave of absence from the King's representative." I am not aware that this case is reported, and the Commissioners do not even take the trouble to state whether it is so or not, or the name of the cause ; but I am quite willing to believe that there is such a case. However, there can be

little doubt that if we had the record before us, we should see that the question, there decided, is one of *civil*, not of *moral* responsibility.

In what precedes I wish it to be distinctly understood that the argument is offered hypothetically, and without the least intention to imply that I attach any belief whatever to the accusations of Mr. Wm. Hands. My only object is to keep the issues raised clear and distinct, and to avoid the inconveniences of the confusion, in which the Commissioners, the *Herald* and the *Mercury* evidently desire to envelope the whole question.

The second question—Was Hands employed as a Clerk and Messenger ?—is of more importance, for the Commissioners, in their laudable endeavor to implicate me, have simply stated what they well knew to be false, in declaring that they have " no evidence whatever of his (Hands) having acted as clerk."

The evidence, which they could not find, I will venture to recapitulate textually.

On the 21st of April, Louis Dominique René Cotret, who was first clerk in the Peace Office *during the whole time Hands was represented to have been second clerk and messenger*, was asked by Mr. Brehaut in cross-examination :—

" Question—Have you not seen Hands employed to go messages, fill up or copy papers, or do other things in our Department, not connected with his duty as constable ? "

" Answer—I have."

No attempt was made to break down, or in the least degree to affect this answer.

Again, Hands himself was obliged to admit, in spite of his denegations, that he " used to fill subpœnas, and might copy some documents for Mr. Schiller, when he called upon me."

Again, in the six pay lists, which were all signed by Hands, the nature of his office is set forth in a printed form, and the signatures are all to be found under this formal certificate : " We do hereby acknowledge having received the amount opposite our respective names in full of salary to date." Again, the receipt given by Hands to Mr. Brehaut on the 28th of July, 1855, the signature to which Hands admits, clearly states that it was for the balance of his salary " as second clerk." As the *Herald* has taken the trouble to *dislocate* this receipt, I will take the liberty of restoring the text :—" Received from Messrs. Delisle & Brehaut, Clerk of the Peace, by the hands of William H. Brehaut, Esquire, the sum of five pounds currency, being the balance in full payment of salary, as second clerk in their office up to 30th June, 1855, and for which I have signed the usual receipts in the pay lists.

Montreal, 28th July, 1855,
(Signed)   Wm. HANDS."

In the face of all this evidence, what are we to say of the statement of the Commissioners, that they find " no evidence whatever of his having acted as such clerk ? "

In addition to this, we have Mr. Brehaut's statement under oath, in which he says :— " That he (Hands) acted as clerk and messenger." We have also Mr. Schiller's statement, likewise under oath, in which he says :—" I can say, as regards Mr. Hands, that I frequently employed him in the office in making subpœnas and copies of official documents at the time he refers to in his evidence and to do messages."

To what is above I may add my own statement, likewise under oath, which probably will be considered, by most of my readers, as being quite equal in value to the deposition of Mr. Wm. Hands. It is as follows:—

" As to Mr. William Hands, who has deposed that, although returned in the Pay List to Government as a Clerk, he never was such and never received any of the salary represented to have been paid to him, I can only say, that, after the departure of Mr. Baby, then second clerk in the office, because the salary of fifty pounds he was receiving was not sufficient to maintain him, and was wholly inadequate to the duties of a second clerk, Mr. Brehaut spoke to me, one day, on the subject and expressed his intention to employ the said William Hands, who was then a Constable under the High Constable, alleging, to the best of my recollection, that as an efficient Clerk could not possibly be obtained for fifty pounds a year, he had the intention of employing the said Hands, who wrote a good hand, to fill the vacant office, and mentioned also, that he could be used as a messenger, having no such officer, which would be very useful. I told Mr. Brehaut, to the best of my memory, that, as it was a matter properly connected with his department as agreed between us, he might do as he pleased, and from that day I supposed that the said Hands had been engaged by Mr. Brehaut, for I saw him constantly about the office, and I also saw his name in the pay-lists returned every quarter to Government. As my department was separate and distinct from the office of the Peace, I cannot say particularly, at this distance of time, how Mr. Hands was employed, but I frequently employed him myself to do messages for me, and I would hardly have taken that liberty with him, if I had not supposed that I could fairly do so and that I had some control over him."

Having alluded to the case of Mr. Auguste Delisle, (which I treat of in the next chapter,) I go on to say :—

" With reference therefore to both Mr. Hands and Mr. Auguste Delisle I can only say, and most solemnly affirm, that neither Mr. Brehaut, nor any one else, ever directly or indirectly in any manner, shape or form whatever, paid me one farthing beyond my legitimate salary as it was received, and that I never received in whole or in part, any portion of the salaries alleged to have been paid either to Mr. Hands or Mr. Auguste Delisle, and which those persons deny having received ; on the contrary, Mr. Brehaut assures me that he paid both those persons the full amount for which they gave him their receipts on the pay lists transmitted to the Government quarterly with our accounts. I would add that neither Mr. Hands nor Mr. Auguste Delisle ever complained to me on the subject."

We find thus that five statements under oath are looked upon as "no evidence" by the Commissioners, who are pleased to accept instead, the single testimony of Hands, formally contradicted as it is by the cross-examination, and by no less than seven receipts.

But it may be said that the Commissioners have not relied on Hands' testimony, and that in fact they have rejected it, in so far as it is not supported by corroborative evidence, as, for instance, by refusing to believe that he had not been paid ; that there is another class of evidence, in support of the assertion that he was not a clerk, namely, that derived from the fact, that he was constable during the whole time it was alleged he was a clerk in the Peace Office. This fact only gains importance by the disingenuous manner in which it has been presented. We are told that, as he had acted as constable, " he could not be second clerk in the office of the Joint Clerk of the Peace, Messrs. Delisle & Brehaut." To destroy all this reasoning, it is only necessary for me to remark, that his work as a constable was not permanent but by the piece, and provided it did not interfere with what Hands was required to do for the office, there could be no objection to a man, who had a family to support, eking out his means of subsistence by acting as a constable. There is no evidence to show that Hands' employment as a constable occupied any considerable portion of his time, though it has been maliciously said, that he was employed "day and night." He was certainly not required during the night at the Peace Office. As well might it be pretended that Hands could not have been a constable, because I employed him as an agent to collect my rents.

While speaking of Hands' employment as a constable, it is worth while to remark that when I attempted to prove, by the evidence of Bissonette, what the nature and extent of that employment was, the Commissioners ruled the evidence to be illegal. The Commissioners afterwards found it necessary to enter into this class of evidence, which they did in their own fashion.

It has been also said that Hands could not be messenger, as Fraser declares he filled that office; but this is evidently a mistake on the part of Mr. Fraser. He was messenger and crier of the Police Court, but not of the Peace Office. If he had been attached to the Peace Office, his name would have appeared in the pay-lists, which it does not!

There are no conclusions more unreliable than those that are based on probable incompatibilities.

CHAPTER III.
Mr. Auguste Delisle.

A futile attempt was made to leave the impression that Mr. Auguste Delisle had not been paid the whole of his salary, beause his final receipt, given to Mr. Bréhaut, did not state " whether it was for salary or otherwise." To give any point to this coup d'epingle of the Commissioners, it would have been necessary to show that Mr. Brehaut had other dealings with Mr. Auguste Delisle, and even then it would have availed nothing, for the receipt expresses a " final settlement for all accounts up to this date."

I have only alluded to this matter, to show the spirit in which the Commissioners reported.

CHAPTER IV.

The Books in the Peace Office.

Under this heading there is a rigmarole story, which seems to establish that the Commissioners did not understand the books of the Peace Office when they saw them, and that they did not remember how many they had seen, when they reported about them. I am sorry to waste time treating about such trifles ; but as the Commissioners have made a separate article on the subject, I could not well pass it over without notice.

CHAPTER V.

Stolen Goods.

A moment's glance at Chap. 104 of the Consolidated Statutes of Lower Canada, will show how utterly idle is the prosy dissertation of the Commissioners. Section I is as follows : " The Clerks of the Peace, &c., shall keep a book in which shall be regularly entered all goods or effects *brought to their respective offices* as having been stolen or suspected to be stolen, &c."

Is it not clear, that if no goods were brought to the office, there could be no book kept ? Now it is proved, beyond a doubt, that no goods were ever brought to our office, and moreover that by the very nature of the duties we had to perform, it was impossible for us to give effect to the Statute, and consequently they were left in the custody of the High Constable. That my readers may not suppose I am trying to make that appear impossible which is not so, I will copy a portion of Judge Mondelet's evidence, which is not to be found in the *Herald's* version of the report, although much of his evidence is quoted in close connection with the part I now reproduce. He is asked : " Question, In your experience will you please state whether you consider it feasible- or practicable that the Clerk of the Peace should be the custodian of stolen goods, and at the same time be entrusted with the prosecution of offenders before the Court of Quarter Sessions, and whether in practice it is not necessary that the custody of such goods should be vested in the High Constable as being the proper officer to produce such goods in Court, whenever required ?" "Answer. It would not only be highly indecorous in the Clerk of the Peace, acting both in the keeping and the producing in Court of the stolen goods. It would also be impracticable, at least in such a district as Montreal, where there is so much criminal business. I believe it to have been the constant practice for the Clerk of the Peace to conduct the criminal business before the Court of Quarter Sessions, and it will at once be suggested to any one's sense of propriety and knowledge of the regular and safe administration of Criminal Justice, that this functionary neither could nor should be transformed into a witness ; go for or cause to be brought into Court stolen goods, which he should not allow to go out of his possession, and then stand in the witness box and be interrogated as a witness touching the coming into his possession, his safe keeping of, and his producing into Court the stolen goods, *and all that upon the self-examination of himself by himself.*"

I shall conclude this chapter by citing an instance of the great care and good faith displayed by the Commissioners in carrying out the instructions of their employers. With the view of catching me in a contradiction they say :

"Mr. A. M. Delisle, in his statement marked No. 9, made under oath on the 1st day of May, 1863, ' with reference to the charges preferred against him, and explanatory of his position and of the facts connected with said charges,' refers to this sale as follows : ' As to the sale of unclaimed stolen goods which, it appears, took place in July, 1858, I can only say that I never had any knowledge of it, nor that Mr. Schiller was in possession of the proceeds of that sale for so long a time.' "

The contradiction is then exposed by the Commissioners as follows :

" For the purpose of effecting this sale, a list of unclaimed goods was submitted and filed on the 1st of April, 1857, in the Court of Queen's Bench, Crown side, and the order was given in open Court as above stated in the extract of proceedings from the Register of the said Court, *kept by Mr. A. M. Delisle as Clerk of the Crown.*"

It so happens that on the 1st day of April, 1857, I was absent, at Quebec, on Government business, and the register in question was signed by Mr. Brehaut, as my Deputy, and not by me !

The first of April is a day fatal to a certain class of persons.

CHAPTER VI.

Postages.

A nasty little snarling attempt has been made to affix on the Department, if not on me personally, the 3rd item of the charges which the Commssssioners drew up—"3rd—That large frauds have been carried on in the way of postage." This is not proved, but the Commissioners say :—

"How or whether any distinction was made between the amounts of postage as *properly* chargeable to the Offices of the Peace and the Crown, and those of the private correspondence of those gentlemen and their families, the undersigned have no means of determining beyond the fact, that the above bills would seem large for offices in relation to which most communications were and are official ; and have been incurred since the passing of the act 13 and 14 Vic Chap. 17, in 1850, by which a considerable reduction was made in the rates of postage."

It is difficult to say what the Commissioners intend to convey by the words " postage properly charged to the Offices of the Peace and the Crown ;" or what means they had of judging whether the postages were large or small ;

but in order that there may be no doubt as to the real state of the case, which the Commissioners had no means of determining, I may remark that, almost invariably, private letters are prepaid; but the few that may not have been so were charged to the Department, and the evidence given by the Post Office authoritise establishes conclusively, that the accounts of the two Departments were, in that respect, on the same footing as every other in the Province.

CHAPTER VII.

Fees not Accounted for.

An accusation is attempted to be substantiated by the Commissioners, in rather a confused manner, to the effect that I had not accounted for the fees collected on recognizances, writs of *certiorari*, and of *habeas corpus*. In other words, it is an accusation of embezzlement. Now as I have already said in these remarks, by the admission of the Commissioners, there can be no ground for an accusation against me of inefficiency. Therefore, the whole complaint must break down, and the justification of the Government for my dismissal must fail, unless some criminal or quasi-criminal offence be proved against me. I have also established, what will not be denied by any one less interested or prejudiced than the Commissioners, that criminal liability cannot be substantiated against me for any act that is not my own.

Having laid down these principles, I cannot do better than repeat so much of my statement as has appeared in the *Herald*, in relation to this matter. It is as follows :—

" Considering this question of the Commissioners is predicated upon the assumption that fees were received and not accounted for to Government, and virtually embodies a charge of embezzlement, I desire to record my solemn protest against the course pursued by the Commissioners in interrogating me in relation thereto; but as I feel that my character has been most unjustly and injuriously assailed, I shall waive all formality and give the fullest information in my power—and speaking on my own behalf, I beg to say, that at the period referred to and subsequently, so long as I continued to hold the office of Clerk of the Crown, Mr. Charles E. Schiller acted as my Deputy, and In that capacity, collected all fees and moneys received in the department, and this duty he invariably performed."

This is fully admitted by Mr. Schiller, who will in his turn explain how utterly unfounded are the charges which the Commissioners brought against him.

" I paid over to the Government everything, Mr. Schiller accounted to me for, and having every confidence in his integrity and honesty, I never had any reason to doubt for one moment that his accounts were not faithful and correct.

" If in any case no fees were collected on any such proceedings, Mr. Schiller is in a position, I have no doubt, to give a satisfactory explanation of it, as for instance, that the judges had directed that the process should be issued gratuitously."

CHAPTER VIII.

Commission of Ten Per Cent.

In order that this charge and its answer may be fully understood, it is necessary for me to give the history of the legislation affecting the office of Clerk of the Crown. In 1850, the fees of the office, which were formerly my remuneration, were funded, and my salary was fixed at £250, afterwards raised to £300, a-year. In addition to this, I was entitled to take 10 per cent on the balance of fees, over and above the expenses of the office. In the dislocated version of the report, it is impossible. clearly to understand what the point is the Commissioners wish to make; but it would seem that they hold that I *had not collected the money, and that the sums on which I charged the commissions did not remain in my hands.* The Statute cited by the Commissioners, and by which the fees were funded, 13 and 14 Vic., cap. 37, section 3, states "That . . . all salaries fees, emoluments, and pecuniary profits, whatever, &c., shall continue to be, and shall be, demanded and collected as heretofore by the officers aforesaid respectively, &c." This is exactly what I did. I carried to the account of the fee fund, exactly the same fees which I had previously received for my own profit; and when there was a surplus over the expenses—which, during 12 years, only happened twice, I believe, and then for very small amounts,— I took the 10 per cent. off the balance, as the law allows. The Commissioners seem to think that I ought not to have charged to the fund certain fees formerly payable by the Government to me; but I had no choice, the Statute is precise—" All salaries, fees, emoluments and pecuniary profits whatsoever, which are now, or may hereafter be attached to the said offices respectively, *under any authority whatsoever, shall form a special fund,* &c."

I suppose if I had not charged them so, the Commissioners would have attributed some corrupt reason for my not obeying the law, or would have declared that grave irregularities had been committed by me, although an able, energetic and *efficient* officer.

It would be a curious circumstance if all the Receiver Generals since 1850, and the Auditor General, should have misunderstood a Statute so well known to them as the Official Salary Funding Act, and that the same interpretation of it should have been reserved for two such legal luminaries as MM. Lafrenaye and Doherty, thirteen years after it had become law.

But what renders this charge of the Commissioners sovereignly ridiculous is, that the whole profits accruing to me from this pretended fraud, were two sums, one in 1851, of £6 5s. 2d., and the other in 1854, of £2 7s. 9d. ! So that if we are to believe the laboured statement of the Commissioners on this point, it must be supposed that I went on making up my accounts illegally for twelve years, for the chance of a trifle, perhaps to be realized once in six years; and what would be more curious still, that the Receiver and Auditor Generals joined in the fraud; for it is impossible to presume that they were ignorant of the mode in which the fees were charged, or of the mode in which they should be charged.

It would be interesting for the public to know how much this wonderful discovery of the Commissioners has cost the Public Treasury.

Conclusion.

And now I have brought to an end a defence, not of one or of any number of precise charges, but of many years of my life; and I flatter myself that, however difficult such a task must be to the most innocent, I have succeeded so as not to leave the slightest stain on my character; and may, therefore, fairly conclude that the accusations against me are the excuse for my dismissal, but that the reason is, that my political opinions do not accord with those who, for the moment, hold the executive power.

We are accustomed to reproach the Government of the United States with the wholesale dismissals which accompany each change of administration; but although objectionable, how much more respectable and honest is such a system than the one recently inaugurated here. There they admit the political motive of the dismissal; here it is denied, and the object is obtained by a deep laid conspiracy, false accusations, supported by false oaths, falser reports and perjured counsels.

A. M. DELISLE.

Montreal, Jan. 16th, 1894.

REMARKS OF MR. BRÉHAUT

ON THE LETTER ANNOUNCING TO HIM THE CAUSES OF HIS DISMISSAL.

To the remarks of Mr. A. M. Delisle, on so much of the report of the Commissioners as appeared in the *Herald*, I had intended to add a few observations on some points in which it seemed to me my friends might think I ought to give further explanations. This task has been rendered unnecessary, for after three weeks delay, and after, as it is no doubt expected, the public mind has been sufficiently prejudiced by the, unwarrantable attacks of the ministerial press, the Government has put me in possession of such motives as it can assign in justification of my dismissal. Late as this act of justice comes, and I think few even of the most zealous supporters of the Administration will approve of this lengthened delay in telling me the cause of my removal from office, I have every reason to congratulate myself on a piece of good fortune which is not shared by my late colleague, Mr. Delisle. He has been obliged to defend himself, and in so doing he has defended the Department, against the vague calumnies of irresponsible Commissioners and dishonest party writers ; but I am now in a position to meet my adversaries on the much narrower field presented by the Secretary's letter of the 12th, received by me on the 14th. In that letter I am told, that I was removed "from the office of Clerk of the Peace at Montreal in consequence of the inquiry lately made into the office by Messrs. Lafrenaye and Doherty, by whose report it was established that fraud and grave irregularities were attributable to me and to the other Joint Clerk of the Peace in the management of the office. As far as regards me, the facts complained of are, that I was a party to obtaining from the Government the salary of one William Hands, as a second clerk employed in the office, from March 1854, to the 30th of June, 1855, while the said William Hands was never so employed, and that through a total disregard of the provisions of the law concerning stolen goods, grave irregularities had accrued both in the disposal of the goods and in not accounting for the same, and for moneys received in the office for the Government by the Deputy Clerk of the Peace."

The simple perusal of this communication will convince most people of the utter groundlessness of the charges, the investigation of which has occupied almost a whole year, and cost the country no inconsiderable amount of money. Neither the Executive Council nor the Attorney-General adopts any responsibility as to the truth of the allegations against me. The whole *onus* is thrown on the Commissioners, whose report, and not the evidence, *establishes &c*. There is a kind of accidental truth in this phraseology ; but the report maintains what the evidence does not establish.

As hard words and rude expressions convince no one, and as above all, they break no bones, I shall not imitate the language of my correspondent, who speaks in the name of the Governor General; but I may ask my candid readers what they think of a general accusation of "fraud and grave irregularities?" The charges were utterly wanting in precision, and consequently very unfair; but one would have expected that when men, sworn as to the counsel they were to give to the representative of their Queen, undertook to pass sentence upon another officer, like themselves holding a Commission from their Sovereign, the dictates of honor would have told them that vagueness was no longer tolerable, and that they must be ready to precise the offences which they pretend are proved. "Fraud and great irregularities were attributable " to me and the other Joint Clerk of the Peace, but, so far as regards *me*, the facts *complained of* (proved is probably meant) are :—

1st. That I have drawn and paid (for that he was not paid is abandoned, as a proposition altogether too preposterous, in face of the seven regular and very formal receipts) Wm. Hands as second clerk, he never having been employed as such.

2nd. That through a total disregard of the provisions of the law concerning stolen goods, grave irregularities have *accrued* (whatever that may mean,) both in the disposal of the goods and in not accounting for the same ; and,

3rd. That monies received in the office for the Government by the Deputy Clerk of the Peace had not been regularly accounted for.

So the fraud reduces itself to the payment to Wm. Hands of a salary which he did not earn ; a fraud for the benefit and advantage, not of myself, but of a third party, a stranger to me, with whom I had absolutely nothing to do. This is the incredible story which it is expected the public will believe. So long as it could be pretended that my colleague and I had divided the salary, or rather a part of the salary (for this was the original charge) between us, there might have been some possibility of inducing very warm partisans to believe the story. A motive for crime is an inducement to believe it possible ; where there is no motive, it is hardly possible to credit a crime of the nature of the one alleged. But, however little the Commissioners and law officers of the Crown value their reputation when there is a political object to be gained, they were staggered at the idea of declaring that they believed Hands had not been paid, when *quarter by quarter, for a year and a half, six times,* he had signed the regular pay lists sent in to the Government, and the general receipt shortly after he had left the office. It was not easy however to give up the Hands' affair altogether. His deposition had been triumphantly sent to Quebec, (see Mr. Doutre's letter of the 26th April, 1863,) and the public had been so fed with the belief that the Hands' affair was a great scandal and fraud, that to give it up altogether, would have been a death blow to the whole conspiracy. Between these contending reasons, like weak people, the conspirators took a middle course and told a tale which no sane man can believe. Had the Commissioners persisted in the charge as laid, I should willingly have shewn the contradiction in Hands' evidence, which would have established his utter incredibility ; but as the point is given up by the Commissioners, and with it necessarily the credibility of the witness Hands, I shall confine my remarks, which will be very short, to the question of whether he was employed as a clerk and messenger. Even upon this matter I shall avoid entering further than shortly to recapitulate the evidence, which is fully discussed in Mr. Delisle's remarks, and add one or two considerations which, it seems to me, he has overlooked.

In support of the Commissioners' statement, that there is " no evidence" to shew that he was employed, we have Hands' testimony alone ; and that, as has been shewn, and indeed as it must be admitted, is valueless. On the other hand, we have Coteret, an admission of even Hands himself, that he did work for the office, Schiller's statement,

which is a good deposition for us in this matter, he not being implicated, and Mr. Delisle's statements and mine, both under oath; and last, but not least, the six pay lists and the general receipt, in all of which he takes the quality of second clerk. To this I would add, that the time during which we allege that he was employed, fills exactly the period from Mr. Baby's leaving the office up to the time of Mr. Auguste Delisle taking the place of second clerk. There was then a vacancy to fill, and a man to fill it. Hands was no increase of the staff of the office.

As for the secondary evidence, by which the Commissioners attempt to support their one-sided proposition, namely : 1st, That Hands was a constable, and therefore could not be our clerk and messenger ; and 2nd, That Fraser was our messenger and that therefore Hands could not be so too, it can all be demolished in an instant. Hands' work as a constable was only occasional, and it could not interfere with the duties he was required to perform for us. A calculation from the evidence shows that the greatest number of services made by him in any month, was 31, equal to one service a day. Such services, it may be remarked, are generally made in the morning before the Justice comes into Court, or in the evening. If Hands had not had any other means of subsistence than what he gained as a constable and from his pension, it is hardly possible to conceive that he could have purchased a house for £170 cash, which he had accumulated since his arrival in Montreal. Again Fraser was mistaken, when he stated that he was our messenger. This is proved beyond a doubt by the pay-lists, in which his name does not appear. Had he been on our staff, he would have been paid through us.

I think I may compliment the conspirators on the demolition of their first false accusation against me.

The second is even more easily disposed of. Mr. Delisle has shewn the misrepresentation of the statute, out of which they have spun the charges about the irregularities which had occurred in the disposal of stolen goods ; and the attempt to hold us, the Clerks of the Court, alone responsible for a practice, whether legal or not, which was sanctioned by all the judges and the prosecuting officers for the last thirty years, and which is still practised, will not recommend itself to the public mind. People will hardly be disposed to blame us for not doing what Judge Mondelet, supported by all the best authorities on this point, declares to be "impracticable." There is a maxim which used to be well known, *Impossibilium nulla obligatio est ;* and even if this one were not applicable in the present case, in view of the thirty years practice we might invoke the equally familiar maxim—*Communis error facit lex.* But our self constituted judges despise the rules of law as well as the principles of justice.

The following quotation from Mr. Schiller's statement will show that any trifling blame which may attach for the delay in sending up the only proceeds of the sale of stolen goods, which ever came into the Office of the Peace, was not mine. If it had been, I should not have been much ashamed to own what, at most, is only a trifling negligence. Mr. Schiller says, in his letter of the 27th of January, 1863, addressed to me, "although often desired by you to prepare and forward those accounts, I was, from a pressure of business, prevented from so doing for a sufficiently long time, so that I at length thought it would be as well to account for the amount in my hands when the next sale took place." (See the letter published at length, *supra* p. 73.)

The third justification put forth for my dismissal is, that monies received by the Deputy Clerk of the Peace had not been regularly accounted for. I presume that this charge refers to the £50 illegally taken by Mr. Schiller for bail, *under the order of the Judge of Sessions.*

It is a curious exemplification of the absence of good faith which is manifest in all the proceedings of the Government in this matter, that the bail was taken by Mr. Schiller, as Deputy Clerk of the Crown, a department with which I had nothing to do, and not as Deputy Clerk of the Peace. This is an error which could not have been made by a conscientious man, desirous of rendering justice, but a very likely mistake for any one to fall into in an endeavour to find an excuse to justify wrong-doing.

It is not necessary for me to offer any apology for Mr. Schiller's conduct in respect of this £50, for his justification, which follows, is complete and incontrovertible.

As we have heard much of *grave* irregularities, and some little of fraud, let me ask, on the review of the whole case, whether fraud attaches to those who have robbed me of my livelihood on such flimsy excuses, or to me?

In spite of the powerful and unscrupulous attempt made to ruin my character, I would not willingly exchange it for that of any of my detractors.

W. H. BREHAUT.

Montreal, January 16th, 1864.

REMARKS OF MR. SCHILLER

ON

SO MUCH OF THE REPORT OF THE COMMISSIONERS—M. M. LAFRENAYE & DOHERTY—AS HAS APPEARED IN THE MONTREAL HERALD.

I did not hesitate, before the Commissioners, to state all that I knew relative to the Department, and to give such information as to myself as would satisfy the most morbid curiosity; and I do not fear now, before the public, to question the justice of the decision at which the Commissioners have arrived.

It has been made a reproach that I petitioned for a writ of *quo warranto* in order to arrest the proceedings of the Commissioners, because I was afraid of their investigations. Nothing can be further from the truth. I tried to stop the proceedings of the Commissioners because I considered them illegal then, as I do now; and I was anxious to give the Courts an opportunity of putting an end to a system of persecution and oppression, by which their particular attributes are invaded; but whatever I had to fear from the injustice of the Commissioners, I had no reason to dread their investigations, as the issue has proved. Had it been otherwise, will it be believed that I should have written to Mr. Abbott the memorandum of the 28th January, 1863, or to Mr. Brehaut the letter of the 27th January, 1863? With my experience of Criminal Courts of Justice, those who have the poorest opinion of my abilities, will readily believe, that if I had had anything to hide, I should have contented myself with pleading "Not Guilty," and have left the Commissioners to find their way to a conclusion as best they could. Instead of that, I *divulged*, before they were appointed, all that they have since *discovered* about me, except that I was a marvellously efficient officer. Under ordinary circumstances, modesty would have prevented me from marshalling my own praises; but when one is exposed, as I have been, to unmerited abuse and calumny, it seems to me that I have a right to call the attention of my friends to the certificates of good conduct and capacity which I have received from the Chief-Justice, Justices Mondelet, Badgley and Monk, the Hons. L. T. Drummond and L. S. Morin, MM. Driscoll, Johnson and Judah, Queen's Counsel; Mr. Coursol, Judge of the Sessions of the Peace, and Mr. Devlin, Advocate. Among these expressions of approbation, I may particularly cite the evidence given by Mr. Drummond, for as he is a supporter of the present Administration, and was even a member of it, his opinion in my favor will not be liable to the suspicion of being colored by any party bias against my persecutors. He was asked —

Q.—Would you have the kindness to state your opinion of the manner in which Mr. Schiller discharged his duties as Deputy Clerk of the Peace, and Superintendent of Witnesses?
A.—I have already expressed my opinion as to the highly satisfactory and I should have said admirable manner in which Mr. Schiller performed his duty as Superintendent of Crown Witnesses. He was equally efficient as Deputy Clerk of the Crown and of the Peace, as also in the arduous duties performed by him before the Grand Jury, where he usually relieves the Prosecuting Crown Officer from all trouble, and thereby enables the latter to continue his attendance in Court without interruption. From Mr. Schiller's prodigious memory, from his admirable talent for organization, extraordinary powers of endurance, and his experience about the Criminal Courts since he was a mere child, I came to the conclusion, at a time when from seventy-five to one hundred and twenty-five Indictments were brought up before the Criminal Courts here, that no other person in the country could fill his place, and it would at least require two other men to perform the work he was in the habit of going through.

Considering then that the Government was in possession of all the facts that the Commissioners pretend have been found against me by my own admission in writing, as early as the middle of January of last year, how ridiculous is it to say that I moved for a writ of *quo warranto* three months later, in order to prevent discoveries? The only discovery that then remained to be made was, that I did the work of two men, and that I saved thousands of dollars annually, if not pounds, to the Government.

The Commissioners have entered "with considerable labor" upon a calculation to establish that I had cleared "in the aggregate a large amount for which no service was performed" by me, as they, the Commissioners, consider that $4 a day, during the sitting of the Criminal Court, "was fair and sufficient for the services I was called upon to perform."

Before entering upon an examination of

the results of this "considerable labor," it is proper for me to observe, that it is purely a work of supererogation, as under their Commission, they had not even a color of authority for making any inquiry or report into the duties of my separate office of Superintendent of Crown witnesses. These gentlemen must, therefore, either have performed this work as a labor of love, or because they found it profitable ; and in the latter case I trust they may have measured the value of their labors at the low rate they have appreciated my services.

The whole question of whether I had a right to charge the full mileage allowed by law, and to make such profit as I could on the transaction, is not to be examined by any abstract principle which the Commissioners or the *Herald* choose arbitrarily to adopt. My pretension is that I was justified not only by a long usage, which of itself presumes an authorisation ; but also by the implied permission of the Crown, the Government having been fully informed, so far back as 1849, of the manner in which my bills were made out.

So clearly did the Commissioners see that the question of authorization or no authorization was the matter to be decided unfavorably to me, in order to justify their predetermined report against me, that they have used the whole of their ingenuity to destroy the evidence of this knowledge on the part of the Government. They say, " It cannot be said that Mr. Schiller's mode of charging mileage has been sanctioned by the Government upon such reports."

From Mr. Drummond's evidence, it appears that whilst he was Solicitor General for L. C., he was "called upon to investigate charges made against Mr. Schiller, that he paid less for the service of subpœnas than he charged the Government, and that he sometimes sent subpœnas by mail to country bailiffs, and subsequently charged the Government mileage from the city as if a constable had been sent to the country to serve such subpœnas." Mr. Drummond then refers to a letter in which he communicated the result of this investigation to the Deputy Inspector General on the 10th August, 1849. I have not a copy of that letter by me, but it is hardly possible to suppose that Mr. Drummond was not then informed precisely as to how the matter stood, for it is not denied that, on the 30th July 1849, Mr. Delisle reported to the Deputy Inspector General on the same subject, in the following words : " The representations that Mr. Schiller charges more than he gets the service performed for seems highly unjust and might with equal propriety, be made against every public officer in the Province. To those who are familiar with the nature of his duties, it will be evident, that as he must be in personal attendance upon the Court and, upon the officer prosecuting for the Crown, both before and after the Court, he can devote very little of his time to the service of subpœnas in person, and it would be hardly

fair to expect that he would pay to Bailiffs and constables all he received and have nothing left for his responsibility and labor. He is, in that respect, very much in the situation of all other public officers whose incomes are derived from fees, and who procure the cheapest possible assistance."

Observe that the communication to which the above was an answer, was a circular letter addressed to the then Solicitor General Mr. Drummond, Mr. Driscoll and Mr. Delisle, and that Mr. Drummond's letter of the 10th of August, 1849, was his answer to it.

To this evidence I may add the testimony of Mr. Judah, Q.C. As to the practice in another district, he says, " I certified similar accounts during six years, &c."

And again, (I copy from the *Herald's* version of the report.)

Mr. Schiller having put the following question :—
Are you aware how charges are made for services of subpœnas by Constables and Bailiffs in the Criminal Courts ?

Mr. Judah gave the following answer :—
The system alluded to in this question existed to my knowledge in the District of Three Rivers 30 years ago. The duties performed for which the charges alluded to were made were performed by the High Constable, who invariably obtained the subpœnas from the Crown Office and caused their service to be made by Bailiffs and Constables at a remuneration agreed upon between them, charging the Government with the full distances. In 1849 I was selected by the Attorney General, Sir Louis Hypolite LaFontaine, Baronet, Chief Justice, to conduct the criminal business of the Crown for the District of Three Rivers, and to report particularly on the charges made by the High constable for the services of subpœnas. Accordingly at the close of the Term when called upon to give my certificate of the correctness of the charges for the service of subpœnas made by the High Constable, I ascertained from him that the services had been made by different parties, paid for in sums less than those charged. *I thereupon granted the usual certificate, and on my return to Montreal reported the fact to the Government.* It is to my knowledge that the system existed for many years before, and it is undoubtedly true that it is continued to the present day, however objectionable it may appear to persons not conversant with criminal matters, in the absence of any officer whose special duty it is to attend to these matters, that this is an improper mode of remunerating the officer. In fact it is only a fair way of indemnifying him for his labour, and as the fact was known to all Governments for the last 30 years, it is but fair to presume that they sanctioned it."

Mr. Eleazar Clark, High Constable of the District of St. Francis, was examined as a witness, and gave evidence of the same practice as that followed by me, being also followed in that District.

I am hardly required, for my defence, to justify the practice complained of ; but as the Commissioners have sententiously advanced an opinion as to the effect of such a practice, I will venture to place the evidence of experience against their theory. In his evidence Mr. Drummond says :—

The result of this system under **Mr. Schiller's** superintendence has been *to diminish the cost of the administration of justice, especially at Montreal, to a very material extent.*
Since it was inaugurated I remember one instance of the Criminal Court in Montreal having been compelled to adjourn before the usual hour for want of a witness. The instructions received by Mr. Schiller from me in 1848, obliged him to clear a sufficient number of benches in the court-room under the accommodation of the witnesses required, in at least three cases,

besides the one that was under trial, and to watch over them constantly, so as to secure their services when required, and this part of his duty he performed in a manner so satisfactory as to secure the result above mentioned.

[Notwithstanding the annonymous complaints conveyed to me through the Deputy Inspector General, I did not deem it my duty to enquire whether Mr. Schiller did or did not, in a legitimate way, add a few dollars to his yearly salary as Deputy Clerk of the Crown.]

He had then no salary for the distinct and separate office of Superintendent of Crown Witnesses, nor as Clerk of the Grand Jury, before whom he marshalled the witnesses, *in carrying out a system under which thousands of dollars, if not pounds, were annually saved to the Government.* If Mr. Schiller received from Government more than he paid his constables. I take it for granted that he did so under arrangements made with them, and with which they were satisfied, *else the work would not have been done as efficiently as it was.* I held Mr. Schiller personally responsible for the appearance of all Crown witnesses, and their attendance before the Court until duly discharged.

In order to carry out my orders, it doubtless became necessary for Mr. Schiller to secure permanently the services of a certain number of active constables, upon whom he could depend at all times and under all circumstances. If Mr. Schiller paid these constables in some cases less than he received from Government, if his charges against the Government were not beyond the tariff rates, *I can see nothing more reprehensible in his conduct, in that respect, than in the conduct of the Prothonotary or other officer at the head of a department paid by fees, who takes $5 as a fee upon a Writ, the labor of getting up of which does not cost him more than a quarter of a dollar.*

It is a fact, the significance of which will hardly have escaped the attention of any intelligent reader, that from all this evidence of Mr. Drummond, so favorable to me, and, indeed, I may say, so laudatory, the Commissioners should have only extracted the sentence between [ ], and which, taken alone, might be construed unfavorably to me.

Mr. Drummond continues :—

Whether Mr. Schiller has been reprehensible or not in making such charges, (the details of which I know nothing,) it would be unjust to make him the victim of a system which has been acted upon and tolerated, if not approved of, by the Government in this, as well as in other districts in Lower Canada, for at least a quarter of a century.

Burke says, "Where there is an abuse of office, the first thing that occurs in heat is to censure the officer. Our natural disposition leads all our inquiries rather to persons than to things."

The superior intelligence of Mr. Drummond led him intuitively to establish this distinction, which the more vulgar minds of the Commissioners were unable to understand.

The other complaints against me are four in number :—

1st. That I illegally kept the proceeds of sales of unclaimed stolen goods—£29 14s. 2½d.

2nd. That I illegally kept the unclaimed monies—£27 5s. 7½d.

3rd. That I illegally kept £50, paid to me by Mr. Ennis for bail.

4th. That I did not account for all the monies received by me for fees.

The first two of these items I shall remark upon together. The Commissioners say :—

"The net proceeds of that sale amounted to the sum of £29 14s. 2½d, as appears by statement marked No. 36, *which sum Mr. Schiller has ever since retained in his possession*, with

also a further sum of £27 5s. 7½d., which, he alleges, he received from the High Constable in September, 1859, being unclaimed moneys, as appears by a list of such moneys furnished by himself, and marked No. 37." This statement contains a deliberate falsehood. Both the amounts in question were paid, under instructions from Mr. Abbott, then Solicitor General, on the 2nd of April, 1863 ; it was, therefore, untrue that, when the report was written, the sum of £29 14s. 2½d. was still "retained in my possession." And it was a persistence in the same falsehood, when, later, the Commissioners said :—"The undersigned submit that the reasons given by Mr. Schiller are insufficient, as he was bound to remit that sum to his principals *at once*, so that the same might be by them transmitted to the Receiver General, according to section 3 of the said Act."

The third section does not limit any time as to the payments to the Receiver General, so that the words "at once" are an intensification of the Statute, which owes its place in the report to the imagination of the Commissioners.

The reasons submitted by me for the delay, which the Commissioners think insufficient, are to be found in my letter to Mr. Brehaut of the 27th January, 1863, printed with the evidence, and upon which I am quite willing to rely. That letter plainly shows that I had no dishonest intention in the delay ; and after the commendations I have received for my diligence and capacity, I can afford to endure the condemnations of Messrs. Lafrenaye and Doherty.

But the *great wisdom* of the Commissioners only shows itself fully when they venture to offer a suggestion of what we ought to have done in this or that circumstance. We are then reminded of the saying. "*la critique est facile, l'art seul est difficile.*" Under an order of the Police Magistrate, Mr. William Ennis deposited in my hands, in lieu of bail, a sum of £50, for the appearance of one John Greene. Being called on his recognizance, Greene made default. The taking of the money for bail was, under the circumstances, unquestionably illegal ; but what was to be done ? I could not give the money to any one, for no one had a right to receive it, and I could not give it back to Mr. Ennis on my own authority. The only course was for Mr. Ennis to make application to the Magistrate or to the Government for authority to me to give back the £50. The evidence establishes that I told Mr. Ennis what he had to do, and he didn't do it. What follows is the evidence of Mr. Ennis, as it appeared in the *Herald's* version of the report :—

"I deposited, as aforesaid, the said sum of money ; firstly, £45, and two or three days afterwards, the balance of £5, into the hands of Mr. Charles E. Schiller. The said Greene did not appear at the following Term, and his recognizance was forfeited. Four or five months afterwards, Mr. Schiller met me and told me that I ought to make an application to Government to get back my money, or get an order from justice saying that he did not consider it right to give up the money to Government, that he still had it in his possession, and if I could get an order from Government or from justice he would give up the money."

In face of this evidence, the Commissioners "lost the horse, but not the saddle." They made a suggestion, which it is only fair to give in their own words. They say :—

"Under any circumstances this sum ought to have been transmitted to the Government. But if any doubt existed as to the proper disposition to be made of this sum, it might have been paid over to the Sheriff of the district of Montreal immediately after the 19th October, 1859, in accordance with the provisions of Chapter 109 of the Consolidated Statutes for Lower Canada, Section 21, which enacts "that all monies arising in any District from fines and penalties paid into the hands of the Clerks of the Peace or of the Crown from the forfeiture of bonds or recognizances, and not forming part of the Consolidated revenue fund of this Province, shall be paid over to the Sheriff of such District," &c., &c.

Why ought it to have been transmitted to the Government? If illegally taken, it was not the property of the Crown, and consequently the Receiver-General had just as little right to possess himself of it, as I had to dispossess myself of it. The other proposition, to pay it to the Sheriff, is still more ridiculous ; it was neither a *fine* nor a *penalty*, nor the forfeiture of a bond or a recognizance.

Is it not clear that in telling Mr. Ennis what to do, I had done all, and more than all, than duty required of me. And is it not equally evident that the course I suggested was the only legal one, and that those proposed by the Commissioners serve only to exhibit their ignorance as well as their malice ?

Here follows the rest of Mr. Ennis' deposition, which the Commissioners *forgot* to insert in their report :—

The next time he afterwards spoke to me on the subject, was about the time Lord Monck first came to Montreal, about July, 1862. This happened in Notre Dame Street. Mr. Schiller remarked that the Governor was an Irishman, and that it was a good opportunity for me to apply to get back my money. *I told him that I would but I never did.* The next time was when I heard that the said Greeno was in Hamilton, and I went to Mr. Schiller about twelve or thirteen months ago. Mr. Schiller told me to go to O'Leary, the detective ; and I went to his house in George Street, where I found him. I told him that Greeno was in Hamilton. He said he would go after him if the captain would let him, and that he would let me know the next morning. He told me next morning that the captain would not allow him to go. On that occasion also, Mr. Schiller told me that if I brought back Greeno, he would give up the money. About six or seven months ago Mr. Schiller, again, on meeting me in Great St. James Street, spoke to me on the subject of the said money, and told me that I ought to apply to the Government to get it, or that I should sue him to get it back, and get a judgment for that purpose, and that he would give me the money, that it was in his hands still, that I would get my money in ten minutes after the judgment was rendered.

On the occasions I refer to Mr. Schiller was always the first to introduce the subject.

The last of the charges against me is, that

I did not account for all the fees I collected. A most minute scrutiny has established that, in 5 years and a half, I forgot to enter fees on three writs of Habeas Corpus, at 11s. 8d. each, and on one recognizance, 5s., making in all the enormous amount of £2, and forming A LITTLE OVER ONE ERROR IN A YEAR AND A-HALF.

Whatever may have been the intention of the Commissioners in writing their report, I have really to thank them for building me up a reputation for order and exactitude, without a parallel. But justice obliges me to mention two or three omissions, which, if they increase the average of errors, at least show that I was not always a gainer by them.

I went to Three Rivers on the 12th September, 1850, on public business, and staid there a week, at a cost of about $20. I forgot to charge it.

In 1852 I brought several witnesses from Boucherville to give evidence as to the sanity of Lacoste dit Languedoc, for whom I paid about $6, which I forgot to charge.

From 1853-7 I spent much for cab-hires, in sending to the houses of the Judges, for which frequently I forgot to charge.

And from 1852 to 1857, at the request of the Law Officers of the Crown, I did special night duty, in order to aid in the detection of the dangerous gangs of counterfeiters, who were then doing so much mischief (see Clarke's Evidence), and for which I ought to have received remuneration from the Government, but I never asked for any.

I do not set these things off as an equivalent against the fees on the three writs and the one recognizance, but only to show that my *numerous* errors were not all interested.

C. E. SCHILLER.

Montreal, January 16, 1864.

———

P.S.—In the foregoing remarks I have not alluded to the accusation of C. M. Delisle, that I had got $500 from him to settle his affairs, and that I had not done so, because it formed no part of the accusations brought against me by the Government. But as it might appear strange my leaving such a charge unanswered, I may state that I got $400, not $500, from C. M. Delisle, to pay two parties whom he had defrauded, namely, $300 to Mr. G. B. Muir, in Notre Dame Street, and $100 to Mr. Olivier Gadbois, Mr. Joseph Beaudry's bookkeeper. This accusation is not, therefore, more difficult to answer than those urged by the Government, and the profit I gained by the transaction was the loss of my travelling expenses and $4, as the sum due to Mr. Muir was $304, and not $300.

C. E. S.

SUPPLEMENT.

CORRESPONDENCE WITH THE GOVERNMENT SUBSEQUENT TO THE 22ND DECEMBER, 1863.

THE GOVERNMENT VIRTUALLY ABANDONS THE ENNIS ACCUSATION.

[*Letter of Mr. A. M. Delisle to Provincial Secretary of 2nd January, 1864, the substance of which is given in the letter to Lord Monck.*]

SECRETARY'S OFFICE,
Quebec, 4th Jan., 1864.

SIR,—I have the honor to acknowledge the receipt of your letter of the 2nd instant, and to inform you that it has been referred to the Honorable the Attorney General for Lower Canada, in connexion with your letter of the 22nd ultimo, already before him for report.

I have the honor to be, Sir,
Your most obd'nt Servant,
E. PARENT.

A. M. DELISLE, Esq., Montreal.

SECRETARY'S OFFICE,
Quebec, 9th Jan., 1864.

. SIR,—In reply to your application for copies of papers relating to your dismissal from the office of Sheriff for the District of Montreal, I have the honor, by command of His Excellency the Governor General, to inform you *that a copy of the report of Messrs. Lafrenaye and Doherty will be furnished to you as soon as it can be made, which will be done without delay*; but that the report of the Attorney General cannot be furnished, as it is not usual to furnish such reports, nor *the Orders in Council based on them*.

I have the honor to be, Sir,
Your most obd'nt Servant,
A. J. FERGUSON BLAIN,
A. M. DELISLE, Esq., Montreal. Secretary.

MONTREAL, 11th Jan., 1864.

MY LORD,—On the 22nd ultimo I was informed by letter of the Assistant Secretary, in date of the 21st, that your Excellency had been pleased to revoke my commission as Sheriff of this District, by an instrument bearing date the 19th day of December last. As the letter of the Assistant Secretary gave me no information as to the causes of my dismissal from office, I immediately wrote to the Provincial Secretary, and among other things said,—" As the cause of the revocation of " my commission is not stated, and that I feel ex-" tremely anxious to be informed upon that sub-" ject, as it must, I presume, be the result of the " investigation made by Messrs. Lafrenaye and " Doherty, the Commissioners, who have enquired " into the charges made against Mr. Brehaut, Mr. " Schiller and myself, by Mr. C. M. Delisle, may " I request to be furnished with the report of the " Honorable the Attorney General to the Execu-" tive Council upon that subject, as well as upon " the petition I had the honor of addressing to his " Excellency on the 5th November last, accompa-" nied by copies of letters from Joseph Doutre, " Esq., Q.C., to the said C. M. Delisle, and the

"order and proceedings of Council had there-"upon. May I also take the liberty of requesting "to be furnished with a copy of the report of "Messrs. Lafrenaye and Doherty."

The receipt of my letter was acknowledged by the return of mail.

On the 2nd of January, not having been informed of these reasons, I again addressed a letter to the Provincial Secretary, when, in reiterating my request, to be informed as to the causes of my dismissal, I stated,—" I respectfully sub-" mit that the reference of my prayer can only be " a matter of form, as there can, I apprehend, be "no doubt as to my right to know the cause of " my dismissal, and that it is doing me a serious " injustice to withhold from me, for a single week, "information which I do not ask as a favor, but " which I claim as a right, and which, in common "fairness, should have been communicated at "once.." On the 5th January I received a letter from the Assistant Secretary, acknowledging the receipt of my letter of the 2nd instant, and informing me that it had been referred to the Honorable the Attorney General for Lower Canada, in connexion with my letter of the 22nd ult., already before him, for report. This morning I received a letter from the Provincial Secretary, in reply to my application for information as to the cause of my dismissal from office in which I am informed by command of your Excellency; that a copy of the report of Messrs. Lafrenaye and Doherty will be furnished to me, " as soon as it can be made, which will be done without delay," but that the report of the Attorney General cannot be furnished, as it is not usual to furnish such reports nor the orders of Council based thereon. To this statement of facts I have to add, for the information of your Excellency, that the report of Messrs. Lafrenaye and Doherty, which I am promised will be furnished to me as soon as it is made, was in the possession of the Editor of the *Quebec Mercury* previous to the 31st of last month, as an article in the issue of that paper of the morning of the 31st, contained allusions and citations from the said report, and I have a similar reason for knowing that this report was also in the hands of the Editor of the *Montreal Herald* in the early part of last week, while it appears that it is only found convenient to furnish me with a copy, so soon as it can be made, after the 9th of January, nearly three weeks after my dismissal. I have further to remark to your Excellency that the report of the Commissioners alone, without that of the Attorney General, will not furnish me with the facts which, I respectfully submit, I have a right to be informed of; the reasons for which your Excellency has been pleased to revoke my Commission as Sheriff. It is in vain for your Excellency's constitutional advisers to pretend that I can gather from that report, which applies to three persons, and which, I am informed, fills one hundred pages, the reasons of my dismissal. I maintain that it is my right to know the causes of my dismissal specifically, and not by conjectures, and, as I can only conclude, from the tenor of the Provincial Secretary's letter of the 9th, that that is to be denied me, and from the extraordinary proceeding of withholding from me the Commissioners' report, until after it has been for weeks in the hands of the Ministerial press, and unfairly used against me, that I can expect no justice at the hands of your Excellency's advisers, I am now obliged to appeal personally to your Excellency to obtain the information I require. In taking this step I trust your Excellency will do me the credit to believe that, in addressing your Excellency directly, I do not desire to cause you any personal embarrassment, but solely to save me from the necessity of carrying my demand for justice to a tribunal where all concerned in this matter will appear on a footing of equality as British subjects.

I have the honor to be,
My Lord,
Your Excellency's most obedient servant,

A. M. DELISLE.

To His Excellency LORD MONCK,
Governor General, Quebec.

SECRETARY'S OFFICE,
Quebec, 9th January, 1864.

SIR,—I have the honor to inform you, by command of His Excellency the Governor General, that an instrument has been issued revoking your Commission as one of the Harbor Commissioners of Montreal.

I have the honor to be, Sir,
Your most obt. servant,

A. J. FERGUSSON BLAIR,
Secretary.

A. M. DELISLE. ESQ.,
Montreal.

MONTREAL, 12th January, 1864.

SIR,—I have the honor to acknowledge the receipt of your letter of the 9th inst., which only came to hand this day, informing me, by command of His Excellency the Governor General, that an instrument had been issued revoking my Commission as one of the Harbor Commissioners of Montreal, without assigning any reason whatever, or stating that any complaint has been made against me in the discharge of the duties of that office.

This course of proceeding is so unprecedented and unusual, and, I may add, unfair and unjust to me, that I feel in duty bound solemnly to protest against it. I respectfully submit, for the consideration of His Excellency the Governor General, whether withholding from me the causes which have led to this extraordinary step, and which I cannot but look upon as most oppressive and arbitrary, is a course which should receive the sanction of Her Majesty's representative.

As a British subject, living under British institutions, I have a right to be informed of the causes of my dismissal; and I now take the liberty of respectfully demanding the information I desire at the hands of His Excellency the Governor General.

I have the honor to be Sir,
Your most obt. servant,

A. M. DELISLE.

The Hon. A. J. FERGUSSON BLAIR,
Prov. Sec., Quebec.

GOVERNOR GENERAL SECRETARY'S OFFICE,
Quebec, 13th January, 1864.

SIR,—I am directed by His Excellency the Governor General to acknowledge the receipt of your letter of the 11th instant, and to inform you that it has been referred to the Provincial Secretary.

I have the honor to be, Sir,
Your obedient servant,

FRANCIS RETALLACK,
Governor's Secretary.

A. M. DELISLE, ESQ.,
&c., &c., &c.

SECRETARY'S OFFICE,
Quebec, 23rd January, 1864.

SIR,—I have the honor to inform you that His Excellency the Governor General soon after the receipt of your letter of the 11th inst., addressed to him, referred it to me for the consideration of His Excellency's Constitutional Advisers. I am now desired by His Excellency to communicate for your information, that your removal from the office of Sheriff of the District of Montreal was forced on His Excellency by the charges of fraud and gross mismanagement, which were proved by the report of Messrs. Lafrenaye and Doherty, and the evidence accompanying it, to have taken place in the offices of Clerk of the Peace and Clerk of the Crown whilst those two offices were held by you; that these charges, as far as proved against you are: 1st. That while being Joint Clerk of the Peace with Mr. Brehaut you falsely represented to the Government that one Wm. Hands was employed from March 1854, to the 30th June, 1855, as second clerk in your office, and that you drew for him from the Government a salary at the rate of £50 per annum for 1854, and of £125 for 1855, although he was never so employed. 2nd. That you kept no proper register of the stolen goods brought to your office, as required by law, that you allowed those goods to remain in the possession of the High Constable, who kept no account of them until 1861; that they were often delivered without any order from the Court, and sometimes to other than the owners; that you had no lists of unclaimed stolen goods, since the 1st April, 1857, before the Court of Queen's Bench, although the law requires that such should have been done at each session of the Court; that no sale of those goods has taken place since the 8th of July, 1858, that a large proportion of those goods are missing, in 60 cases out of 104 they being totally unaccounted for; that Mr. Schiller, your Deputy, received the sums of £29 14s 2½d, as being the proceeds of a sale of unclaimed stolen goods made on the 8th of April, 1858 ; £27 5s 7½d unclaimed monies which he received in 1859, from the High Constable, and £50 received in lieu of bail on the 20th August, 1859, which sums were never paid over to the Government. 3rd. That from the 10th September, 1850, when the fees of the office of Clerk of the Crown were funded, to the 1st April, 1856, you make no return of the fees paid into your office, and which you were bound to collect for the Crown, and that from the 1st April, 1856, you have accounted for only part of what you received or should have received. 4th. That you have charged to the Government annually, on certain pretended balances of fees which you never collected, a commission of ten per cent; to which you were not entitled. 5th. That as Clerk of the Crown you certified Mr. Schiller's accounts for disbursements for services of subpœnas to Crown witnesses, by means of which he obtained from the Government large sums of money to which he had no right, the Commissioners having approximately established that in five years from 1853 to 1857, those overcharges amounted to £1088 7s 3¼d, or £217 13s 5¼d per annum, and that it is impossible to suppose you could have been ignorant of the manner in which Mr. Schiller did, for a period of twenty years practice such an imposition on the Government. His Excellency, desires me further to add that although the above grounds were considered sufficient to justify your removal, his attention was also drawn to reports made by the officers of the audit Branch of the Finance Department, whereby it appeared that gross mismanagement existed in the Montreal gaol, attributable to a systematic disregard on your part of the Regulations prepared by the Prison Inspectors, and sanctioned by His Excellency in Council ; that large sums of money had been charged by the jailer under the head of "medical comforts," and that, for the six months ending on the 30th of June, 1863, a sum of £453 16s 9d had been charged for tea alone, supplied to about eighty patients, although no officer employed in the jail should, according to those re-regulations, have any participation in the profits arising out of supplies furnished to the Jail, and that these and other extravagant charges had been paid by you and included in your accounts without any remark ; that in this, as in the case of Mr. Schiller's accounts, you have shown a total disregard of the duties imposed upon you for the protection of the public interests.

His Excellency, in conclusion, commands me to add that, as regards the communications to the newspapers, of which you seem to complain, he has no power to prevent parties, whoever they may be, from expressing through the newspaper press their views on any matter which they may deem of public interest, nor any inclination to interfere, had he such power.

I have the honor to be, sir,
Your most obed't and humble serv't,
(Signed)   A. J. FERGUSON BLAIR, Sec'y.
A. M. DELISLE, Esq., Montreal.

SECRETARY'S OFFICE,
QUEBEC, January 23rd, 1864.

SIR,—In reply to your letter of the 12th instant, I have the honor to inform you, by command of His Excellency the Governor General, that you were removed from the Montreal Harbor Commission in consequence of your removal from the office of Sheriff, for the reasons stated in my letter of this day, in answer to your letter of the 11th instant to the Governor General.

I have the honor to be, sir,
Your most obedient servant.
A. J. FERGUSON BLAIR, Sec'y.
A. M. DELISLE, Esq., Montreal.

MONTREAL, Jan. 27, 1864.

SIR,—I have the honor to acknowledge receipt of your letter of the 23rd instant, informing me, by desire of His Excellency; that my removal "from the office of Sheriff of the District of Montreal was forced on His Excellency by the charges of fraud and gross mismanagement, which were proved by the report of Messrs. Lafrenaye and Doherty, and the evidence accompanying it, to have taken place in the offices of the Clerk of the Peace and Clerk of the Crown. while those two offices were held by me."

Such grave accusations call for a detailed remonstrance from me, as I utterly deny that the evidence, taken before the Commissioners, supports in any degree whatever, all or any of the instances of fraud or mismanagement set forth in your letter of the 23rd, or justifies the conclusion at which His Excellency has been advised to arrive.

But before proceeding to answer. one by one, the false allegations of your letter of the 23rd, and entirely apart from the consideration of the merits of these accusations, I must protest in the most formal manner against the unjust and tyrannical mode of proceeding adopted against me.

1st. By withholding from me, during one month and two days, any information as to the cause of my dismissal from office, in spite of my reiterated demands to be informed of such causes, the first of my letters asking such information being of the 22nd ultimo.

2nd. By the communication of the Report of the Commissioners to the writers in the Montreal Herald and in the Quebec Mercury, at least three weeks before the causes of my dismissal were made known to me.

3rd. By the publication in the said newspapers, under the direction (as I have good reason to believe) of the Executive Government, or of some member of it, having access to the private documents of the departments, of garbled extracts of the said Report of the Commissioners, the real text of which was withheld from me.

4th. By withholding from me, even up to the present moment, the Report of the Commissioners, a copy of which had been promised to me by your letter of the 9th instant.

5th. By attributing, as a reason for my dismissal, a complaint which was never officially communicated to me, but which was privately communicated to an anonymous writer in the Quebec Mercury previous to my dismissal, for the evident purpose of writing me down, without affording me an opportunity of defending myself; and thus, by prejudicing the public mind, to prepare it for my predetermined dismissal.

6th. By the tone of your letter of the 23rd, which is injurious in expression and jeering in its style.

On the merits of the charges as articulated in your letter of the 23rd, it will be my business to establish that they are not only unsupported, but even contradicted by the evidence, and, consequently, that they form the excuses for, and not the causes of, my dismissal.

In so far as respects the offices of Clerk of the Peace and of the Crown, while held by me, the charges are divided into two categories. First, those of "gross mismanagement"; and, secondly, those of "fraud."

As regards any general accusation of mismanagement, it must be apparent to the most cursory observer, if he be unbiased by the resolution to maintain a foregone conclusion, that such a charge is unsustainable, in face of the evidence of all of those who have spoken as to my energy, ability and efficiency in the discharge of my duties—evidence which the Commissioners themselves have been obliged to admit as conclusive..

Again, mismanagement in the discharge of my duties (had such mismanagement been proved) as Clerk of the Crown and of the Peace, would not justify the dismissal from a totally different office ; and it may be also remarked that official promotion, such as that from the office of the Clerk of the Peace and the Crown to that of Sheriff, is a waiver—a giving up—of any complaint of incapacity or mismanagement. This proposition is elementary in the administrative code, and so far is this the case that, where the service is of a military character, it would be a complete bar to any further proceeding before a court martial to prove, that since the fact complained of was within the knowledge of competent authority, the accused had received promotion, or even that he had done duty. Ignorance of gross mismanagement in a Home Department during a series of years cannot be presumed ; besides it is contradicted by the unanimous evidence of all those who were examined as to my efficiency. One cannot be able, energetic and efficient, and at the same time guilty of "gross mismanagement." I have, therefore, established the first step in support of my proposition that His Excellency was ill advised in coming to the conclusion that I was deserving of dismissal from the office of Sheriff, owing to gross mismanagement in the offices of Clerk of the Peace and of the Crown, formerly held by me.

From the wording of your letter of the 23rd, I presume that the mismanagement is included under the second item of the cause of my dismissal, thus covering the complaint of our not having the custody of stolen goods, that Mr. Schiller had never paid over two sums—one of £29 14s. 2¼d., proceeds of sale of unclaimed stolen goods, another of £27 5s. 7¼d., unclaimed monies, and a sum of £50, received in lieu of bail. In adverting to accusations of this sort, it is right to be scrupulously exact as to the statement of facts, and I will therefore take the liberty of correcting some rather important inexactitudes in this part of your letter.

In the first place the Statute only obliges the Clerk of the Peace to keep a register of such stolen goods *as are brought to his office*, and the evidence establishes, beyond a question, that none were ever brought to our office, and this for reasons held to be fully sufficient by those whose competency to decide in the matter will hardly be questioned—namely, the Judges of the Criminal Courts and the prosecuting officers. And, I may also add, what scarcely can be unknown to those who have advised his Excellency that this was a sufficient cause of my dismissal from the office of Sheriff, that the practice condemned in my colleague and myself is still continued.

In the second place, it is untrue that the two sums of £29 14s. 2¼d. and £27 5s. 7¼d. "were never paid to the Government." They were paid to the Government under the directions of the late Solicitor General, Mr. Abbott, on the 2nd day of April last. It is also in evidence that there was no concealment about these monies; that Mr. Brehaut knew that Mr. Schiller had them, and that Mr. Schiller had stated to Mr. Abbott in writing on the 28th of Jany., 1863, that he had those monies. It is further in evidence that nothing obliged Mr. Schiller to mention having received one of these sums, as he got it from the High Constable, who had no recollection of the transaction. From all this, then, it is plain that the retention of these two sums was, at most, an act of negligence on the part of an officer who has obtained the reputation from one of your late colleagues, the Hon. Mr. Drummond, of doing the work of *two* men, of having saved thousands of dollars, if not pounds, annually to the Province, and being the only person in Canada who could fill the place he did. And it is for the reflection of the negligence of such an officer that His Excellency has been advised to dismiss me from an office other than that in which the alleged negligence took place.

As to the £50 received in lieu of bail, it is abundantly established by the evidence of Mr. Carter, that Mr. Schiller, was not legally entitled to take that money, however much he might be justified in so doing under the directions of the Police Magistrate, Mr. Coursol, and consequently he could not be acting as my mandatory. His taking such sum was not within the scope of his functions, and therefore as Clerk of the Peace I could not relieve him of the money, nor could he dispossess himself of it except on the application of the person by whom it was paid, Mr. Ennis, who being finally examined as a witness, admits that Mr. Schiller repeatedly told him so, and invited him to ask for the money in a legal way. (V. pp. 36-65.)

The charges which seem more particularly to include fraud, are to be found classified under the items of your letter 1st, 3rd, 4th and fifth. I propose to answer then *seriatim* and in as few words as possible.

1st. That we drew Hands' salary although he was never employed as second clerk and messenger. In the version of the report which appeared in the *Herald*, the Commissioners are made to say:— "Whether he (Hands) received the salary affixed to his name on such pay list or not, *the fact of his not having been a clerk in that office for and from the month of March*, 1854, *to the thirteenth day of June*, 1855, *is undoubted*, and the return of his name as such in accordance with the provisions of the 10th section of the act 13th and 14th Vic., chap. 37, or the payment to him of such salary, was, in the opinion of the undersigned, unwarrantable, *the Commissioners finding no evidence whatever of his having acted as such clerk.*"

By the wording of this portion of the report it appears that the Commissioners abandon the idea of pretending that Hands' was not paid ; and they would therefore have it believed, that we drew a salary for a stranger, and committed a fraud for his sole advantage. The improbability of such a story will probably be considered as a sufficient refutation ; but in deference to the Commissioners I cannot fail to meet their distinct declaration that they find " no evidence whatever of his having acted as such clerk." The evidence which the Commissioners could not see, is of several kinds, testimonial, documentary and of a presumptive character.

1st. Rene Cottret who was first clerk in the Office during the whole time Hands was represented as having been second clerk, declares that he saw him doing work for the office, as the following question and answer establish :—(V. p. 31.)

"Question—Have you not seen Hands employed to go messages, fill up or copy papers, or to do other things in our Department, not connected with his duty as constable ?"

"Answer—I have."

2nd. Hands admitted that he "used to fill subpœnas, and might copy some documents for Mr. Schiller, when he called upon me." (V. p. 18.)

Again, in the six pay lists, which were all signed by Hands, the nature of his office is set forth in a printed form, and the signatures are all to be found under this formal certificate : " We do hereby acknowledge having received the amount opposite our respective names in full salary to date." (V. p. 19.)

Again, in a check receipt taken by Mr. Brehaut from Hands, when he paid him a small balance still due him a short time after his engagement as second clerk and messenger ceased, he took the quality in which the Commissioners found no evidence of his ever having acted, This receipt is as follows :—(V. p. 23.)

"Received from Messrs. Delisle & Brehaut, Clerk of the Peace, by the hands of William H. Brehaut, Esquire, the sum of five pounds currency, being the balance in full payment of salary, as second clerk in their office up to 30th June, 1855, and for which I have signed the usual receipts in the pay lists.

"Montreal, 28th July, 1855.
(Signed)   Wm. Hands."

3rdly. In addition to this, we have Mr. Brehaut's statement under oath, in which he says :—(V. p. 72.) "That he (Hands) acted as clerk and messenger." We have also Mr. Schiller's statement, likewise under oath; in which he says :—"I can say, as regards Mr. Hands, that I frequently employed him in the office in making subpœnas and copies of official documents at the time he refers to in his evidence and to do messages." (V. p. 76.)

To this I cannot do better than repeat the statement under oath ; which I filed before the Commissioners, and which is as follows :—(V. p. 40.) "As to Mr. William Hands, who has deposed that, although returned in the Pay List to Government as a Clerk, he never was such and never received any of the salary represented to have been paid to him, I can only say, that, after the departure Mr. Baby, then second clerk in the office, because the salary of fifty pounds he was receiving was not sufficient to maintain him, and was wholly inadequate to the duties of a second clerk, Mr. Brehaut spoke to me, one day, on the subject and expressed his intention to employ the said William Hands, who was then a Constable under the High Constable, alleging, to the best of my recollection, that as an efficient Clerk could not possibly be obtained for fifty pounds a year, he had the intention of employing the said Hands, who wrote a good hand, to fill the vacant office, and mentioned also, that he could be used as a messenger, having no such officer, which would be very useful. I told Mr. Brehaut, to the best of my memory, that, as it was a matter properly connected with his department as agreed between us, he might do as he pleased, and from that day I supposed that the said Hands had been engaged by Mr. Brehaut, for I saw him constantly about the office, and I also saw his name in the pay-lists returned every quarter to Government. As my department was separate and distinct from the office of the Peace, I cannot say particularly, at this distance of time, how Mr. Hands was employed, but I frequently employed him myself to do messages for me, and I would hardly have taken that liberty with him, if I had not supposed that I could fairly do so and that I had some control over him."

Fourthly. We have secondary evidence of Hands being a clerk in the office, derived from the fact that he filled the place left vacant by the resignation of Mr. Baby, and that his place was in turn filled by Mr. Auguste Delisle. It is also significant that Hands gives the reason why he was not permanently engaged as second clerk; namely, because he could not fill up the registers. This also explains why he did not do any work, a record of which remained in the office.

It is curious that the Commissioners should have looked upon all this as being "no evidence whatever." In order that I may not be accused of a similar over-sight, I may add, that the only direct evidence of Hands not being employed as second clerk is his own statement; and that, as I have already said, he pointedly contradicts on cross-examination, and it is also contradicted by the pay-lists signed by himself. Again, I further pretend that the contradictions of Hands' testimony render his evidence unworthy of credit. At first he denied having signed more than *two* pay-lists; it is proved that he signed *six*. He then excused himself by saying "two that I called pay-lists." They were printed forms and identical. He said first, that he never gave a receipt in full to Mr. Brehaut; when it was produced he admitted his signature, and excused himself by saying he did not know how it got there. His account of himself, too, was contradictory and evidently false. I therefore maintain that the reverse of the Commissioners' statement is the truth, and that they should have said that they "find no evidence whatever of his *not* having acted as such clerk."

3rd. This item accuses me of not having accounted for the fees of the Crown Office from the 10th September, 1850, up to the 1st April, 1856, and from that date for only a portion of the fees I received or *ought* to have received. This charge leaves me in perfect ignorance as to whether it is intended to affirm that I collected fees and kept them, or only that I ought to have collected fees and that I had neglected to do so. The judgment against me is therefore almost, if not quite, as vague as the original accusation. In common justice I should have been told, item by item, the particular fees which were not charged ; but since that is too much to expect, I will tell you that

the evidence only establishes four instances in which Mr. Schiller neglected to enter fees received, in five years and a half, making in all an amount of only $8. I may also add that Mr. Schiller has established, in a communication to the *Montreal Gazette*, that during the same period he had also forgotten to charge several items in his favor of much greater amount than $8. On this head I defy comparison between Mr. Schiller and any officer in the Province, whose duty it may have been to collect, and account for, small sums of money, often taken in Court, or in the hurry and bustle of other and more important business ; and I maintain that in making less than one omission of the kind a year, he has reduced error to the minimum of what is conceivable in beings not infallible. (V. p. 91.)

4th. The accusation that I charged a commission of ten per cent. on balances, to which I was not entitled, exhibits a lamentable ignorance of the most ordinary administrative acts, on the part of those who have assumed the responsibility of advising His Excellency in this matter. The Fee Fund Act, 13 and 14 Vic. cap. 37, sect. 3, enacts: "That, &c., all salaries, fees, emoluments and pecuniary profits whatsoever which are now, or may hereafter be attached to the said offices respectively, under *any authority whatsoever*, shall form a special fund, &c." In obedience to this Statute, I charged to the credit of the fund exactly those fees which, before the Funding Act, I charged to my own credit; but the Commissioners pretend that I should not have charged such fees as were payable by the Crown. To this, I answer, that I had no choice, the Statute says, that all salaries, fees, emoluments and pecuniary profits which, at the time of the passing of the Act, were attached to the office, should form the special fund. The interpretation which I thus gave to the Statute, was the same it received from all the Receiver and Auditor Generals since 1851. I may, therefore, conclude, that my interpretation was not so faulty, nor my conduct so inexcusably fraudulent, as to merit my dismissal nearly ten years afterwards from another office.

5th. This item charges me with having certified Mr. Schiller's accounts as Superintendent of Crown witnesses, and you say it is impossible that I could "be ignorant o†the manner in which Mr. Schiller did for a period of twenty years practice such an imposition on the Government." It is certainly impossible that I could be ignorant of the manner Mr. Schiller charged his accounts for mileage ; but I deny that he practised any *imposition* on the Government. On the contrary, so far back as 1849, the whole question was fully ventilated. A complaint of the way in which mileage was charged by Mr. Schiller having been made, the Deputy Inspector General addressed a circular letter to the then Solicitor General, Mr. Drummond, to Mr. Driscoll, Q. C., and to me, asking about this very practice, and I answered in the following words on the 30th July, 1849 :—" The represent"tations that Mr. Schiller charges more than he "gets the service performed for seems highly "unjust and might with equal propriety be made "against every public officer in the Province. "To those who are familiar with the nature of "his duties, it will be evident, that as he must "be in personal attendance upon the Court and, "upon the officer prosecuting for the Crown, "both before and after the Court, he can de-"vote very little of his time to the service of "subpoenas in person, and it would be hardly "fair to expect that he would pay to Bailiffs and "Constables all he received and have nothing "left for his responsibility and labor. He is, in "that respect, very much in the situation of all

" other public officers whose incomes are derived " from fees, and who procure the cheapest possi- " ble assistance." With such evidence as this it is hardly possible to suppose that His Excellen- cy's advisers should not feel themselves in honor bound to retract the injurious expression that, in this matter, there was any imposition on the Government. Can there be such an imposi- tion without concealment?

. But if not, and I am so blameable for having cer- tified these accounts, and if every public officer is to be held, to all intents and purposes, liable for the acts of his Deputy, where will the responsi- bility end? I shall not be condemned alone or in bad company. The accounts of mileage for the service of subpœnas for the last term of the Court of Queen's Bench were made up on the same system as those I have been dismissed for having certified; and those accounts were certi- fied by Mr. Laflamme, who was acting as the re- presentative of the Attorney General. There is no escape from the dilemma, if I have connived at an "imposition," so has the Hon. A. A. Dorion, Her Majesty's Attorney General for Lower Canada, and his representative, Rodolphe Laflamme, Q. C. But the matter does not stop there, for my guilt, or rather I should say, our guilt, is shared by the Honorable Mr. Justice Sicotte, who certified such accounts, in the same manner, yet he was placed on the Bench by your Administration, and I was dismissed.

These remarks, I conceive, will be held by every rational person to be a conclusive refutation of all the accusations in your letter of the 23rd, in so far as regards the offices of the Peace and of the Crown; and I come, at last, to the accusation connected with the office of Sheriff, which is now officially communicated to me for the first time, more than four weeks after my dismissal. I say that it is the first *official* notice I have had of this charge, for a newspaper, curious to say, some time ago conveyed to the public the charge in the same words as it is now communicated to me by your letter. It is said that gross mismanagement existed in the Montreal Gaol, "attributable to a systematic disregard on my part of the Regula- tions of the Prison Inspectors, and sanctioned by His Excellency in Council"—the very expressions of an article in the Montreal *Herald.* The facts, which are not unknown to His Excellency's Ad- visers, I shall take the liberty to recapitulate, so that I may not be supposed to acquiesce in these gross misrepresentations. Previous to my becom- ing Sheriff, my predecessor, Mr. Boston, had re- presented to the Government that the dietary proposed would be most objectionable, and, pend- ing the correspondence, he did not put the new regulations in force. Finding the matter in this position when I was appointed Sheriff, I did not feel myself entitled to alter the regulations, until the Government answered Mr. Boston's remon- strance. However, to expedite the matter, I ad- dressed two letters to the Government, asking for a decision, but never received any answer. One of these letters was dated the 15th November, 1862, and the other the 10th October, 1863. It appears, therefore, that those who ad- vised the Governor-General that this is a suffi- cient cause for my dismissal, are themselves wholly to blame for the continuance of this sys-

tematic disregard of the regulations of the Prison Inspectors. Again I may argue, if I, the Sheriff, should be dismissed for having paid these ac- counts during a year and a half, how can Dr. Beaubien be held guiltless, since he certified them for the last ten years? If there be any fault, his is certainly greater than mine, both in gravity and in duration. I may also add, that Messrs. Sims and Ferres' report does not blame the officers but the system; yet it is on this report the govern- ment relies for my condemnation. They say :— " Mr. McGinn is not perhaps in fault in presenting such accounts, seeing that no remark has ever been made upon them by the government, and that his claim has been duly acknowledged and paid for a long series of years. But we beg res- pectfully to give it as our opinion, that steps should be taken at the earliest possible date, to make an entire change in the system by appoint- ing a hospital steward, to superintend all matters connected with the hospital, under such regula- tion as the government may see fit to establish." You conclude your letter with the following words : " His Excellency . . . . has no power to prevent parties, *whoever they may be,* from expressing through the newspaper press their minds on any matter which they may deem of public interest, *nor any inclination* to interfere, if he had the power."

Whatever may be the merit of this conclusion in a literary point of view, it will not be denied that in an official document, written in the name of the Governor General, wit is but a sorry substi- tute for truth.

My complaint to the Governor General was not that parties wrote against me in the newspaper press; but that the parties in question, "whoever they may be," wrote respecting me on information obtained from official documents reflecting on me, which had neither been communicated to me nor the public. The communication of such docu- ments, for such a purpose, I consider to be dis- honorable and dishonest, and I conceive I had a right to complain to His Excellency of a practice which even now I feel satisfied His Excellency personally never sanctioned.

I might fairly, within the limits of decency, re- tort upon the Advisers of His Excellency some of the injurious expressions they paid to me, but here recrimination is unnecessary. By your letter of the 23rd, you distinctly raise several indictable issues, which you allege as the causes of my re- moval from office. If the Advisers of His Excel- lency are sincere in the advice they have given, there is but one course left for them, to proceed at once by indictment. The result of such a course will be the condemnation, or justification, of them or me.

I have the honor to be, Sir,
Your obedient servant,
(Signed,) A. M. DELISLE.
To the Hon. A. J. Ferguson Blair, M.L.C.,
Provincial Secretary.

P.S.—While preparing the above, on the 28th instant, I received your letter of the 26th instant, transmitting me a copy of the Report of MM. La- frenaye and Doherty.
(Signed,) A. M. D.

ARTICLE from the Montreal Gazette of the 16th February, 1864, and CORRESPONDENCE relative to the £50 paid by Mr. Ennis as bail to Mr. Schiller.

Our readers will recollect that one of the accusations against Mr. Delisle and Mr. Schiller was, that the latter had received a sum of £50 in lieu of bail from Mr. Wm. Ennis, for the appearance of a man of the name of Greene, and that this sum had "never been paid over to the Government." The answer to this charge was very simple, namely, that Mr. Schiller was not legally authorized to take this amount, although justified in so doing under the order of the Police Magistrate, Mr. Coursol, and that in consequence he could not pay it over without an order of the Court or the Government. The evidence establishes that Mr. Schiller had frequently told Mr. Ennis so ; and the legal position of the case was also made known to the Commissioners by the evidence of Mr. Carter, who took the trouble of giving the Commissioners the whole law of bail, and the principles out of which it arose that a payment of money could not be made in lieu of bail for the appearance of any one accused of crime. Nevertheless the Commissioners in their report, (page 90 of the copy furnished to Mr. Delisle,) declare that "under such circumstances this sum ought to have been transmitted to the Government," and the Provincial Secretary in his letter of the 23rd, enumerates the non-payment of this same £50 to the Government, as one of the acts of fraud, which were the reasons of Mr. A. M. Delisle's dismissal. In his remarks on this letter, Mr. Delisle very clearly showed the absurdity, not to say the dishonesty, of this charge ; but now we have the admission of the Attorney-General himself, "that the Government has no claim on the £50 deposited by Mr. Ennis in the hands of Mr. Schiller, and cannot interfere in the matter."

So Mr. Delisle and Mr. Schiller have been dismissed for not paying to the Government a sum of money to which the Government has "no claim." We live in strange days. Oh! Mr. Dorion,—"What trick, what device, what starting hole, canst thou (or the organs) find out to hide thee from this open and apparent shame ?"

The evidence of this admission on the part of the Attorney-General, as also of Mr. Schiller's having at once paid the £50 to Mr. Ennis, so soon as he had in hand a justification for his so doing, is to be found in the following correspondence which Mr. Schiller has requested us to publish :—

Montreal, 13th February, 1864.

To Charles E. Schiller, late Deputy Clerk of the Crown and of the Peace :—

Sir,—With reference to the sum of fifty pounds deposited by me on the 26th August, 1859, in the case of John Greene, in lieu of bail, you not only frequently told me to apply to Government for the amount, but also at a late period to sue you for the recovery of it, as the Government had made your retention of the money one of the charges to be investigated by the Commissioners. I preferred, however, to apply to Government instead of suing, which I did by letter addressed to the Honorable A. A. Dorion, Attorney General, on the 21st January last. Yesterday I received an answer to my application, by letter, dated Quebec, 11th February instant, signed by George Futvoye, Esq., Clerk Crown Law Department, informing me, by direction of the Honorable Attorney General, that the Government had no claim to the said sum of £50, so deposited by me in your hands.

Under these circumstances I renewed my application to you this day, handing you Mr. Futvoye's letter as your justification for paying me the amount, and you thereupon promptly paid me the same in full, for which I return my best thanks.

This acknowledgment will avail to you as a receipt, and you are at liberty to use it and Mr. Futvoye's letter in any way you think proper.

I am, Sir,
Your much obliged servant,
(Signed,)   William Ennis.

(No. 3,851.)
Crown Law Department,
Quebec, 11th February, 1864.

Sir,—I am directed by the Honorable the Attorney General for Lower Canada, to acknowledge the receipt of your letter of the 21st ult., and, in reply, to inform you that the Government has no claim on the £50 deposited by you in the hands of Mr. Schiller, and cannot interfere in the matter.

I have the honor to be Sir,
Your most obedient servant,
(Signed,)   Geo. Futvoye,
Clerk of Cr. Law Dept.

To Mr. William Ennis,
Montreal.

INDEX.

www.ingramcontent.com/pod-product-compliance
Lightning Source LLC
Chambersburg PA
CBHW030547270326
41927CB00008B/1557